Adobe
InDesign CS/CS2
Breakthroughs

Adobe
InDesign CS/CS2
Breakthroughs

David Blatner
Anne-Marie Concepción

BLATNER
BOOKS

Peachpit
Press

David: For Allee Blatner, whose spirit
of play has always been an inspiration

Anne-Marie: To my daughter Nicole,
who grew up to be my best friend

ADOBE INDESIGN CS/CS2 BREAKTHROUGHS
David Blatner and Anne-Marie Concepción

Copyright © 2005 by David Blatner and Anne-Marie Concepción

Blatner Books are published in association with
PEACHPIT PRESS
1249 Eighth Street
Berkeley, California 94710
(800) 283-9444
(510) 524-2178
(510) 524-2221 (fax)

Find us on the World Wide Web at: http://www.peachpit.com
Peachpit Press is a division of Pearson Education

Editor: Nancy Davis
Production editor: Lisa Brazieal
Indexer: Caroline Parks
Cover design: Charlene Charles-Will
Cover photograph: ©2005 Laurence Chen, www.Lchenphoto.com
Interior design and production: David Blatner (moo.com) and Jeff Tolbert

ISBN 0-321-33413-2
9 8 7 6 5 4 3 2 1

Printed and bound in the United States of America

Overview

Contents

Introduction

HEY BUDDY, WHAT'S YOUR PROBLEM? No, wait, we're not trying to be obnoxious; we really do want to know what your problem is—well, as long as it involves Adobe InDesign. After all, that is our job: listening to problems and coming up with breakthrough solutions.

In fact, we've spent much of the past couple of years listening to seminar attendees talk about their problems, teaching new and advanced users, working with clients, reading online InDesign forums, and talking with other InDesign trainers. We discovered that there are certain questions that are asked over and over again—questions about importing Microsoft Word documents, putting guides on master pages, using transparency effects, printing and exporting PDF files . . .

This book is a compendium of those commonly encountered problems, and—more importantly—their solutions! Some solutions are simple, such as pointing out a feature that you might never have known about. Other solutions are complex, requiring multi-step procedures and waving witchbane around your head while standing on one foot.

A few solutions involve problems with InDesign CS which were fixed in InDesign CS2, while some are more concerned with new problems that popped up in this most recent version. Most of the solutions in this book are applicable to both CS and CS2.

Of course, with all this talk about problems and solutions, you might get the feeling that we think InDesign is buggy or causes headaches. No way: We love InDesign and it is among the most stable, functional pieces of software we own. But we've been around long enough to know that *all* software has bugs—and they usually bite you just before a big deadline. And *every* major application can cause you to reach for the Ibuprofen at the end of a long day.

InDesign is the best page-layout software we've ever used (and we've used a lot of them), but if you don't encounter any frustrations with it, then you're just not working hard enough.

How to Read This Book

As much as we'd love to fly out to [insert name of your city here] and sit by your side as you work, we just can't right now. That's where this book comes in: Each chapter of this book covers an area we know people have problems with—text, for instance, or exporting PDF files. We don't expect you to read the whole thing cover to cover. Rather, skip around the book, gathering what you need when you need it.

You might strategically leave this book wherever you go when you have a major problem: For David, it's next to the refrigerator. Anne-Marie prefers the deck where she can face away from her office.

For More Information

Note that we have no intention of this book covering every feature in InDesign. Sure, we cover a lot of ground, and we take an in-depth look at some areas that often cause confusion with users. But we expect that you'll use this book in conjunction with other resources on InDesign. For example, we don't cover how to script InDesign or import/export XML. Fortunately, there are other resources out there. Here's a few places you can go for more information.

- *Real World Adobe InDesign CS2.* While we are a bit biased (this book was written by David Blatner and our friend Olav Martin Kvern), this is also the book recommended by members of the InDesign development team at Adobe.

- *Adobe InDesign CS2 Visual QuickStart Guide.* Sandee Cohen offers a wonderful step-by-step introduction to InDesign. We tend to like this better than the *Adobe InDesign Classroom in a Book*, though that one is good, too.

- **Adobe InDesign Web Site.** Most corporate Web sites are filled with marketing materials. You'll find plenty of that at Adobe, but it's alongside excellent useful information, too. It's definitely worth a trip to *www.adobe.com/products/indesign*. Also, the answers to many of your most puzzling InDesign questions can often be answered by the knowledgeable and helpful volunteers in the InDesign User to User Forums at *www.adobe.com/ support/forums/main.html*

- **InDesign Magazine.** There's only one magazine in the English language that focuses solely on InDesign issues. Creativepro.com, in conjunction with our own David Blatner, launched *InDesign Magazine* in July, 2004. The PDF-based magazine is packed with in-depth features, reviews, and tutorials. You can find more information at *www.indesignmag.com*

- **InDesign Users Groups.** At the time of this writing, there are InDesign Users Groups in San Francisco, Seattle, Chicago, Atlanta, Portland, Reno, Minneapolis, Milwaukee, Boston, Tampa, Washington, DC, New York City, and Melbourne, Australia; we expect more soon. See *www.indesignusergroup.com* to see if you've got one near you.

Acknowledgements

Just like our *bubbe* used to say: It takes a village to write a book. We'd like to give special thanks to a few of our favorite Village People who helped us turn a quivering mass of digital notes into the book you're now holding.

First, many thanks to the folks at Adobe who produced a great product and have helped support this book, including Will Eisley, Michael Wallen, Chad Siegel, Mark Neimann-Ross, Dov Isaacs, Thomas Phinney, Olav Martin "Ole" Kvern, Eric Menninga, Matt Phillips, Tom Petrillo, Patty Thompson, Nick Hodge, Paul Sorrick, Zak Williamson, Tim Cole, Molly Ruf, and Whitney McCleary.

Thanks to Peachpit publisher Nancy Ruenzel, who liked the idea of making this the first Blatner Books title. To our editor, Nancy Davis, for her extraordinary patience and (usually) gentle nudges to get it done. And to Lisa Brazieal for her astonishing calm in the face of chaos. To Pamela Pfiffner, our champion embedded inside the Peachpit fortress. To Don Sellers, for his excellent copyediting and proofing and to Jeff Tolbert for his blindingly fast production work and design sense. And to Caroline Parks, our indexer extraordinaire.

Our sincere appreciation goes to Sandee "Vector Babe" Cohen, Joe Grossman, Clint Funk, Scott Citron, Steve Werner, Diane "DTP *no haha*" Burns, Eda Warren, Cari Jansen, Peter Truskier, Jim Birkenseer, Branislav Milic, Chris Murphy, the InDesign beta testers, and participants in the BlueWorld InDesign mail list and the InDesign User to User Forums.

David: "My profound admiration and gratitude goes to my patient wife, Debbie, and to our sons Gabriel and Daniel, who encourage me to stop, breathe, and play. And thanks to Ted Falcon and Ruth Neuwald Falcon, for lunch, inspiration, and humor."

Anne-Marie: "I couldn't have done this without the enthusiastic support and abiding patience of my StudioB agent, Lynn Haller; and of my clients, DesignGeek readers, colleagues, family and friends. Thank you!"

1

*Palettes and Menus
and Windows, Oh My!*

Palettes and Menus and Windows, Oh My!

AT SOME POINT IN MICHELANGELO'S CAREER, BEFORE HE PAINTED the Sistine Chapel, he had to learn how to use brushes and oil paints, right? How to stretch a canvas, how to keep charcoal from getting all over everything. And surely, Jimi Hendrix stumbled for at least a few months (okay, days) while his fingers learned where to press on the strings to get the sound he wanted. Every artist has an interface they need to master before they can get down to creating.

With a program like InDesign, graphic designers are confronted with an interface that is daunting at best. Take the palettes. Have you ever *counted* how many there are in the program? 38! (That in itself can be a problem — what are we, mission control specialists?)

With all the features in those palettes, not to mention all the tools and their variations, preferences, shortcuts, and page navigation methods — everything that you could roll up into one big glob called an *interface* — you'd think there can't possibly be any room for improvement.

Actually, we can think of quite a few things that need improving. Oh my, yes. This chapter will show you how to avoid interface challenges lying in wait, detour around the ones you can't avoid, and when possible, wreak havoc upon the rest, leaving you the victor, the Almighty King! (or Queen!) of InDesign. *Bwaaa-ha-ha-ha*!

Then you may return to your quiet pursuit of creative expression.

Palette Madness

Collapse those Palettes

? I've opened up so many floating palettes, I can barely see the document! I try to turn them into side tab palettes (the kind that collapse into tab-only mode on the side of the screen) by dragging them to the right edge of my monitor, but they refuse to collapse. They just sit there, hanging off the edge of the screen, laughing at me.

☑ You're probably dragging the palette from its title bar. That's fine for moving it around, but to make a collapsed side palette, you have to drag it from its "special place" — its *tab* (where the palette name is). Or, you may not be dragging it far enough. Right before it feels like you're about to drag it off the edge of the screen (Mac users) or application window (PC users), just a few pixels away, you'll see the palette outline preview flip up, showing its collapsed position. Then you can release the mouse button to collapse the palette.

Don't forget that you can collapse palettes on the left side of the screen or window, too, turning you into a two-fisted InDesign geek.

Palette Groups that Make Sense

? I don't understand the logic behind the palette groupings that Adobe sets up by default. For instance, why is Swatches grouped with Paragraph Styles and Character Styles? Wouldn't it make more sense for Swatches to be grouped with Color and Gradient? It's bothersome to have to open two different palette groups to work with color.

☑ Those groupings are just suggestions, and they're easy to rearrange and recall as you work. Start by figuring out which palettes you want to combine into a group — let's say it's Color, Swatches, and Gradient — and get each one open as a individual floating palette on your screen. If a palette is currently part of another group, release it from bondage by dragging it by its tab to somewhere else on your screen and dropping it anywhere other than over another palette.

Now you can group your "onesie" floating palettes together. Drag the tab of one palette (Color, in our example) over another (Swatches) and hover there for a second. When you see a black outline around the palette you're hovering over, that's your signal to release the mouse button. They're now grouped. Continue dragging and dropping palettes in the same manner until you've got the group you want (**Figure 1-1**).

Once you get the hang of grouping and ungrouping palettes, you may find it more convenient to do so while the palettes are collapsed, it works there too (and you get the same cue — a black outline around the collapsed palette — when it's "ready to receive").

Note: InDesign offers another way to group palettes, called "docking." For details, see "Text Style Palettes a la QuarkXPress," later in this section.

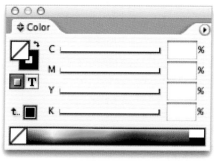

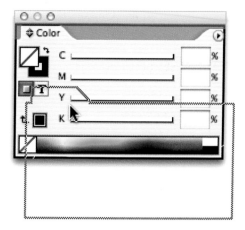

Part 2: Hover over the "receiving" palette until you see a temporary black border appear around it. That's your cue to release the mouse button if you want to group the palettes.

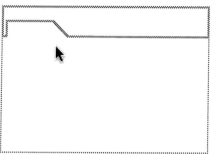

Figure 1-1, Part 1: Starting with two floating palettes, drag one by its tab toward the other one. As you drag, an outline of the palette follows the cursor.

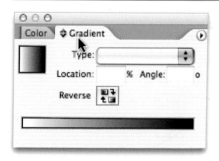

Part 3: Release the mouse button and the palettes are grouped.

Keep Grouped Palettes Grouped

? I've got a palette group that's driving me crazy. When it's floating, I want to be able to collapse the entire group at once to turn it into a side tab group; and when it's a side tab group, I want to be able to drag it out again so it's a floating group. No matter where I drag, though, for either maneuver, I can only do this one palette at a time. Doesn't that defeat the whole purpose of grouping palettes?

✓ Hold down the Option/Alt key when dragging on any of the tabs in the palette group, and they'll stay grouped no matter what.

Trim Up Those Side Tabs

? Some of my side tab palettes take up way more room than necessary when they're completely tucked away. Behind the tab(s) there's a tall gray vertical area, completely devoid of anything useful. Why can't I use that space to add more side tab palettes?

✓ If you look closely at the bottom of that grey twilight zone area, you'll see a darker gray horizontal

Figure 1-2: Drag the little horizontal handle at the bottom of a collapsed palette to resize it without opening it.

on the tab as close/open commands. Clicking on any other part of the palette you can see will pop it to the front without collapsing it.

Pressing a palette's keyboard shortcut will pop it to the front too.

Text Style Palettes à la QuarkXPress

? It's bothersome having to jump back and forth between two palettes—Paragraph Styles and Character Styles—to format text, or to figure out how someone else formatted it. I miss QuarkXPress's single, comprehensive "Style Sheets" palette, where I could see all styles applied to a given selection of text at once.

line, about two pixels deep. Position the cursor over this line and it turns into a double-sided arrow (InDesignese for "drag me!"). Now you can drag the bottom edge, shrinking the height of the collapsed palette and freeing up space for more side tab palettes (**Figure 1-2**).

✓ Dock the Character Styles palette to the bottom of the Paragraph Styles palette, and you'll have a solution

Pop Them to the Front

? What are you supposed to do to get an open side tab palette appear in front of another one that's overlapping it? When I click on the tab in back, it comes to the front but then immediately collapses into "tab only" mode. I have to click the tab a second time to reveal the palette.

✓ Clicking on the tab area to bring a palette to the front is fine for floating palettes. When they're in side tab position InDesign interprets clicks

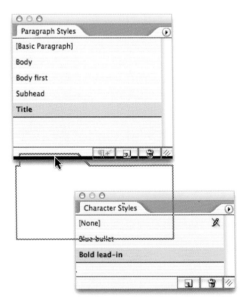

Figure 1-3: Look for a heavy horizontal rule below the target palette when docking another one to it.

that'll make you forget whozit's Style Sheets palette in a San Jose minute. To dock a palette, drag its tab close to the bottom edge of another floating palette. When you see a heavy horizontal line appear between the two, release the mouse button. The palette you were dragging "snaps" into position below the one above it and stays there (**Figure 1-3**).

When two (or more) palettes are docked, they move as one unit. So now you've got a Styles palette that looks and functions a lot like what's-his-face's. You can't turn docked palettes into side tab palettes, unfortunately. But when you press the keyboard shortcut to open one of the palettes, they both open now.

Make More Room for Left Side Palettes

❓ I'd like to use all the left edge of my screen/application window to hold side palettes, but the Tools palette keeps getting in the way.

☑️ Open the Preferences dialog box (on the Macintosh, choose InDesign > Preferences; in Windows, it's Edit > Preferences), look in the General Options area and change the Floating Tools Palette setting from the default Double Column to Single Row. Now you can dock the Tools palette right underneath the Control palette, nice and neat, and the left edge of your window is completely accessible for more side palette fun.

TIP: Some folks really like Microsoft Word's toolbar across the top of their screen. If you're one of these types (we won't ask for a show of hands), you might want to change the Floating Tools Palette setting (in the Preferences dialog box) to Single Row. The palette then nests nicely directly underneath the Control palette.

Create Custom Workspaces

❓ I just spent half an hour getting the palettes arranged just so. But two hours into my project, I've messed them up again. How can I get InDesign to reset the palettes to how I arranged them?

☑️ Once you've got your palettes "perfect," hie thee to the Window menu and choose Window > Workspace > Save Workspace. Give it a name and click OK. From now on, whenever you're in the middle of a project and you find yourself with palettes scattered all over the place, go back up to Window > Workspace and choose the name of the custom Workspace you saved. InDesign resets all the palettes to that arrangement.

If only we could do the same in real life (Window > Workspace > Clean Kitchen... Window > Workspace > Me, Age 22)... now, *that* would be a useful feature.

Share Custom Workspaces

? I've got a great custom Workspace I created at work, and I want the same one on my laptop. I can't figure out how to get it over there.

✓ Custom workspaces are saved as .xml files on your computer in a folder called, mysteriously, "Workspaces."

To copy custom Workspaces from one computer to another, drop a copy of one computer's workspace.xml file into the other computer's Workspaces folder, and relaunch InDesign.

- On the Mac, look here: [username] > Library > Preferences > Adobe InDesign > Version 4.0 > Workspaces > yourworkspace.xml

- In Windows, look here: [username] > Application Data > Adobe > InDesign > Version 4.0 > Workspaces > yourworkspace.xml

Preferences Pains

Change the Default Measurement Unit

? I don't know picas from pigeons, but that's what InDesign insists I learn. My colleagues and I are used to using inches for specifying measures, have been for years. Are we hopelessly out of touch with the professional design world?

✓ You obviously live in the United States, where inches seem to have permeated almost every aspect of culture. (Even spam! We keep getting emails that want to help us add inches to one part of our anatomy or another.) Of course, in Europe the most common graphic design measurement unit is the millimeter. Fortunately, you can change

InDesign's default measurement unit to just about anything you want. For your tastes, open the Preferences dialog box, choose the Units and Increments panel, and pick Inches from both the Horizontal and Vertical popup menus. If you want this setting to be the default for all documents you create from now on, make the change *with no documents open* (for more info, see the sidebar, "Customizing InDesign's Application Defaults" below).

TIP: You can easily change the measurement unit on the fly for the current document. Put your cursor on top of the horizontal or vertical page ruler and right-click (or Control-click if you're on a Mac with a one-button mouse). Choose your preferred measurement unit from the contextual menu (**Figure 1-4**).

Customizing InDesign's Application Defaults

An application *default* is a software program's "suggested setting" for a given dialog or palette field, menu choice, checkbox, radio button and the like. Back in the factory, before the program started shipping, software engineers and user interface experts had to go through each area of the program that offered a choice and decide on a starting setting.

Imagine this conversation:

Mary Engineer: "Most people want hyphenation on, so let's turn it on by default."

Jim Interface: "Yeah, if they don't want it, they can always turn it off."

Mary: "Okay, but what should we use for the minimum number of letters a word should have before auto-hyphenation kicks in? Five letters?"

Jim: "Six letters. No, five. No, six, definitely six. I don't know, let's toss a coin."

Mary: "Okay... Hey, how 'bout them Mariners?"

Fortunately, you don't have to live with their suggestions for all of eternity. To change InDesign's default settings, close all open documents. Though some features are now grayed out (such as the File > Export command), many will be accessible, including every tool and palette. Go ahead and modify whatever you want. For example, if you add a color to the Swatches palette, that color will be in every new document you create from here on out. If you turn on the Apply Leading To Entire Paragraphs checkbox in the Type panel of the Preferences dialog box, it'll stay on for all new documents. And so on.

When you're done, save your changes by quitting the program. (For some reason, defaults only get saved when you quit.) The next time you launch InDesign, you'll enjoy the pleasant experience of the default settings reflecting your personal choices right from the start.

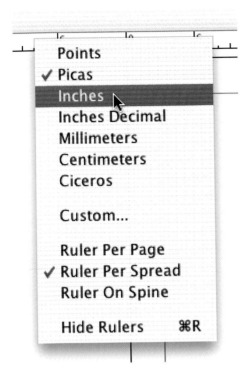

your hard drive to locate the file(s), move them to your Trash or Recycle Bin and then restart the program, forcing it to rebuild a default set of preferences.

InDesign offers a more convenient way to do the same thing, via a keyboard shortcut. Quit InDesign if it's running, start the program again, and immediately press the appropriate "rebuild preferences" keys *as it's launching*:

- Windows: Ctrl-Alt-Shift
- Macintosh: Command-Control-Option-Shift

If InDesign launches without showing you an alert asking if you want to delete your preference file, then you didn't hold down the modifier keys early enough. If you do see this alert, click the "Yes" button, and InDesign builds itself a fresh one as it completes the start-up process.

Rebuild InDesign's Preferences

? InDesign is acting sort of flakey. Every time I [fill in simple action here], it "unexpectedly quits," and/or it won't let me drag out a ruler guide, and/or the pasteboard is five times normal size, etc.

✓ Try rebuilding InDesign's two files that together constitute its preferences: InDesign Defaults and InDesign Saved Data. The normal way to rebuild preferences is to root through

> **WARNING:** If you rebuild InDesign's Preferences, you lose any custom glyph sets (see page 93) you may have made. If you're a glyph set kind of guy or gal, be sure to back up the Preferences file (while it's a healthy file) for safekeeping.

Shortcut Aggravations

Super Multiple Undo

? I love the fact that I can undo multiple times in InDesign, but sometimes I want to undo a bunch of stuff all in one fell swoop. Why doesn't InDesign have a History palette like Photoshop?

☑ Why Adobe didn't give us a History palette is a question for the oracle. How to deal with this limitation is a question of finding the right third-party developer. If you want a palette, check out 65bit Software's EasyHistory or DTP Tools' History plug-ins. They're both relatively inexpensive and offer cool features like taking snapshots of your document in any current state.

65bit Software also offers a free plug-in called Multido, but it uses a menu instead of a palette (more awkward, but free).

Here's where you can find these three plug-ins:

- *http://www.65bit.com*
- *http://www.dtptools.com*

Where's a List of Shortcuts?

? I'm used to getting a printed "cheat sheet" of keyboard shortcuts when I buy a program, but I didn't get anything like that with InDesign. It's difficult to figure out which keyboard shortcuts do what without a printed reference. At least for me, anyway.

☑ There are a couple of ways to get a printout of InDesign keyboard shortcuts, if the ones InDesign displays in its menus and tool tips aren't enough for you.

First, you can open Online Help (Help > InDesign Help) and after it loads, scroll down the list of Contents in the left-hand pane. Towards the bottom you'll see a link called "Keyboard Shortcuts." Click the link (and then click Default Keyboard Shortcuts in InDesign CS2) and you'll see a long list of other links leading to subcategories. Click any one of *these* links — "Keys for Selecting Tools," "Keys for Using Palettes," and so on — to open a printable page of Windows and Macintosh keyboard shortcuts for that category.

Another way is more sneaky. Choose Edit > Keyboard Shortcuts and click the "Show Set" button at the top right. InDesign creates and opens a text file listing every menu item, palette and tool, organized into the same categories as the "Product Area" popup menu. If an item has a keyboard shortcut, it's listed here; if it doesn't, it says "[none defined]." You can print out the text file or save it for future reference on your hard drive. It'd be nice if it formatted the shortcuts (like made the headings bold), but no, if you want this list formatted, you'll have to do it yourself.

A Better Selection Tool Shortcut

? The Selection tool's keyboard shortcut, "V," is hardly ever useful to me since most of my time in InDesign is spent edit-ing text—pressing "V" in this case just inserts the character wherever I'm typing. I'm developing a bad case of tennis elbow from having to mouse over to the Tools palette to click the Selection tool a hun-dred times a day. What possessed Adobe to give the tool a single letter shortcut?

☑ The method to Adobe's madness of assigning single letter key-board shortcuts to items in InDesign's Tools palette lies in their desire for The Holy Grail of Creative Suite Consistency. Photoshop and Illustrator's tools used single letter shortcuts as far back as we can remember, so it does make some sense for InDesign to share the trait. And many tools, including the Selection tool, are almost exactly the same between InDesign and Illustrator, even as far as sharing the same slot in the Tools palette. Of course, Photoshop and Illustrator users don't normally spend as much time as InDesign users spend editing text.

The good news is that InDesign has a number of ways to skin this cat. When you're editing text with the Type tool, you can switch to the Selection tool without visiting the Tools palette via any of the following methods:

- Click outside of the text frame onto an empty area (not on top of a different frame), then press "V".

- If you can't find any empty real estate nearby, press Command-Shift-A/Ctrl-Shift-A (the keyboard shortcut for Edit > Deselect All), then "V".

- Hold down the Command/Ctrl key to get a temporary Selection tool; releasing the key reverts to the Type tool (Note: This is the only method where InDesign remembers your text cursor loca-tion in the text frame after using the Selection tool). You can also Command/Ctrl-click on the text frame with the Text tool to select the frame itself (rather than the text inside it); now you can press V to switch to the Selection tool.

- You can press Control-Tab/Ctrl-Tab (same on Macintosh and Windows) when editing text to select the text frame as though you clicked on it with the Selection tool. Now you can press another key (like "V") to switch tools, turn on preview, or whatever.

Here's an even better solution: Add a new keyboard shortcut for the Selection tool. Choose Edit > Keyboard Shortcuts, and pick "Tools" from the Product Area popup menu. Click on the entry for the Selection tool to see its current shortcut appear at the bottom of the dialog. Now, type a new keyboard shortcut, such as Command-Option-V/Ctrl-Alt-V. This one is usually reserved for the Paste Into feature, so choose Text from the Context popup menu—that tells InDesign that this keyboard shortcut should switch to the Selection tool *only* when the cur-sor is in text (when you're never going to use Paste Into). Don't forget to click the Assign button before pressing OK, or else the shortcut doesn't take affect. Now the Selection tool has two different shortcuts, one of which only works when you're editing text.

Lock the Default Keyboard Shortcut Set

? Some of the designers in my department have been modifying the Default Set in Edit > Keyboard Shortcuts instead of creating their own custom set and leaving the Default alone. This makes it difficult when more than one person shares the same computer; they don't understand why sometimes the default keyboard shortcuts don't work. I tried rebuilding the InDesign preferences on the affected computers, but it didn't restore InDesign's Default keyboard shortcut set.

☑ As far as we're concerned, making the Default keyboard shortcut set "writable" is a bug. The Default Set was locked in earlier versions, and if you tried to make a change, you'd get an alert stating such (and suggesting you create a Custom set). Unfortunately, there is no way to rebuild the Default keyboard

shortcut set once it gets changed. You can reinstall the program, or you can copy over a pristine Default set from another copy of InDesign to replace the modified one (you might need administrator privileges for this).

- On Windows, you'll find the Default file here:
  C:\Program Files\Adobe\Adobe InDesign CS\Presets\InDesign Shortcut Sets\Default.indk

- And on Macs, it's here:
  [Hard Drive Name]/Applications/ Adobe InDesign CS/Presets/ InDesign Shortcut Sets/Default

To prevent the problem in the future, lock the Default file — that is, set it Read Only — using your operating system's method of doing so (Get Info on the Mac; Properties in Windows).

Purposefully Previewing

? I keep bouncing into or out of Preview mode without meaning to. I know it's because of Preview's one-key shortcut, a "W," which I sometimes hit by mistake. It's driving me crazy!

☑ Do yourself a favor and change the shortcut from just plain 'W' to something that requires a few more keys (and thus more intention) in Edit > Keyboard Shortcuts > Product Area: Tools > Toggle View Setting Between Default and Preview.

Page Navigation

Yes Virginia, There is a "Go To Page" Command

? I can't believe that there's no "Go to Page [n]" command, let alone a keyboard shortcut for it, in the Layout menu where all the other page navigation commands are listed. If I have a short document, using the shortcuts for "Go to Next/Previous Page" is doable, but for long files, they're virtually useless.

☑ The keyboard shortcut you're looking for is the same as it is in QuarkXPress: Command-J/Ctrl-J (think: "*J*ump to Page"). It's right there in Edit > Keyboard Shortcuts: choose the "Views, Navigation" Product Area, and then find "Access Page Number Box." With such an obscure title, it's not surprising you didn't notice it.

When you use the shortcut, the current page number at the lower left of the document window becomes selected. Type the page number you want to "jump" to and hit Return/Enter to go to that page.

TIP: The Command-J/Ctrl-J feature is great for jumping from one page in your document to another, but most people don't realize it also works to jump to a master page. If you want to go to master page "A," just type A into the page field and press Return/Enter.

A Hand Tool Shortcut That Always Works

? I've been using InDesign for months and find the Hand tool indispensable for dragging the page around my window without having to use the scroll bars. But why didn't they give it a shortcut I can use all the time? If I'm not editing text, then I use the spacebar — logical, as that's what Photoshop and Illustrator use. But if I have some text selected, then I have to hold down the Option/Alt key to get Mr. Grabby!
Aaaugh!

☑ Let's use the belt-and-suspenders method. From now on, every time you want to access the temporary Hand tool to scroll your document around, regardless of what you're doing in the program, hold down *both keys*, the Option/Alt key *and* the Spacebar. Make sure to press Option/Alt slightly before you add the Spacebar. It works every time.

TIP: If you've got a mouse with a scroll wheel, you already know that you can use it to scroll up and down through your pages. Did you know you could also use it to scroll left and right? Keep the Shift key held down when you scroll the wheel: Shift-wheel up scrolls the window to the left; Shift-wheel down scrolls the window to the right. Oh yeah baby, work it.

Zoom In/Out Madness

? I know that InDesign's keyboard shortcut for the temporary Zoom tool is Command-Spacebar/Ctrl-Spacebar (adding the Option/Alt key to that for Zoom Out). Normally it works fine, but sometimes it leaves a trail of empty spaces in my text. What's going on?

☑ You need to hold down the Command/Ctrl key at least a nanosecond before you add the Spacebar. If you're editing text, that tells InDesign "ignore what's happening with the Spacebar, it doesn't concern you." If you're not editing text, it actually makes no difference which one you press first, but why torture yourself. Get in the "Command/Ctrl first" habit and move on to more interesting things.

You might also consider using an alternate keyboard shortcut. For example, Command/Ctrl-+ (plus sign) and – (minus sign) zoom in and out just as nicely.

TIP: If you've got a mouse with a scroll wheel, you can use this little-known trick to zoom in and out of your page. Hold down the Command/Ctrl key and scroll up (forward) to zoom in, down (backward) to zoom out. Scroll slowly, because every "tick" of the wheel jumps at least one 25% scaling increment, increasing to larger increments the more you're zoomed in. (In CS2, they reversed the direction: scrolling back zooms in and scrolling forward zooms out.)

2

Making Pages and
Taking Names

Making Pages and Taking Names

*T*HE FUNDAMENTAL PURPOSE OF A PAGE LAYOUT PROGRAM IS just that: laying out pages. Above all else, the application ought to make it easy for users to get pages to appear *where* they want them to be, and to get the objects on those pages arranged *how* they want them arranged. These tasks are the main course, the meat of a page layout program. Everything else is a side dish.

If you're hankering for some protein, InDesign's feature set for basic page production is a carnivore's feast. For example, take the concept of a master page. Providing an editable master page in each document is not enough for InDy. It also provides multiple masters, pages that convert to masters, parent/child masters, spread masters for non-facing page documents, overridden master elements, hidden masters, and masters with multiple layers.

The same welcome flexibility and power is evident in other layout-centric aspects of InDesign, such as the options it offers for new document creation; combining documents; adding and rearranging pages; duplicating, grouping and aligning objects; margin, column and ruler guides; and using layers to keep things organized.

Yet lurking in this roast beast are a number of perplexing issues — call them bits of gristle — [Editor: Are we about done with the meat thing? Authors: Can't talk. Eating.] that need to be worked around or removed.

Designers, man your steak knives!

Document Setup Hassles

Bypass the New Document Dialog

? Back in the old days, choosing File > New Document would give you just that: a new document. Now none of the programs I use, including InDesign, will do this simple task. Why does InDy force me to Suffer the Tortures of a Thousand Fields (my nickname for the New Document dialog box) every single time I want to create a new file?

✓ You're absolutely right. Here's what to do: If you press Command-Option-N/Ctrl-Alt-N, InDesign will skip the New Document dialog and slap up a new document right quick-like. It uses the same specifications (margins, page size, and so on) as the last document preset you chose (we'll talk about document presets in just a moment). If you haven't made any document presets, you get the defaults: either a letter-size or an A4 page (depending on where you live). If you're not happy with the specs, you can always change the margins on your master page (Layout > Margins and Columns), and everything else in File > Document Setup.

Change the New Document Defaults

? At my company, very few of the documents we create in InDesign require facing pages. I don't remember the last time I did one, in fact. Yet every time I open the New Document dialog box (File > New > Document), "Facing Pages" is checked on by default.

✓ Start up InDesign, but don't open any InDesign files. You'll note that many menu items and palettes are accessible, even though there's no document to apply the menu command or palette setting to. Interesting, eh? That means everything you do now will apply to all future documents.

Let's take advantage of it. Open the File > Document Setup dialog box and turn off the Facing Pages option. Click OK, quit InDesign, and then relaunch it again. Now when you open the New Document dialog box, the Facing Pages checkbox is turned off.

Create Your Own Document Presets

? There are about four or five different types of documents I create in InDesign, and each one has its own particular settings for margins, facing pages, bleed guides, and so on. I keep a cheat sheet of the settings on a Post-It by my desk, but it's still a pain to enter them one by one.

✓ Don't worry, you'll just have to enter them one more time, we promise. Go to File > New > Document, and enter all the settings for one of these types of projects. Don't forget to click the More Options button to set up any bleed and slug guides as well. Now, resisting the urge to click OK yet, look for one

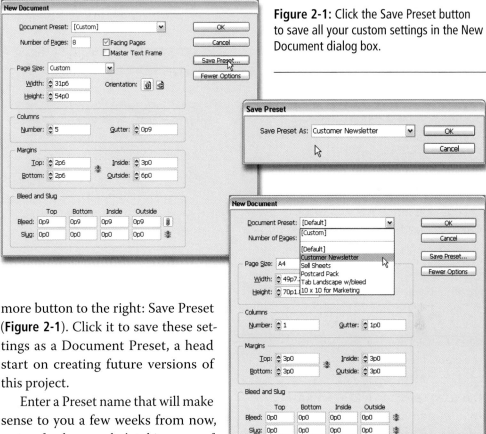

Figure 2-1: Click the Save Preset button to save all your custom settings in the New Document dialog box.

Figure 2-2: Now you can just choose your settings from the Document Preset popup menu.

more button to the right: Save Preset (**Figure 2-1**). Click it to save these settings as a Document Preset, a head start on creating future versions of this project.

Enter a Preset name that will make sense to you a few weeks from now, or to a freelancer who's taking care of your projects while you're slurping up mango daiquiris on Maui.

When it's time to churn out the next newsletter (or whatever), you can open the New Document dialog box and choose the name of your Preset from the popup menu at the top (**Figure 2-2**). All your settings appear in the appropriate fields, just as you first entered and saved them. Click OK to create your document with these settings.

You can create as many Document Presets as you want. They're saved in your InDesign Preferences file on your hard drive, so be sure to keep a back up copy handy in case you ever need to rebuild your Preferences (see page 10).

TIP: You can pick a document preset and bypass the New Document dialog box altogether by holding down the Shift key while selecting a document preset from the File > Document Presets menu.

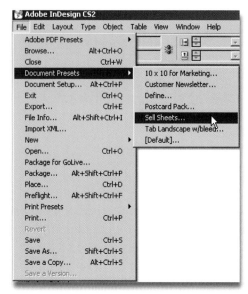

Figure 2-3: Presets in alphabetical order! What a country!

Alphabetize the Document Presets

? My Document Presets menu lists about 30 different presets that I've created over the past few months. Since they appear in the order I created them, and not alphabetically, it's a pain finding the one I want.

✓ You can force any InDesign menu to temporarily appear in alphabetical order by pressing Command-Option-Shift/Ctrl-Alt-Shift when you click on the menu bar name. To see these menus' *submenus* appear in alphabetical order as well, keep the modifier keys held down while you drag down the menu to open the submenu (**Figure 2-3**).

In other words, you can get your Document Presets to appear in alphabetical order if you access them via the File > Document Presets submenu while holding down these modifier keys. The

"force alpha" trick doesn't work for popup menus inside dialog boxes, so you can't use it on the Preset menu in the New Document dialog box. Bummer.

> **TRIVIA QUIZ:** What's the smallest custom page size you can create in InDesign, and what's the largest?
>
> **ANSWER:** Smallest is one inch square, largest is eighteen feet square (that's 1,296 picas, for you designer-geeks).

Turn Off Facing Pages

? I thought my document should be set up as facing pages, but now, halfway through the project, I'm thinking it's more trouble than it's worth. Do I have to start all over again with a new document (that's set to *non*-facing pages), and copy everything over?

✓ Nope. Just open your current document, go to File > Document Setup and turn off the Facing Pages checkbox. All the 2-page document spreads in your Pages palette change to 1-page spreads.

> **WARNING:** If you had anything on the right-facing page of your 2-page master when you turned off the Facing Pages option, your old right-facing pages are no longer linked to it and may look different. See the "Reapply Right-Facing Masters to Non-Facing Pages" tip on page 33.

Merge Two Documents

? I need to add pages from one document into another. When I worked
in QuarkXPress, I would do this via a
"thumbnail drag" (put both documents in
Thumbnail view and drag pages over). But
there's no Thumbnail view in InDesign! My
workaround is to copy all the items from
one page of Document A, and use Edit >
Paste in Place to paste the items in the
right position in Document B. But as far
as I can tell InDesign only lets you Paste
in Place one page at a time.

✓ It's true that Paste in Place only
works one page (or spread) at a
time. If you've got more than a couple
pages to bring over, though, don't even
bother. There's an easier way. Let's call
it "icon drag."

Open both Document A and
Document B. You may want to tile them
(Window > Arrange > Tile) so you can
see both documents at the same time on
your monitor. There's no need to change
your current document view. The two
documents don't even need to be the
same page dimensions! (Though if they
aren't page objects may shift around.)

Add Custom Page Sizes

Want to edit the options in the
Page Size popup menu in the New
Document dialog box? Perhaps you
use poster-size pages. No problem.

Look inside the Adobe InDesign
CS application folder on your hard
drive for a file called "New Doc Sizes.
txt" (it's inside the program's Presets
folder; in CS on the Mac it was called
"New Page Sizes.txt"). Double-click
the text file to open it in your default
text editor.

This file contains both the instructions on adding new page sizes and the
data InDesign uses to build this menu.
The instructions are simple: You add
one line of information to the end of
this file for each new page size you
want to add to the New Document
dialog box. Each line should state
three things, separated by multiple
spaces or tabs: The Preset name
(which can include spaces), its width,

and its height. Be sure to include the
InDesign shorthand for measurement
units in the width and height specifications, such as "20in" or "60p9" with
no spaces. These will get converted to
whatever default measurement unit is
in effect in InDesign.

Here are some example lines you
can add, lifted right from the text file:

Certificate   11"   9"
Poster   17in   22"
Postcard   15cm   100mm

As soon as you've saved your
changes to the file, InDesign learns
about it and includes them in the
Page Sizes popup menu in the New
Document dialog window. You don't
have to quit the program first or anything.

We can't figure out a way to *remove*
the existing Page Sizes that you don't
use (they're not part of the New Doc
Sizes.txt file). But we're working on it.

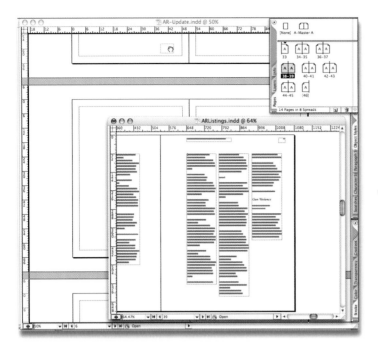

Figure 2-4: Drag a page icon and drop it onto the document you want to add the page to.

And Merge Their Master Pages, Too

? **When I add a page from another InDesign document to my current file by dragging its Pages palette icon over (see previous solution), its master page doesn't come along with it.**

When the master page names are identical in the two documents, the dragged-over page gets re-linked to

To bring pages from Document A into Document B, open the Pages palette and select the page(s) you want to copy over. (Shift-click to select contiguous pages; Command/Ctrl-click to select non-contiguous pages.) Then drag the actual little icons of your selected pages from Document A's *Pages palette* and drop them onto Document B's *window* (not its Pages palette—it has no Pages palette of its own, when you think about it. There's only one, and you're using it to drag the icons out of; **Figure 2-4**).

It makes no difference where you drop the page icons onto the receiving document, they always get added after the last page. Click on that document to make it active, and use the Pages palette to rearrange the pages as necessary.

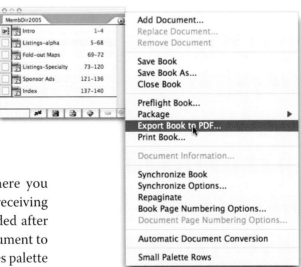

Figure 2-5: The Book palette menu contains some powerful batch functions.

the one in its new document. That behavior would be really useful if it were what you wanted to happen. But in this case it's not. So, before you drag over the page icon, rename that document's master page so it doesn't match the names of any of the master pages in your current document. This time when you drag the page icon over, the uniquely-named master will come along for the ride.

By the way, if you want to copy a master page from one document to another, you can just drag the master page icon from the Pages palette.

Herding Pages

Mix Page Sizes in the Same Document

❓ **The one feature I wish InDesign had of QuarkXPress 6.x's is the ability to combine different page sizes and orientations in the same document. In InDesign, I have to maintain a separate file for the tabloid landscape documents that will be folded and bound into my letter-size, portrait-oriented engineering reports. It's hard to keep style sheets consistent among the files, and it's a pain having to repeat every Print, Preflight, and Export to PDF command for each document.**

☑ Don't feel like you're missing out, because you wouldn't be able to do much of that in QuarkXPress 6.X anyway. While you can create multiple layouts with different page sizes and orientation in the same XPress project file, you can't run a Print or Export to PDF command on all of them at the same time, you have to do them one-by-one. And of course you can't run a single Preflight on all the layouts, since XPress doesn't offer a Preflight command.

However, you *can* get what you want in InDesign. Just take a trip to the File menu and create a new Book document (File > New > Book). After you name the Book file and choose a location to save it, the book opens in InDesign looking just like a palette. Use the commands in its palette menu or the "plus" icon at the bottom of the palette to add two or more InDesign documents to it — each file can have a different page size or orientation.

And here's the money shot for you, bub: By using the Book palette menu commands, you can Print, Package, Preflight, or Export to PDF the entire "book" (all the files you added) at once. Bingo! And if your paragraph or character styles change, you can propagate those changes to all the documents in the book using the palette's Synchronize button (**Figure 2-5**).

The "Book" name for this feature is unfortunate. As you can see, it's useful for lots of different kinds of projects, not just chapters of books. A better name would be something like "Collection" or "Group" (of documents).

Fit More Page Icons in the Palette

? When I'm working on a long docu-ment—anything beyond, say, six pages—the amount of scrolling I have to do in the Pages palette becomes ridiculous. I'm seeing a lot of wasted space here!

☑ Open the Pages palette menu and choose Palette Options. To fit the most number of icons into the space allotted, opt for Small icons and turn off the "Show Vertically" checkbox. When you click OK, you'll find that the palette real estate is being used far more efficiently, though it takes some getting used to.

> **TIP:** Modify your Pages palette options with no documents open, then quit InDesign to save your modifications as an application default. The next time you work in InDesign, the Pages palette will look the way you want it to look, by default.

Add a Page to the Right Spot Quickly

? When I click the Create New Page icon at the bottom of the Pages pal-ette, it gets added after the last page in my document. I want the new page to go elsewhere, but I can't figure out how to tell InDesign.

☑ By default, the new page is inserted directly after the cur-rent, active spread. That means that you need to double-click the spread immedi-ately preceding the spot where you want the pages to go before you click the New Page icon. (Or, use the keyboard short-cut for adding a new page: Command-Shift-P/Ctrl-Shift-P.)

Alternatively, you could drag a master page icon to the spot you want the page in the Pages palette. Or Option/Alt-click the New Page icon, which is a shortcut to the palette menu's Insert Pages dialog—which lets you choose not only the loca-tion of the new page (regardless of which page is currently active), but also which master page it should be based on.

Also, in InDesign CS2, you can use the Layout > Pages > Insert Pages menu item. Many users miss this submenu.

> **TIP:** In InDesign CS, to move one or more pages to a different location in your document you have to drag icons around the Pages palette. In CS2, it's easier: Just choose Move Pages from the Pages palette menu or the Pages submenu (under the Layout menu).

Add Multiple Pages Quickly

? Where's the Pages menu? How am I supposed to add multiple pages, by clicking on the little icon at the bottom of the Pages palette a hundred times?

☑ You're right; there is no Pages menu in the main menu bar, which is disconcerting if you're coming from QuarkXPress. You have to remem-ber that InDesign is palette-driven. A

Figure 2-6: InDesign's Insert Pages dialog box

lot of powerful InDesign commands are buried in *palette* menus.

Guess which palette menu contains the Insert Pages command?

Bingo. Use the Pages palette menu's Insert Pages dialog box (**Figure 2-6**) to tell InDesign how many pages you'd like to add. You can specify which master page it should base them on, and where they should be added, as well. As we mentioned above, you can also get to this same dialog box by Option/Alt-clicking on the palette's New Page button.

Alternatively, a quick, "back door" way to add a bunch of pages is by increasing the number in the Number of Pages field in File > Document Setup. But you don't get to specify where the pages should be added (they get added after the last page) nor which master they should be based upon (they're based on the same master as the current, active page). Of course, this might be exactly what you're looking for.

Make a Gatefold Spread

? I'm trying to make a three-page spread in my facing pages document because the third page will be a gatefold advertisement. No matter what I do in the Pages palette, I can't get a third page to

"stick" to the left or right of this spread. When I drag the page icon near the spread, it *looks* like it's going to go in the right place (I see the vertical bar), but when I release the mouse button, the page icon ends up someplace else.

What we have here, my friend, is a-feature-not-a-bug. InDesign usually considers 2-page document spreads to be sacrosanct: Nothing may defile their pure 2-page spreadness. Because of that, a facing pages document will always be made up of 2-page spreads (except for the first right-facing page and perhaps a final left-facing page), regardless of how many odd number of pages the user adds or deletes. It's protecting you from your wicked ways, and from the extra fees your printer will charge when they need to fix your weirdly-imposed file.

But you can tell InDesign to mind its own business. To override a spread's 2-page nature, target it in the Pages palette (double-click its page numbers under the spread icon) and choose Keep Spread Together from the palette menu. Now you can drag and drop page icons to the left or right of the spread and they'll stick there.

TRIVIA QUIZ: After selecting a spread and turning on Keep Spread Together, what's the maximum number of pages it can hold in a single spread?

ANSWER: 10. Master pages can have up to 10 pages in a spread too. You'll need a mighty big printer to print those spreads, though.

Start with a 2-Page Spread

? It would make my life so much easier if I could arrange the simple 4-page newsletter I do into two 2-page spreads: One spread for the outside (back cover/front cover), one spread for the inside (page 2 and 3). But InDesign won't let me put page 4 to the left of page 1! I targeted the first page's icon and turned on Keep Spread Together from the Pages palette menu, but it still refuses to let me do what I want. (Keep Spread Together does allow me to hang page 4 to the *right* of page 1, which just makes no sense to me whatsoever.)

☑ In addition to turning *on* Keep Spread Together for your first spread, turn *off* Allow Pages to Shuffle from the Pages palette menu. That tells InDesign to follow your lead when you insert and rearrange pages, and stop trying to help you so much.

Now when you drag page 4 up to the left side of page 1, let go of it when you see the black bar with the little right-arrow sticking out. Page 4 will sit to the left of page 1. Of course, you'll have to manually number your pages because your page 4 has now become the first page in the document.

Here's another way to get the first page to be a left page, even if you're working with facing pages. Don't turn off Allow Pages to Shuffle, as we mentioned above. Instead:

1. Use the Numbering & Section Options feature (in the Pages palette menu) to make the first page an even number (like 2).

2. Now select all the pages in the Pages palette (click on the first page and then Shift-click on the last one) and turn on Keep Spreads Together from the palette mneu.

3. Finally, select just the first page again and change its page number back to page one.

Identify the Active Page

? There's something screwy about the way InDesign lets you know what page you're on. For example, why is it that sometimes when I paste an object onto my document, it appears on the wrong page? According to my Pages palette, the correct page is selected. I can't figure it out.

☑ If you make a page active by double-clicking its icon (or its page number) in the Pages palette, your Edit > Paste actions should work as expected. To tell which is the active (or "targeted") page or spread, find the icon whose page numbers are highlighted (reversed out of black) in the Pages palette.

For more information about this topic, see the sidebar "Active Pages vs. Selected Pages," on the next page.

Split Facing Pages for Inside Bleeds

? My document is set up as facing pages and will ultimately be spiral-bound. On a few of these pages I want to set up a graphic to bleed into the inside edge, into the "binding." To make the bleed I obviously have to overlap the image into the pasteboard, but in a facing pages document, the inside edges have no pasteboard!

✓ Open the Pages palette menu and turn off Allow Pages to Shuffle. Now, drag one of your right-facing pages a little bit to the right until you see a large vertical bar appear to its right, then release the mouse button. (Or drag a left-facing page a little to the left until a vertical bar appears to its left, and drop it. **Figure 2-7**) That splits the page into its own spread — but still maintains its "facing page-ness" — so you can make either of these split pages active and create an inside bleed.

Active Pages vs. Selected Pages

Watch out! InDesign makes a distinction between the page you're looking at, the selected page, and the active (or "targeted") page. It's confusing at first, but you get used to it (or you go mad). The active page is the page that you're working on. When you press Command-A/Ctrl-A with the Selection tool (to Select All), it's the objects on the active page (or spread) that InDesign selects. When you Paste, the object on the clipboard shows up on the active page.

However, if you're working on page 3 and you use the scroll bars or Hand tool to navigate to page 5, you'll be looking at page 5 but the active page will still be page 3. To make page 5 the active page, just click anywhere on the page. You can also double-click on any page or spread in the Pages palette to make it active and bring the page into view. You can always tell which page or spread is selected by looking at the Pages palette: the page numbers under the icon are reversed out of black.

(If you're zoomed way out and can see multiple spreads in your window, there's no clue which is the active page. Even the Current Page Number field at the lower left can give you a false reading. Trust in the Pages palette, it's always accurate.)

Selecting a page is different. When you duplicate, move, or delete a page, or change the page's margins or columns, InDesign changes the *selected* page, which may not be the active one. To select a page, click *once* on its page icon or its page number in the Pages palette. Note that the page icon highlights but its page number does not. To select additional pages, Shift-click (or Command-click/Ctrl-click for a discontiguous selection) each icon or icon's page number in turn.

Of course, any page or spread can be selected, active, and viewed at the same time. But understanding the distinctions among these is key to avoiding some truly heinous headaches.

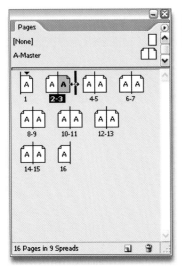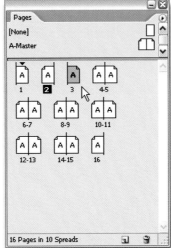

Figure 2-7: Drag the page icon a little bit over until you see a large vertical bar appear.

Master Page Migraines

Select Master Page Items in the Document

? Hey, what's up with this? I put a text frame on my A-Master master page. Now I can't select it on my document pages to put text in it! What's the point of master pages if I can't select those objects?

☑ InDesign is saving you from accidentally changing something you may not want to change. Fortunately, you can Command-Shift-click/Ctrl-Shift-click on the master page object to override it on the document page, then you can edit it.

TIP: To override every master page object on your document spread, open the Pages palette menu and choose Override All Master Page Items.

TIP: Reset Master Items. If, after you have changed a master page item, you come to the conclusion that you'd have been better off leaving it alone, you can select it and reset it by choosing Remove Selected Local Overrides from the Pages palette menu.

Create New Masters Quickly

? QuarkXPress makes it easy to make a new master page; you just drag out a little icon. Why can't I do that in InDesign? I'm tired of having to dig through the palette menu for the New Master command every time I need one.

☑ InDesign lets you make new master pages quickly; it's just not as obvious how. Command-click/Ctrl-click on the New Page icon at the bottom of the Pages palette to quickly add a new, blank, default-named master to your document. Want to customize the name of the master before it gets added? Use Command-Option-click/Ctrl-Alt-click instead, telling InDesign to open the New Master dialog.

You can also make a new master page by duplicating one you already have. Our favorite way to duplicate a master page (or a document page, for that matter) is to Option-drag/Alt-drag the page icon, dropping it in an empty area of the Master Page section of the palette. (Press the mouse button down *before* you add the Option/Alt key to drag a copy of a master page. **Figure 2-8**)

In CS2, you can also duplicate a master page by right-clicking/Control-clicking on it and choosing Duplicate from the context menu.

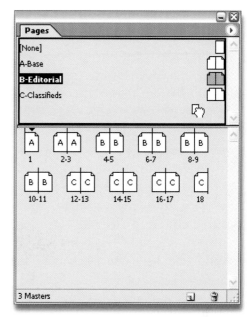

Figure 2-8: You can "peel off" copies of existing master pages to create new ones by Option/Alt-dragging.

Rename Your Master Pages

? **I double-click the name of a master page in my Pages palette, but it never changes to "edit mode." Right-clicking does nothing. It's aggravating that InDesign won't let me name my own darn master pages.**

☑ It *is* aggravating that you can't change the name in the palette. But you *can* change the name. To do so, you need to select the master by doing just what you did — clicking on its name or icon — and then choose "Master Options for [name of selected Master page]" from the Pages palette menu. If you don't like palette menus, try the

shortcut: After selecting the master page, Option-click/Alt-click on it to open the Options dialog box. Here you'll see the field where you can change the name. Make like Shakespeare, then click OK.

Create a Useful Prefix

? **Scrolling through my Pages palette, I see spread after spread of little icons with either an "A," "B," or "C" on them. I know they refer to the master page they're based on, but it's hard to remember that "A" is a Feature Spread, "B" is a page from the Classifieds, and "C" is a full-page ad.**

☑ These little page icons show the first three characters from the prefix of master page's name. By default, InDesign creates one-letter prefixes, and that's what you're seeing. But you can change that.

In the Pages palette, select the master page and then open the Master Options dialog box (from the palette menu or by Option-clicking/Alt-clicking on the master page.) In the Options dialog box, replace the existing prefix with a two- or three-letter prefix that will help you identify the master page when viewing the page icon. Three letters is a tight fit, so you might prefer two letters.

For example, if "A-Master" (or "A-Feature") is the name of the master spread for Features, you could replace the "A" in the Prefix field with "Ft" or "Ftr". Click OK to apply your changes. All document page icons that showed an "A" now show either "Ft" or "Ftr," whichever you entered (**Figure 2-9**).

Make a Gatefold Master

? Many spreads in my document will carry gatefolds. Creating these and formatting them one by one is a mighty tedious endeavor. Is there any way to make a master spread with three pages, so I can apply it to my document gatefold spreads?

☑ You can have up to ten pages in a master spread—just set the number of pages you want in the Master Options dialog box, found in the Pages palette menu. Note that changing the number of pages in a master spread doesn't affect spreads you've already created in your document—that is, applying a three-page master to a two-page doc-

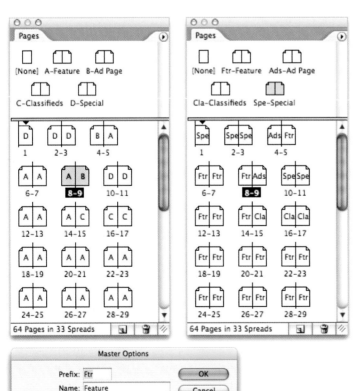

Figure 2-9: Changing the master page prefix in the Master Options dialog box makes identifying pages much easier.

ument spread won't add the additional page, you'll have to do that manually (see "Make a Gatefold Spread" on page 27). However, you can create a multi-page spread by dragging that master out into the document pages section of the Pages palette.

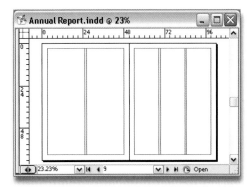

Figure 2-10: Master page spread with different margin and columns settings for each page in the spread.

Asymmetrical Master Spreads

? I want all my left-facing pages to have 3 columns, and all my right-facing pages to have 2 columns. The problem is, when I target my master spread and go to Layout > Margins and Columns, anything I enter there gets applied to both pages in the spread.

✔️ Don't target the entire master spread, just target one page of the spread at a time (click on the page icon, or — if the whole spread is already selected — Command/Ctrl-click on the pages you *don't* want to affect). Now when you make a trip to Layout > Margins and Columns, your change will apply to just that one page of the master page spread (**Figure 2-10**). Don't forget that InDesign doesn't limit you to making margin and column edits to a master page (as QuarkXPress does); you can change margins and columns on your document pages, too!

Reapply Right-Facing Masters to Non-Facing Pages

? After working on my document for a while, I turned off Facing Pages in

File > Document Setup, and now half of my pages look different! The odd-numbered pages are linked to the first page of the 2-page master spread instead of the second, right-facing page.

✔️ Yup, and here's how it went south on you (the fix is coming in a minute). Turning off Facing Pages only splits apart existing *document* spreads, not master page spreads. The master spreads get converted from facing pages to non-facing, yes, but they remain in two-page spread form: Page 1 and Page 2.

All the old pages that were based on that master are now linked to Page 1 (its *left*-facing page) of the master spread, including the document pages that used to be right-facing (and thus used to be linked to the *right*-facing side of the master spread).

It would be great if InDesign would split any existing master spreads into two single master pages when you turn off Facing Pages, maintaining the links between pages and their masters (or at least give you warning of what's about to happen) but alas, nope. Assuming you don't feel like going back to File > Document Setup and turning Facing Pages back on, you have two different options to get your pages looking right:

- In the Pages palette menu, turn off Allow Pages to Shuffle. Now drag page 3 over to the right side of page 2, but don't let go until you see a thick black line with an arrow coming out its side. Now repeat with page 5, 7, and so on. Unfortunately, there's nothing you can do about page 1 with this method.

- Copy the items from the right-facing page of the existing 2-page master. Now create a new, single-page master page and use Edit > Paste in Place to plonk down the objects on your new single master. Finally, apply that new master page (Pages palette menu > Apply Master to Pages) to the pages in your document that need it — the odd numbered pages.

Preview Master Page Changes

❓ I want to make some changes to my master page, but as I futz with it, I'd like to be able to see how my changes would affect the document pages linked to it. InDesign won't let me see both master page spreads and document spreads in the same window, so I guess it's impossible, huh?

 If you just want to change the margin or columns on your

master page, you can do this while still looking at your document pages. Just select (click *once* on) the master page in the Pages palette and choose Layout > Margins and Columns. If you turn on the Preview checkbox in the Margins and Columns dialog box, you can even see the changes in real time before clicking OK.

If you want to do something more to your master pages (add objects, move stuff around, and so on), then create a new, separate view of your document by choosing Window > Arrange > New Window. Making a new window isn't useful unless you can see both windows, so tell InDesign to put the two windows side-by-side by choosing Window > Arrange > Tile. In one window, open the master page; in the other window, view the document page.

As you edit the master page in one window, the other window shows how those changes affect the document pages linked to that master (**Figure 2-11**). When you're done, you can close either window, and go on your merry way.

Begone, Phantom Masters!

❓ My copy of InDesign is haunted, I'm sure of it. Listen to this: I'm working on a facing pages document. I have two different master spreads that I apply to various document spreads. On one of these spreads the left-facing page was based on A-Master and the right-facing page was based on B-Master. All looked hunky-dory in InDesign. But when I printed the document, that right-facing page contained all

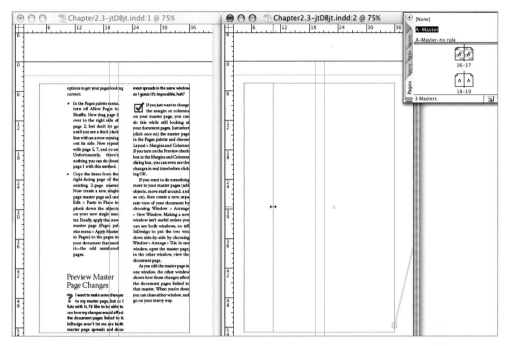

Figure 2-11: Look Ma, a master page preview!

---

the elements from *both* masters! How do I get rid of the Phantom A-Master on the page?

You've hit on a strange, creepy (but easily fixable) bug in InDesign CS's facing pages documents. The phantom master only appears when printing or exporting to PDF, and only if you turn *off* the Spreads checkbox in the Print/Export dialog box.

The cause of the bug appears to lie in the location of the master page objects. The fix is to keep all master page objects (on every master spread) at least 1 point away from the binding spine of the master spread. Masters with objects located within .99 points or less of the spine get the "Phantom" bug, and reappear on output when the circumstances are just as you describe.

Fortunately, this bug has been squashed in InDesign CS2.

One Master, Multiple Headers

The file that I'm working on has 12 chapters, and I'm afraid I might have to build 12 different master pages. You see, I need to put the chapter name as a running header at the top of each page. I know I can base one master page on another, but this still leaves me with the unpalatable idea of making 11 master pages more than I want to.

The solution isn't more master pages, it's setting up sections in your document. Each chapter in your document should begin as a new section (see the sidebar "Sections Step by Step"

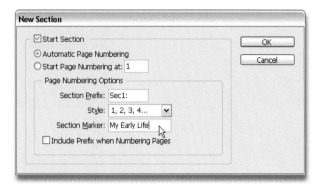

Figure 2-12: Enter the chapter titles in the Section Marker field of the Numbering & Section Options dialog box. Each section of your document can have its own Section Marker.

if you're not sure how to make sections). Once you do that, you can use InDesign's Section Marker feature to control the headers automatically.

In the text frame on your master page, place the cursor where you want the chapter name and then choose Type > Insert Special Character > Section Marker. You'll see the word "Section" appear, and you can format that word any way you want.

Now, for each chapter opener page in your document, open the Numbering & Section Options dialog box (this feature lives in the Pages palette menu), and enter the chapter title (up to 80 characters or so) in the Section Marker field (**Figure 2-12**).

Sections Step-by-Step

Anything having to do with sections in InDesign occurs in the Pages palette, so open that up.

1. Target the document page (click its page icon in the Pages palette) that represents the first page of a section.

2. From the palette menu, choose Numbering & Section Options.

3. In the Numbering & Section Options dialog box, click the Start Section checkbox to enable it. If you've targeted the first page of a document, this will be turned on by default.

4. Set your other options in the dialog box. For example, you can specify a new starting page number (but you don't have to) by clicking the radio button next to Start Page Numbering At, and entering the starting page number in the field. If you've used the Section Marker special character in your file (as described in the "One Master, Multiple Headers" solution on page 35), enter this section's Section Marker text in the field provided.

5. Click the OK button to close the dialog box. To create additional sections in the same document, follow the steps as outlined above.

The Pages palette will add a little downward pointing triangle above each page icon that is the start of a new section. Double-clicking the triangle opens the Numbering & Section Options dialog box and shows the current settings for that section.

Magically, InDesign replaces each occurrence of the Section Marker special character with whatever text you entered in the Section Marker field for that section, maintaining the formatting applied to the special character. That's working smart!

Object Manipulation

Position an Object Precisely

? **Why won't my objects move where I tell them to move? I select a frame and enter "2in" in the X Position field of the Control or Transform palette, meaning I want the object two inches in from the left of the page. Crystal clear, right? But when I click out of the field, the object apparently moves where it wants to; sometimes it even hangs way off into the left pasteboard. I've checked the 0/0 marker of the rulers and they're in the default location (upper left corner of my document), so that can't be it.**

☑ You're a recent QuarkXPress convert, aren't you? You can always tell the type, as they always assume those X and Y coordinates define the upper-left corner of an object. Hey, we've been there. You need to pay attention to the object proxy icon (seen on both the Control and Transform palettes). InDesign looks to this proxy to figure out which part of the object you're referring to when you ask it to transform (move, rotate, resize, and so on). There are 9 possible orientation points on the proxy: the four corners, the center of each of the four edges, and the center of the object (**Figure 2-13**).

Figure 2-13: The proxy icon is used to set a reference point for a selection.

So if you're trying to get the left edge of your object positioned exactly 2 inches from the left edge of the page, you need to click one of the three handles on the left side of the proxy first.

Long-Term Memory for Paste in Place

? **Man, do I love the Paste in Place command. My office has never been neater, because it's no longer littered with little scribbled notes of X and Y positions of the various things I've been cutting and pasting all day. The one fly in my ointment: I wish there were a way that Paste in Place could remember the positions of more than one Cut/Copy operation. I wouldn't need to keep going back to a previous page or open the old document to "reload" the clipboard, saving me mucho time.**

☑ Instead of the Clipboard, use an InDesign Library (File > New > Library). Objects you drag into a Library remember their position on the page you dragged them from. To place a Library item on the current page in the same position as its source, don't drag it out of the Library; instead *select* it in the Library palette and use the Library palette menu's Place Item command. As long as the current page has the same page size, orientation, and facing pages setting as the source of the item, InDesign automatically places it in the remembered position.

Select an Object Behind Another One

? I have a text frame, and behind one of the paragraphs I've placed a tinted rectangle. I need to adjust the tint of the rectangle, but since it's narrower than the frame, I can't get to it! Every time I click on the rectangle with a Selection tool, only the text frame gets selected. I'm so tired of using Arrange > Send to Back/Front… so very, very tired.

✔ Hold down the Command/Ctrl key while you click on the stack of objects with the Selection or Direct Select tool. The first click selects the top-most object, the second click selects the object right behind it, the third click selects the next one down, and so on. When you've reached bottom, the next click cycles back and selects the top-most object again. If you clicked one time too many, you can cycle backwards through the stack by adding the Option/Alt key to the mix.

Another thought: Ever hear of the Layers palette? You could move your text frame to a higher layer, then lock that

layer so you can see its items but can't select them. Target the layer holding your tinted rectangle, and you'll find you can click and drag the "behind" objects with ease.

"Select Next Object Below" Doesn't

? Instead of Command/Ctrl-clicking on a stack of objects to drill down and select the item I want, I thought I'd be smart and use the Select commands in the Object menu. I selected the object that's covering up the one I need, and chose Object > Select > Next Object Below. But the next object down wasn't selected; an object elsewhere on my spread was selected! I don't get it.

✔ Perplexing, isn't it? The problem is that the Select commands aren't "click-aware." They take the entire spread of the current layer into account when figuring out which object is behind or above the currently selected object. When you chose the "Select Next Object Below" command, InDesign probably selected some text frame way off in a corner or something; because according to its computer brain, that was the technically correct choice; it was the next object below *in the entire spread.*

Fortunately, the Select features in the context menu are smarter than the Select features in the Object menu. Select the topmost object, right-click (or Control-click if you use a Mac with just one mouse button) on the topmost object, and choose Next Object Below to select the object immediately below.

Drag an Object That's Behind Another One

? Success! I'm able to select the object I want, even though it's completely behind a bunch of other things. Change the fill and stroke, change the font, change the scale, no problem, the palettes know which object I'm talking about. Everything was going so well, then… failure! I can't drag it to a different position. The "behind" object is selected, but when I drag, I end up dragging the top object instead (even though it wasn't selected, quite weird).

☑ Drag on the "behind" object's *center point* (the little square icon that appears in the center of a selected object's frame) to move it (**Figure 2-14**). If you drag from anywhere else on the object, InDesign interprets it as a drag on the top object, as you've discovered. Another option is to Command-click/Ctrl-click until you reach that object and then — before you release the mouse button — start dragging. The object may not appear to be selected, but when you move the mouse, it moves.

Can't Select an Object in Front

? I *see* the object, the object *prints,* and it's *in front* of any overlapping objects, but I can't select it. What gives?

☑ It's almost certainly sitting on a locked layer. Open the Layers palette and see if there's a layer with a lock icon (a pencil with a red line through it); if so, click the icon to "unlock" the layer. You should be able to select the object

Cum iustin ea faci blam vulput nim num et lorper acidui tatis esse modolortie tie molore magna feumsandit lutatue ero et, con et lutatio dion ute te modiam, ver sum quam vel ea feum ver ad dolo.

DOLOBOREETUM VEL IUREET NIM DELENIM AD MIN ET, SI.

Bor accummo lobortie cortis nonulpu tpatie dio odolore veniat am nonsequat lum ea feuisisit, quatio dolor se molent verilisse dio od do odolorem diat, quipit lutpate moleseq uipisci blan heniat. Agnisi. Ed magnim volorting ex etum et ulputat.
Tum ing esto cortinis dolore modionsenim iusci tisit incinibh esed euismod modolutat dolorpe raesto conulla commy nonullutpat. Ut ulpute modignim irit

Figure 2-14: Drag from the center handle to move an object that's behind another one.

now as usual. You might want to think about it a bit first, though. Perhaps it's on a locked layer for a reason?

Can Select an Object, but Can't Move it

? Here's a strange one. I've got a text frame that I can select, and I can edit the text inside it, but I can't resize it, move it or delete it. And no, it's not on a locked layer.

☑ Are you seeing a little padlock cursor appear when you try to drag a handle on it or drag the item itself to move it? That's telling you the text frame has "Lock Position" enabled. Another quick check is to right-click on the item or look in the Object menu to see if there's an "Unlock Position" menu item, if so, that's what happened. Choose that command to unlock it, and the menu item reverts back to "Lock Position." Now you can move and resize the object.

Keyboard Shortcuts for Align and Distribute

? **Why isn't the Align palette listed in Edit > Keyboard Shortcuts > Product Area: Palette Menus? I click on the palette's align and distribute icons all the time and would like to assign keyboard shortcuts to the ones I use most often.**

✅ The align and distribute functions are hiding in the Product Area: Object Editing panel of the Edit Keyboard Shortcuts dialog box.

Distribute Oddly-Shaped Objects Evenly

? **Hi guys, trying to neaten up a photo spread here. The pictures vary in dimension, and I'd like to space them apart by exactly .25 inches. When I select the pictures, enter ".25in" in the Use Spacing field in the Align palette, and click the Distribute Left Edges icon, the pictures end up overlapping each other. I've tried all the icons and can't figure it out. All I want is .25" of space between each picture in a single row.**

✅ If the pictures were all the same width, you'd be on the right track. For example, if each image was two

Figure 2-15: For some reason, InDesign hides the Distribute Spacing command. Choose Show Options in the Align palette menu to see it.

inches wide, you could enter "2.25in" in the Use Spacing field, and click any of the three Distribute Horizontal icons (Left edge, Center, Right edge). The pictures would space themselves out with .25" of space between each.

However, when you're dealing with objects of varying dimensions, you have to use the *secret* Distribute command called Distribute Spacing (as opposed to Distribute Objects, the one you were using, the default). To see the Distribute Spacing options, choose Show Options from the Align palette menu (**Figure 2-15**).

Enter .25" in Distribute Spacing's "Use Spacing" field, and click the Distribute Horizontal Space icon. Exactly .25" of space separates each object. Voilà.

Overlap Objects Evenly

? The Distribute commands are great, but how about the opposite, some Overlap commands? Am I the only one who'd like to be able to exactly specify by how much a number of objects, currently spread all over the place, should align *and* overlap each other?

✓ Yes, you're the only one. But Adobe cares about you so much, they've included that feature in InDesign. All you need to do is enter a negative number (use a hyphen for the negative sign) in either of the two Use Spacing fields in the Align palette.

Align Selected Objects to a Given Object

? Illustrator lets you choose which object other objects should align themselves to, and I've grown to rely on that feature. But as far as I can tell, you can't do that InDesign. If I select three objects whose top edges are located in different vertical positions on the page, and click Align Top Edges, the object that's "highest" on the page stays put, and the other two jump up to align with it. But what if I want two of the items to align their top edges with the item that's "lowest" on the page?

✓ Select the object you want the others to align themselves to and lock its position (Object > Lock Position) on the page. Now select all the objects, including the locked one, and click the Align or Distribute command you want. Since locked objects can't move, InDesign aligns/distributes the other selected objects to the locked one.

If two or more objects are locked, InDesign decides which one should control the action based on its position (e.g., the "higher" locked object would be the one that all the others align their top edges to). Objects that aren't locked jump into alignment with it, the remaining locked objects stay in their original position.

Guideline Grief

Create a Spread Guide on a Single Page

? I need a guideline that reaches across the whole spread! I know I can drag a guide out of the ruler but sometimes it goes across just one spread and sometimes it goes across just a single page.

✓ You can always create a spread guide in InDesign by dragging a guide out of a ruler and releasing the mouse button over the pasteboard. But that doesn't help when you're zoomed in and can't *see* the pasteboard. Fortunately, if you hold down the Command/Ctrl key while you drag out a guideline, it will always come in as a spread guide.

Snap Ruler Guides to Tick Marks

? A few times in my InDesign life, I've been able to drag a ruler guide and drop it on the page where I want, usually at an even division of the rulers: 12p6, 17.25" and so on. The majority of the time, guides drop at weird locations like 12p6.4215 or 17.6011". I have to select the guide and use the Control or Transform palette X and Y position fields to move it to a more useable location.

✓ This is one of David's favorite InDesign tricks — so simple and yet so helpful: Hold down the Shift key while you drag a ruler guide and it will snap to the nearest ruler increment ("tick mark").

Clear Some of the Guidelines

? I've inherited a document from someone who added too many guides to the page, and I'd like to clear some out — not all, just some. So I grab the Selection tool, click the first guide I want to get rid of, and press the Delete key. Same for the next guide, and the next guide. Three down, 47 to go. Click, delete, click, delete, click, delete, are we having fun yet? No.

✓ After you select the first guide, hold down the Shift key to add guides to your selection, and get rid of them with one hit of the Delete key. That'll save you some steps.

Even better: Use the Selection tool to drag a selection rectangle over a group of guides. You don't have to drag over the entire length of the guides, just a part of them. As long as no part of a page object falls in the selection rectangle, this maneuver will select the guides alone, allowing you to clear them with a tap on the Delete key. (If part of an object does lie within the selection rectangle, only the object(s) are selected, and guides are ignored. **Figure 2-16.**)

A combination of the two techniques will make quick work out of a guideline mess.

But instead of deleting all those guides — they might have been put there for a purpose–consider moving them to a different layer and then hiding the layer.

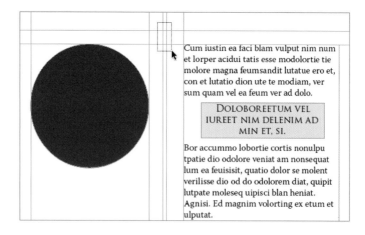

Figure 2-16: Plow a selection rectangle through a bunch of ruler guides to select them all.

Cum iustin ea faci blam vulput nim num et lorper acidui tatis esse modolortie tie molore magna feumsandit lutatue ero et, con et lutatio dion ute te modiam, ver sum quam vel ea feum ver ad dolo.

DOLOBOREETUM VEL IUREET NIM DELENIM AD MIN ET, SI.

Bor accummo lobortie cortis nonulpu tpatie dio odolore veniat am nonsequat lum ea feuisisit, quatio dolor se molent verilisse dio od do odolorem diat, quipit lutpate moleseq uipisci blan heniat. Agnisi. Ed magnim volorting ex etum et ulputat.

Clear All the Guidelines

? I keep searching through the menus for one that says Delete Guides. Sadly, the little elves never add one while I'm sleeping. C'mon, guys! I can't believe Adobe left this one out.

☑ Hey, we agree with you, pal. Smells like an oversight. The good news is that there are at least a couple ways to remove all the ruler guides from the current page/spread, and they're both fast and easy.

Via the menu: Choose Create Guides from the Layout menu. Don't enter anything into the Row and Column fields (or reset them to 0 if there's another number there). Turn on the "Remove Existing Ruler Guides" checkbox at the bottom checkbox and click OK. Bob's your uncle, the ruler guides are gone.

Via the keyboard: Press Command-Option-G/Ctrl-Alt-G to select all the guides in the current page/spread. Press Delete and they're gone.

Via a script: The previous methods only delete one spread's guides at a time. This AppleScript deletes every guide in your document:

```
tell application "Adobe InDesign CS2"
    delete every guide of document 1
end tell
```

Align and Distribute Guides

? I dragged out four guides and need them spaced exactly 14p6 apart. So I have to spend twenty minutes in deep communion with the rulers, Control pal-ette fields and my calculator, trying to figure out things like, "Is 39p3 is an even multiple of 14p6?"

☑ If you haven't noticed it by now, we'll clue you in: Guides can be selected with the Selection tool just like any other object in InDesign. Similarly, multiple guides can be selected (Shift-click to add additional ones to the selection) and acted upon by commands in many of the menu bars and palettes.

Knowing that, here are two possible fixes for your situation:

- Select all four guides, and use one of the Align palette's Distribute commands, with "14p6" entered in the Use Spacing field, to space them out (**Figure 2-17**).

- Drag out one guide and place it exactly where you want the first guide to go. Keep it selected, go to Edit > Step And Repeat, enter "3" for the Repeat Number: field, and "14p6" for the vertical or horizontal offset. Click OK and you'll get the guides you want.

Change Guide Colors on the Fly

? It's nice that I can change the default colors for all the ruler guides (and column/margin guides etc.) in the Preferences dialog box, but I want more. I'd like some ruler guides to be one color, and others to be a different color. I thought I could select a few guides (Shift-click with a Selection tool) and use the Colors or Swatches palette to change their colors, but it doesn't work. What gives?

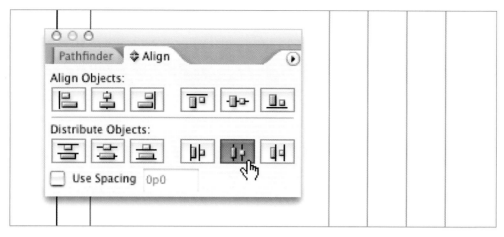

Figure 2-17: The Align/Distibrute commands work on ruler guides too.

✓ It's all possible if you know where to look. To change the colors of certain ruler guides, select them and choose a different color in the Layout > Ruler Guides dialog box (or right-button click and choose Ruler Guides from the context menu).

Create Mixed-Width Columns

? **I want three columns on my pages: Two wide ones for the main stories and one narrow one on the outside for miscellany. The Margins and Columns dialog box doesn't let me do this, it always creates columns of even width.**

✓ Create your base number of columns with Layout > Margins and Columns. Click the OK button to close the dialog box, then use the Selection tool to drag the column gutters (the two vertical guides defining the space between two columns — they move in unison) to the position you want. Note that column guides are locked by default in InDesign CS2, so you must first select View > Grids & Guides > Lock Column Guides to turn that option off.

To drag a column guide, you have to click on one of the two guides, not the gutter space between the guides. Unfortunately, there's no way to position the guides precisely with the Control palette, so remember to hold down the Shift key while you drag (which snaps the guides to the nearest ruler tick mark).

Locking Column Guides

? **I'm finding that it's too easy to move column guides accidentally! How do I lock them in place?**

✓ In InDesign CS2 you can lock column guides by choosing View > Grids & Guides > Lock Column Guides. However, in InDesign CS, you, um, well, er... you can't lock them. You just have to be extra careful when clicking around column guides. Or, forget the column guides feature entirely and drag out your own guides on the master page. Regular page guides can be locked or even placed on a locked layer in either version.

Change Margin Guides Throughout a Document

? I accidentally specified the wrong margins when I created this document, and didn't realize it till I had laid out a bunch of pages. To change the margin settings to what they should be, I tried going to File > Document Setup, but "Margins" is not a choice there. (Yet Bleed and Slug are there—go figure!) So I went to Layout > Margins and Columns and entered the settings I wanted, but that only changed it for the current page I was on. My document has 48 pages, do I have to do this to every single page?

✓ If you ever find yourself about to do the same action to every page in your document, think "master page." Single-click the name of the master page in the Pages palette to make it active (shift-click additional master page icons if you have more than one), *then* go to Margins and Columns, make your changes and click OK.

Since (assumably) all your document pages are based on master pages (even if you never touch a master page, that's the default behavior), changing the margins settings on the master will force all document pages to reflect the same margin and column settings. Note that changes you make to a master page's margins and columns will not affect any document pages already customized by an individual hit from the Margins and Columns dialog box.

Margins and Columns can also affect more than one page or master page at a time; just select the pages you want in the Pages palette before choosing it.

Margins and Columns Don't Change Page Items

? No matter what I do, the changes I make to the Margins and Columns dialog box don't affect the objects on my page. Sure, the margins change, but the text and picture frames on my pages don't! I've even tried chanting "Lorum Ipsum" while burning candles in a dimly-lit room. No dice.

✓ Yes, this one always seems to trip up ex-QuarkXPress users. You need to take a trip to Layout > Layout Adjustment. This is the feature that controls whether changes to your margins and columns (and page size alterations, too) are applied to objects on your page. By default, it's turned off so you don't accidentally mess up your layout. Turn the feature on and InDesign suddenly pays attention to all the frames and lines that are within a couple points from a margin or column guide.

To Delete the Undeletable Guide

? Is it my imagination or do some ruler guides just refuse to leave the building? No matter what I do, including checking the View menu to confirm that Lock Guides is off, there are some I can't delete. How do I get rid of these loathsome undead—and how did they get that way, so I can prevent it from happening again?

☑ If you can select the guide but you can't move or delete it, you or someone else working on the file probably locked the guide into position (Object > Lock Position). To clear a position-locked guide, select it, unlock it (Object > Unlock Position), and delete it. (Note: Turning on the "Remove Existing Ruler Guides" option from the Layout > Create Guides dialog will also remove position-locked guides.)

If you *can't* select the guide, it's probably sitting on a master page or on a locked layer. Still quite fixable. To delete a master page guideline on a document page, Command-Shift-click/Ctrl-Shift-click on the guide to override it and select it in one fell swoop, then press Delete. (Or you could just go to the master page and select it/delete it there.)

Finally, to delete a guide on a locked layer, you have to unlock the layer. Click on the red-slashed pencil icon next to the name of the layer in the Layers palette so it goes away. Now you can select the guide and delete it. Don't forget to lock the layer again (by clicking in the same square in the Layers palette) when you're done. It's common courtesy.

Create Object Guides

? It would make my life so much easier if I could select an object, wave a magic wand, and have InDesign create four guides, one on each edge of the object. Since Harry and Hermione aren't anywhere

nearby, I'm doomed to manual drudgery and have to create the guides myself.

☑ When you drag a guide near an object, it usually doesn't snap to the side of the object. Here's the trick: First select the object with the Selection tool, then drag the guide on top of the object's corner or side handles. Guides *do* snap to those!

However, if you need to quickly add guides to all four sides of an object, it's time for a script. The InDesign CS installation disc comes with sample Scripts that work in both Mac and Windows. One of the scripts, Add Guides, is your magic wand. Install it (drag the script into the InDesign>Preset>Scripts folder) and run it from the Scripts palette on a selected object (**Figure 2-18**).

> **TIP:** Don't have time to shuffle through the office storage closet to find the InDesign CS installation CD-ROM? Most of the sample scripts found there are also posted in the InDesign section of the Adobe Studio Exchange, free for the downloading: *http://share.studio.adobe.com/*

Disappearing Guides

? Help! Suddenly all my guidelines are gone. Not just the ruler guides, but also all my margin and column guides, frame edges, even things I had on the pasteboard! I double-checked the View menu to make sure Hide Guides was off (it was) and that Show Frame Edges was

Figure 2-18: The AddGuides.js script can create a number of different guides for the selected object.

on (ditto). Nothing helps. Is there anything else I can do, other than dragging pages to a new document—which has no problem showing the guides?

✓ You'd be amazed at how many people find themsevles in this predicament. Fortunately, all is not lost. To fix this, you just need to buy a new computer. Just kidding! Most likely you inadvertently switched to Preview mode, which hides all non-printing objects. To get back to Normal View mode, click the icon at the bottom left of the Tools palette, or press the keyboard shortcut that toggles between both views: "W." While in Preview mode, dragging a new guideline from either ruler will also bring you back to Normal View.

Loving those Layers

Move Objects from One Layer to Another

? I wanted to move an object to a higher layer in my Layers palette. So I clicked on the object and then clicked on the layer I want to move it to, but the object didn't jump to that layer, as I expected. Then I tried dragging the object on top of the layer in the Layers palette, but that didn't work either, and a co-worker looking over my shoulder started laughing at me. Finally, I tried cutting the object to the clipboard, selecting the new layer and Pasting in Place (Edit > Paste in Place), but it just ended up back in the same spot in the

original layer. This is so frustrating. (And embarrassing.)

✓ That last method you tried—Cut, target different layer, Paste in Place—would have worked if the "Paste Remembers Layers" command was turned off (unchecked) in your Layers palette menu. Just so you know. However, you don't have to jump through all these hoops to move an object to a different layer though. Otherwise, no one would use the palette!

Here's what your "colleague" knew but was too mean to share with you. When you select an object, the Layers palette shows a little proxy icon to the right of the layer it's currently on, a little

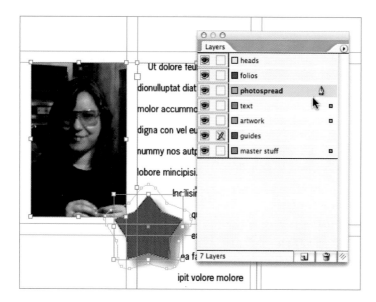

Figure 2-19: Move these objects to the target layer by cut and paste or by grouping.

colored square that's the same color as the layer's selection color. Drag that little icon to another layer, and the selected object(s) that icon represents will move to that layer as well.

Think of the Layer proxy icon as a selection's leash, and the selected objects as the dog(s) they're attached to. The dogs have to follow the location of the leash, so just drag the leash and the dogs will follow. Gently, please.

Move Objects from Many Layers to Another

? **I've got a pile of objects selected on my page — text frames, lines, a couple graphics — and want to move them all to their own new layer. But currently, these guys live on a bunch of different layers, so when I select them all, my Layers palette shows multiple proxy icons. If I drag one of the proxies to the new layer, only that object moves to the new layer. I can think of, oh, about a thousand better ways to**

spend my time than dragging little squares, one by one, from one layer to another.

✓ For this technique, make sure that Paste Remembers Layers is turned off in the Layers palette menu. You don't want objects to remember their layers for now. Select all the objects you want to move, choose Edit > Cut, target the new layer, and choose Edit > Paste or Edit > Paste in Place. All the objects are pasted into the targeted layer (**Figure 2-19**).

Another way to do this (that avoids messing with the Paste Remembers Layers setting) is to drag just *one* of the proxies to the new layer, then choose Object > Group. Since a group of items can only be in one layer, InDesign moves the rest of the selected objects to the topmost layer containing one of the objects and groups them there. Immediately choose Object > Ungroup, and you've got what you want.

Note that the first method works when moving objects to *any* layer, the second works only if you're trying to move objects to a layer that's higher up than their current layer assignments.

Move Objects to a Locked or Hidden Layer

? I want to add an object to a layer that's currently locked, but InDesign won't let me drag the proxy icon to it. Same thing if the layer I want to move it to is hidden. I have to unlock or reveal the layer first, then move, then re-lock or re-hide the layer. Blech.

✓ Hold down the Command/Ctrl key when you drag and drop the layer proxy icon to force a hidden or locked layer to accept the object. Pretty tricky, eh?

Figure 2-20: The Paste Remembers Layers command is the key to importing layers from another document.

Import Layers from Another Document

? There's no Load Layers command in the Layers palette. To recreate my thirty-layer deep, finely-tuned, work-of-art set of layers I created in my old document, I have to reconstruct it, layer by layer, in my current document.

✓ Open the old document and select (via Shift-click) a bunch of objects — one item on each layer you want to bring over. You should see the entire right side of the Layers palette basically filled with a rainbow of layer proxy icons. Copy the selection to the clipboard (Edit > Copy), and switch to your new document. In the Layers palette menu, make sure the Paste Remembers Layers option is turned on. If it's not, select the menu item to toggle it on (**Figure 2-20**).

Now choose Edit > Paste. You'll see both the objects and their layers are added to your document. The superfluous objects are still selected, so press Delete to get rid them in one swoop. The layers they rode in on remain in your Layers palette.

Layers

👁 ▢ ▢ Layer 1

1 Layer

New Layer...
Duplicate Layer "Layer 1"...
Delete Layer "Layer 1"

Layer Options for "Layer 1"...

Hide All Layers
Lock All Layers

Paste Remembers Layers

Merge Layers
Delete Unused Layers

Small Palette Rows

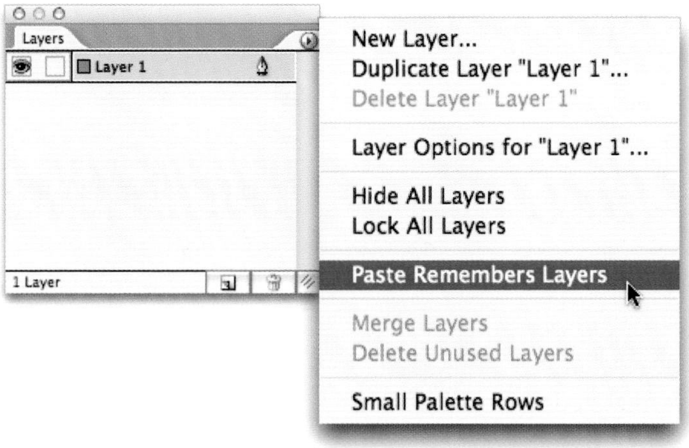

Select Everything
on a Layer

? I need to select every object on one of my layers. The only way I can do this, as far as I can tell, is to choose Edit > Select All and deselect every object with a selection color different than the layer I want.

☑ Wow, that's a lot of work! Try Option/Alt-clicking the layer name next time, which selects all the objects in that layer.

3

Text and Tables

Text and Tables

DROP SHADOWS? WHO CARES. Button states? Big deal. Old school publication designers and production artists — the ones who remember waxers and press-on type — know that the make-or-break feature of any page layout program is how it handles type. Importing, threading, formatting, and tweaking a document's text usually account for the lion's share of layout work. If the program's default way of handling type-related tasks constantly works against you, creating professionally-typeset stories with it is a frustrating journey down a long and weary road.

Thus, InDesign arrives on the pro's desktop as welcome as a tall glass of cold spring water after a long walk 'cross a West-Texas county. Due to the quiet elegance of InDesign's Paragraph Composer and the common-sense justification default settings, type in InDesign simply looks better right from the start. Add to that the power and flexibility of its Open Type support (that cool Glyphs palette!); ingenious time-savers like nested styles and the Story Editor; and the incredibly rich table formatting options (struggles with tabular columns of text fade into distant memory); and you've got yourself a mighty text machine there, my friend.

With so many power features, and the ubiquitous need to work with them, regardless of publication type; it's no wonder this chapter is the longest in the book! Drink well, and drink deeply.

Selecting and Editing

Get a Word Count

? Our authors give us Microsoft Word files for stories, but I can't figure out how to give them the word count they should be aiming for. I can set and style placeholder text in the layout file, but how can I then count the words so I can tell the authors what their target count is before they start to write? InDesign doesn't have a Word Count function like Microsoft Word.

✓ Indeed it do! After you fill your frames with dummy text (choose Type > Fill with Placeholder Text), click anywhere in the frame with your Type tool and look at the Info palette. You'll see a count for that story's characters, words, lines and paragraphs. Or, if you select some text, you'll see a word count for that selected text.

If you install the free TextCount.js script (see page 162 for more on scripts), you can also get a count of all the words in a selection, even across multiple frames — useful if a feature story contains unthreaded text frames — or all the words in an entire InDesign file.

Select Spaces and Punctuation

? When I double-click a word and delete it or cut it to the clipboard, InDesign doesn't remember to delete/cut the word's trailing space; leaving behind two spaces in a row.

✓ We can tell you're probably using InDesign CS because they fixed this in CS2. Yes, it's a pain. Try this: Double-click the word as usual, then press Shift/Left- or Shift/Right-arrow on your keyboard. That adds a single character or space to the selection. Tapping Shift/Right-arrow a couple times is also handy for selecting a comma (for example) and a space to the right of a selected word.

If you are using InDesign CS2, then someone snuck onto your machine and turned off the Adjust Spacing Automatically When Cutting and Pasting Words checkbox in the Type panel of the Preferences dialog box. Turn that back on and you'll be in hog heaven.

Accessing Overset Text

? InDesign shows the same red overset icon whether I'm over by one character or ten thousand. I wish I could quickly select and cut — or even just peek at — what's actually causing the overset, without resizing the frame or creating a temporary threaded one.

✓ If you're pretty sure you want to get rid of the overset text (such as if it's due to trailing empty carriage returns), you can quickly place the cursor at the end of the visible text and then press the "Select to End (of story)" keyboard shortcut: Command-Shift-End/Ctrl-Shift-End. That's the "End" key on your keyboard, usually above the arrow keys by the Home and Page Up/Down

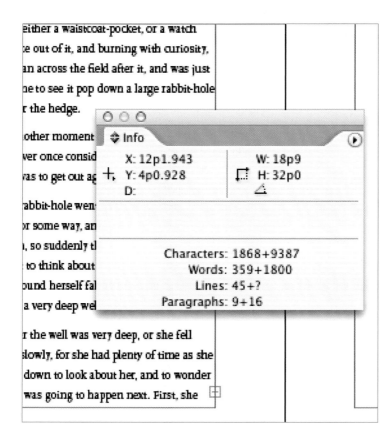

either a waistcoat-pocket, or a watch
te out of it, and burning with curiosity,
an across the field after it, and was just
he to see it pop down a large rabbit-hole
r the hedge.

other moment
ver once consid
vas to get out ag

abbit-hole wen-
or some way, an
, so suddenly th
to think about
ound herself fal
a very deep wel

r the well was very deep, or she fell
slowly, for she had plenty of time as she
down to look about her, and to wonder
was going to happen next. First, she

Info

X: 12p1.943   W: 18p9
Y: 4p0.928   H: 32p0
D:

Characters: 1868+9387
Words: 359+1800
Lines: 45+?
Paragraphs: 9+16

Figure 3-1: The Info palette tells you if and by how much text is overset by adding a + symbol after its usual copy counts (characters, words, lines and paragraphs).

The Info palette also comes in handy here. As long as the Type tool is active in the story—in either Layout or Story Editor—the Info palette shows a live readout of how much text, if any, is overset—it's the number of words after the plus sign (**Figure 3-1**).

ones. Now you can press Delete or cut the text to the clipboard.

More often, though, the overset text has important content you may want to keep. You can see that content—and edit it—without messing with the text frame. Open the Story Editor (Edit > Edit in Story Editor) or press Command-Y/ Ctrl-Y to see all the text in your story, including overset text, in a new, "just for editing" window. InDesign CS2 even offers an easy-to-identify "overset" marker in the Story Editor window.

As you work in the Story Editor, the layout view of the story keeps pace with your edits. Once you've cut enough copy in the Story Editor, the overset icon in the layout's view of the text frame disappears. Perfecto! Close the Story Editor window or press Command-Y/Ctrl-Y again to return to the layout.

Quick Story Editor/ Layout Jumping

? I made some extensive edits to a multiple-page story in the Story Editor window. When I close the window, I always have to spend precious minutes scrolling through the layout to find the copy I just edited.

☑ It's a natural tendency to click on any visible portion of the document page to bring that window to the front, or to do as you did, which was clicking the Story Editor's Close box to close it altogether. Resist the impulse, and instead use its keyboard shortcut to jump back and forth. When you press Command/Ctrl-Y, InDesign jumps to the Story Editor window or the document layout window (whichever is not currently active) *and* automatically scrolls to match the current text cursor position.

Placing and Flowing Text

Take Control of Show Import Options

? It seems that whenever I *want* to see the Import Options dialog box of the text file I'm about to Place, I forget to turn on the Show Import Options checkbox and have to re-Place the file, this time carefully clicking the checkbox; yet when I *don't* want to see the dialog box; the checkbox happens to be checked and bang, there it is, the Import Options dialog box that I don't need and have to click out of. Is this some sort of practical joke?

✓ Yes, it is. Isn't it funny? No, seriously, just keep the checkbox turned off. InDesign maintains the most recent "on/off" state of the checkbox in subsequent trips to the Place dialog box, so you should only have to do this once per document.

Then the next time you *want* to see the Options dialog box, open the Place dialog box as usual and select the name of the file. Hold down the Shift key when you click the Open button to invoke the Import Options dialog box for the selected file. After a few times this method will become an ingrained habit.

Fix Import Problems with MS Word Files

? Some Microsoft Word .doc files import with missing characters, or worse, they don't import at all—the file is grayed out in the Place dialog box.

✓ First, make sure that Microsoft Word's Preferences > Save panel does *not* have "Allow Fast Saves" enabled (in some versions of Word it's on by default). Fast Saves have long been known to cause problems when importing those files into any page layout program.

Then open your document in Word, and choose File > Save As. You should be able to place that new file in InDesign now without any problems. No? Try saving the Word file as an RTF (Rich Text Format) file and make sure the file name ends with ".rtf"; that's often more reliable.

Still have missing text? Some InDesign users have traced the problem to Word files that contain Page Breaks embedded in text paragraphs (instead of sitting in their own paragraph as the Good Lord intended). Open the Word file and check/correct those if necessary, then try again.

(For problems having to do with placing Word and Excel tables, see the Tables section at the end of this chapter.)

Figure 3-2: InDesign's Forgotten Cursor, Semi-Autoflow.

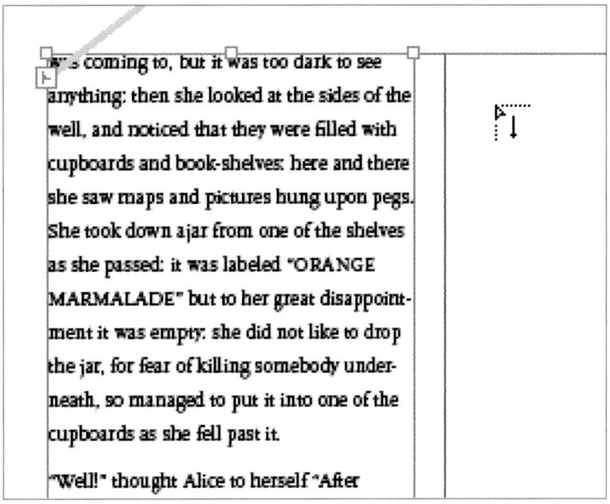

Shake Off that Loaded Cursor

? How do I get rid of the loaded cursor icon? I changed my mind after clicking Open in the Place dialog box, but I can't seem to change the cursor back to a "normal" one.

☑ Clicking any tool in the Tools palette will fix it, but why bother dragging the cursor over there — just tap any letter on your keyboard. Chances are it's a keyboard shortcut to one of the tools. Hit the "V" key (the shortcut for the Selection tool) if you want to be consistent about it.

Get that Loaded Cursor Back

? Half the time that I place a file, it replaces something in my document that I didn't want replaced. Sometimes a text file replaces an image, sometimes an image appears in the middle of text frame, or worse, sometimes I don't know *where* it's gone to. What's going on?

☑ Get in the habit of pressing the keyboard shortcut Command-Shift-A/Ctrl-Shift-A (Deselect All) every time you're about to Place a file. That way, even if the Place dialog box's "Replace Selected Item" is turned on (the root of the problem), the imported file won't replace anything — because nothing is selected.

While you're ingraining that habit into the InDesign grooves of your brain, remember there's always our friend, Undo (Command-Z/Ctrl-Z). That will extract the file from wherever it ended up (un-replacing the original item) and give you back the loaded cursor you wanted. If you Undo one more time, it's as though you had never selected Place in the first place.

Autoflow Without Adding Pages

? I want to autoflow a long text file into a series of pages I've already set up with column guides, but I don't want InDesign to add additional pages. Possible?

☑ The little known "semi-autoflow" function will do exactly that. Load your cursor with the text file, hover over the first empty column, and hold down Shift-Option/Shift-Alt when you click (**Figure 3-2**).

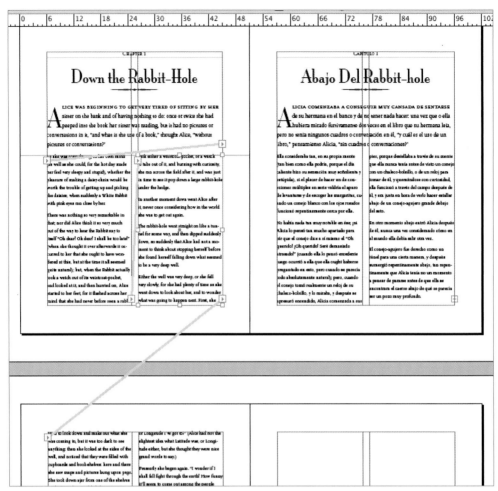

Figure 3-3: Multiple text flows in the same document are easy to set up in InDesign.

Create Multiple Autoflows on the Same Master Spread

❓ In our facing-pages publication, we need the left-hand pages to show an original manuscript in English, and the right-hand pages to show the Spanish translation. The two manuscripts are each hundreds of pages long, so we want to use InDesign's automatic text flow feature. But the Master Text Frame option in the New Document dialog box allows for only one automatic text flow, filling both pages of each spread with the same file.

☑ InDesign automatically flows stories from the left page to the right page of each spread because the two text frames on the master are threaded (linked) by default. To unthread the master text frame, open the facing-pages Master from the Pages palette. Click the left-hand page text frame with the Selection tool to see the In and Out ports, then double-click on its Out port to break the thread.

You end up with two individual, unthreaded frames, one per page. Now go to page 3 of your document, the right-facing page of the first two-page spread, and autoflow the Spanish manuscript (Shift-click with the loaded text cursor). The text fills up all the right-hand pages, creating additional spreads as necessary. Then make page 2 active, the first left-hand page of the document, and auto-flow the English manuscript. The English text fills up all the left-hand pages of the document, creating additional ones as needed (**Figure 3-3**). Note you don't have to start on page 1 and 2; you can begin the autoflow on any page you like.

What if you want two autoflowing threads on the *same* page? No problem. Manually drag out two text frames (let's call them L1 and L2) on the left-facing master and two (R1 and R2) on the right-facing master. Use the Selection tool to thread frame L1 to R1, then thread L2 to R2. InDesign is smart enough to know that in the document, when L2 becomes overset, it should continue on the next spread by linking to L1.

> **TIP:** Even if your facing-pages master has no text frames at all, InDesign will autoflow text from the left page to right page in auto-generated frames in the document because it assumes that's what you want. You can override the default left-to-right autoflow by manually adding frames to the master spread as described.

Superfast Frame Threading

? Is there a faster way to create a series of empty threaded text frames other than drawing each one out, one by one, with the Type tool; then switching to the Selection tool and threading them one by one?

Create the first frame with the Type tool as usual, then click on its Out port with the Selection tool. Your cursor is now loaded with "phantom" text. If you hold down the Option/Alt key while you drag out additional text frames with that cursor, each frame will be threaded to the previous one. A text file placed into the first frame will automatically fill up each additional frame you threaded to it.

This also works with actual text. Starting with a text frame that's over-set, click on its overset icon to load the cursor with the additional text. Then Option/Alt-drag a series of text frames until all the text is placed.

Add Pages Automatically as You Enter Text

? It's quite aggravating that InDesign doesn't automatically add another page when I'm entering text at the bottom of a text frame and need to continue typing in a new frame threaded to it. I made sure to set up a Master Page text frame just so it would. But it won't.

 For this you'll have to turn to one of two InDesign plug-ins: Inflow, from EmSoftware; or EasyFlow, from 65bit. Both work about the same; except EasyFlow is a little cheaper and you can turn its "auto page insertion" feature off if necessary from the Pages palette menu. With InFlow, you'd have to disable the plug-in and restart InDesign to turn it off. (On the other hand, why would you ever want to turn it off?)

Inflow: *http://www.emsoftware.com*
EasyFlow: *http://www.65bit.com*

TIP: To see InDesign's thread connectors—lines connecting the In ports and Out ports of threaded text frames—you need to set three options correctly: 1. Be sure you're in Normal view (not Preview mode); 2. Turn on Show Text Threads from the View menu; and 3. Select any of the frames in the threaded story with the Selection tool (not the Type tool).

Text Frames

Fit Frames to Text Perfectly

? I hate extraneous space at the bottom of my text frames. Since I want the frame to hug the text as tightly as possible, I'm constantly dragging on the frame to resize it after every edit. While I'm undergoing treatment for this compulsion, my psychotherapist would like to know if there's an automatic way to do this in InDesign?

☑ At any time while you're working in a single-column text frame you can press Command-Option-C/Ctrl-Alt-C. That reduces the frame to hug the text content (same as choosing the command from the Object > Fitting menu).

A couple caveats: It doesn't work on frames with more than one column, even if there's plenty of extraneous space at the bottom of each column due to forced column break(s).

Also, if the frame is only one line deep and its last character has any negative tracking or kerning applied to it, an obscure bug causes InDesign CS to shrink the frame too much, resulting in an overset frame. (This was fixed in CS2, thank goodness.)

Keep the Descenders Inside the Frame

? A text frame that's been set to vertically align on the bottom (via Object > Text Frame Options) aligns the *baseline* of the characters to the bottom, leaving their descenders hanging out in the breeze below the frame. Same thing happens when I choose Object > Fitting > Fit Frame to Content.

☑ This is InDesign's normal behavior and just takes getting used to. It's a little jarring, though, if you're recovering from a 10-year QuarkXPress

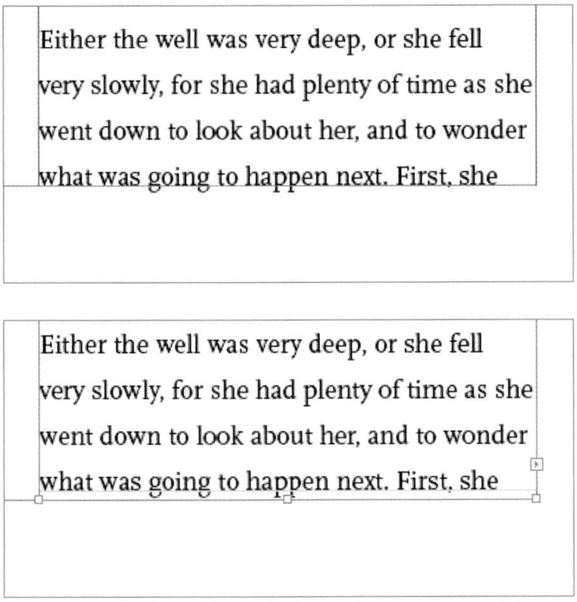

> Either the well was very deep, or she fell very slowly, for she had plenty of time as she went down to look about her, and to wonder what was going to happen next. First, she

> Either the well was very deep, or she fell very slowly, for she had plenty of time as she went down to look about her, and to wonder what was going to happen next. First, she

Figure 3-4: If you don't like how InDesign lets the descenders of text dangle below the bottom edge of a text frame (top), add a bit of Text Inset to the bottom (bottom).

jag. That program uses a line's leading amount, not its baseline, for the bottom of a text box; so the descenders were always inside the frame. That may be useful if the text frame has a stroke!

To force an InDesign text frame to act like a QuarkXPress text box in this regard, apply a dose of Text Inset (in Object > Text Frame Options) to the bottom the text frame. That will keep your descenders neatly tucked into the frame (**Figure 3-4**).

The Side Handles Haven't Gone Anywhere

? When I click on a shallow text frame (like one with just a line or two of type) with the Selection tool, the side handles of the frame disappear under its In and Out ports. If I need to drag a side handle to change the width of the frame without changing the depth, I have to zoom way in to reveal the handles.

☑ Hate to break it to you, but all that zooming was for naught. As long as you *drag* (not click) on those In and Out ports, they act just like side handles. Dragging on the In and Out ports doesn't work if you *can* see the side handles, though —only when the frame is so shallow the side ones "disappear."

Create a Text Frame On Top of Another One

? Having one tool, the Type tool, do double-duty as both a text frame creator and a text editor is a blessing and a curse. A blessing, because it's one less tool to worry about. A curse, because it's impossible to create a new text frame when the cursor's over an existing frame. If I want to drag out a small frame for a callout inside a larger frame that holds article text, InDesign won't let me. The Type cursor goes into text-edit mode because I'm over the article frame.

☑ Yes, it's a tragic case of feature-not-a-bug-itis. To get the Type tool to create a new frame, you'll have to at least *start* your dragging over any empty area of the page, even just a micron outside any existing text frame.

As soon as you start dragging, though, you can move the frame into position by holding the spacebar down (while the mouse button is still down, too). Let go of the spacebar and you're back to sizing the new frame.

On the other hand, if you're zoomed in and there's no "empty" page area in sight, you can try this:

1. Press Command-Shift-A/Ctrl-Shift-A to Deselect All.

2. Tap the 'F' key (selects the Rectangle Frame tool).

3. Drag out an empty image frame as though it were your text frame.

4. Tap the 'T' key (which selects the Type tool).

5. Click inside the rectangle and start typing. Clicking inside the empty image frame with the Type tool immediately converts it to a text frame.

Since the Frame tool has a default zero-point stroke, just like a text frame, it's a better choice than the Shape tool, which has a 1-point stroke by default.

Straddle Heads in a Single Text Frame

? I'd like the title and body of a single story to exist in a single frame. No problem, right? Sure, unless the title needs to be in one column spanning the full width of the frame; while the body text has to flow into multiple columns. InDesign doesn't let you mix numbers of columns in a single frame.

☑ InDesign maven Dave Saunders wrote about this procedure in depth in the Oct|Nov 2004 issue of *InDesign Magazine* (see Introduction for more information). His technique is obscure, but powerful:

1. Assign the text frame the number of columns you want for the body text.

2. Enter your headline as the first paragraph of the story.

3. Convert the title paragraph into a one-celled table by selecting the heading (excluding that paragraph's carriage return character) and choosing Table > Convert Text to Table.

4. Drag the right edge of the table all the way to the far right edge of the text frame, across the columns. Voila, a single column title and a multiple-column body in the same text frame.

   Unfortunately, the body text in the remaining columns doesn't automatically wrap under the bottom of the title's table. You'll have to increase the text frame's First Baseline Offset setting, which is 0p0 by default, to push the misbehaving text down.

5. Place the cursor in the first line after the heading and open the Info palette.

6. Open Object > Text Frame Options and move the dialog box so that you can see the Info palette.

7. Change the First Baseline feature's offset Method to "Fixed" and change the offset amount to the

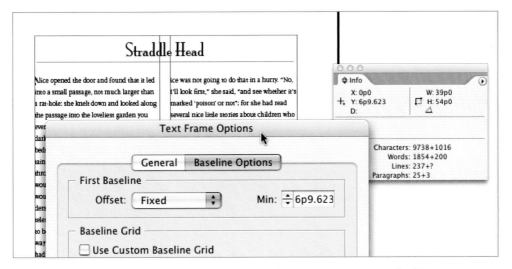

Figure 3-5: Use a one-cell table to create straddle heads in your text frames.

same number listed in the Y field of the Info palette. That's the current distance from the top of the frame to the baseline of that first line (**Figure 3-5**).

8. Click OK and the effect is done.

However, if you later change the height of the heading's table cell or add/remove lines from the title, you'll have to change the offset amount to match. Just go back and repeat steps 5–8.

Don't feel like repeating all those steps? Or found yourself in a fix when the text frame has a text inset? Fortunately, Mr. Saunders wrote HeadStraddler.js, a shareware script that creates straddle heads in InDesign with a single keystroke. It's worth every penny. Check it out for yourself at *www.pdsassoc.com*

Quick Work of Equal Frame Insets

? **There's no "Make All Settings the Same" link icon in the Inset Spacing area of the Text Frame Options dialog box. Maybe I'm spoiled, but I really hate having to enter the same measure over and over again for each of the four text inset fields when I want them all to be the same.**

☑ You're not spoiled, you're just used to the finer things in life. Indeed, 'tis a puzzlement why this area of InDesign lacks the useful icon found in other parts of the program.

Here's a trick that will help. Select the frame and choose Object > Corner Effects. Choose the Rounded style, but set the amount of the "rounding" to 0. The frame appears the same, square corners and all. However, since frames with Corner Effects applied to them can only have one text inset (applied to all sides of the frame), you just need to enter your inset once.

You can put such a frame in an InDesign library for use in other documents. That way you don't have to keep going back to Corner Effects every time.

And of course in InDesign CS2 you can create an object style that does little but turn on the text insets at the values you want. Then you can apply those insets with a single click.

Fix Inexplicable Oversets in Narrow Frames

? Typing merrily away in a somewhat narrow text frame, with plenty of empty space for more text, InDesign suddenly forced an overset. There's room for at least another 50 lines of type in the frame, why did this happen?

✓ Most likely you entered a word that was longer than the width of the text frame and InDesign didn't know how or wasn't allowed to hyphenate it. Perhaps it wasn't in its hyphenation dictionary, or it's a capitalized word and you turned off the option to hyphenate those, or you turned off hyphenation altogether.

Whatever the reason, InDesign's reaction to the situation is to throw up its hands and say uncle. It won't break words at arbitrary points (as QuarkXPress would), instead it pushes the word — and anything you typed or placed after it — into an overset state. You might encounter the same symptom if you reduce the width of an existing text frame — suddenly you have an overset even though there's room for more text.

Remember you can always access overset text in the Story Editor (Edit > Edit in Story Editor), so one solution, other than widening the text frame or changing your hyphenation rules, would be to open Story Editor and add a hard or discretionary hyphen to the word caus-

ing the problem. The layout view immediately updates and you should see your text reappear in the frame.

Fix Inexplicable Oversets in Normal-Width Frames

? My text frame has plenty of vertical *and* horizontal space to hold the text without having to break a word (so it's not the situation described above), but I'm getting an overset nonetheless.

✓ Is the frame near, beneath, or on top of an object that has a Text Wrap enabled? Remember that in InDesign, the default is that *all* nearby or partially overlapping/underlapping objects are affected by another object's Text Wrap setting; stacking order in a layer or multiple layers is ignored.

If that's the problem, select the overset text frame and turn on Ignore Text Wrap in Objects > Text Frame Options. You should see the text reappear in the frame, because it's no longer being pushed away by the Text Wrap setting.

If that's *not* the problem, select the text you can see in layout (or select it in the Story Editor) and check the Keep Options settings in the Paragraph palette menu. Perhaps a Keep Lines Together setting is turned on, and InDesign can't keep all the lines of your paragraph together in that frame. Turn the option off or thread the frame to a new one to reveal the text (**Figure 3-6**).

Other causes might be an accidental tap on the number keypad's Enter key, which is the keyboard shortcut for "jump [the text] to next column or frame;"

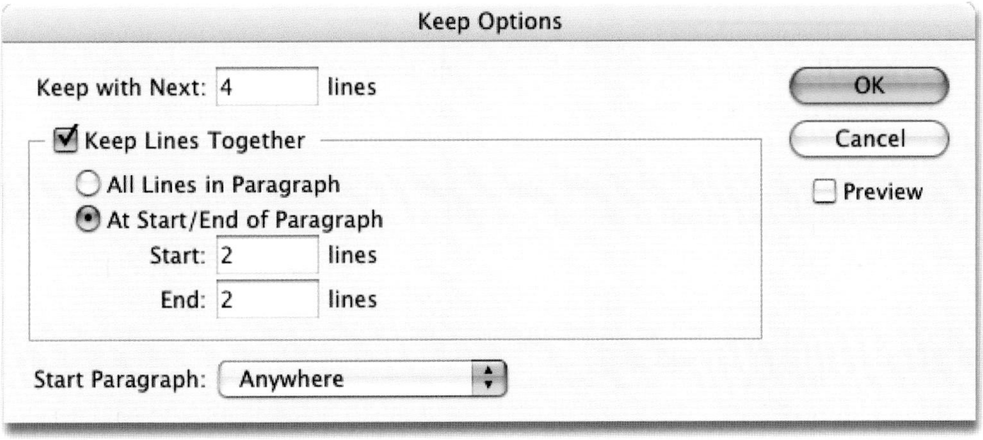

Keep Options

Keep with Next: 4 lines

☑ Keep Lines Together
　○ All Lines in Paragraph
　● At Start/End of Paragraph
　　Start: 2 lines
　　End: 2 lines

Start Paragraph: Anywhere

OK
Cancel
☐ Preview

Figure 3-6: Certain Keep Options settings sometimes cause unexpected oversets. Even if you don't remember setting anything special here in InDesign's Keep Options dialog box, perhaps the author set it up in the equivalent dialog in Word.

an embedded Page Break from a word processing file, which InDesign also interprets as a "jump" command; or an accidental pasting/placing of an image into the text frame, resulting in an inline image that is too large to reveal at 100% in the text frame.

For any of these possible causes, click an insertion point after the last visible character and type a forward delete (a special key on Mac and PC keyboards) one or more times to get rid of the character/image that's forcing the overset. Or, you may want to open the Story Editor to help you identify the culprit and get rid of him.

One more thing to check: Make sure the No Break feature (in the Character palette menu) is not turned on for the text you're editing. If it's enabled for a whole paragraph of text, you're essentially saying the whole paragraph is a single word. Oops.

Inline Frames that Don't Overlap Text Above

? Even though I made sure to paste an inline graphic on its own paragraph, it's still overlapping the text above it.

☑ Click an insertion point in the same paragraph as the inline frame and change the Leading amount to Auto. InDesign figures out the frame's height, goes, "Whoa! I was *way* off," and adds enough breathing room (leading) so the inline frame has room to stretch.

If you're adding a number of inline frames that sit in their own paragraph, you might want to create a paragraph style just for them. Make sure that the Leading in the style is set to Auto, of course.

Wrap Paragraph Text Around Inline Frame

? The first character of my paragraph is actually an inline frame, a decorative drop cap I made in Illustrator and pasted in the text flow. I can drag the frame down

with the Selection tool so the top of it aligns with the cap height of the first line of the paragraph, but since the subsequent lines of text don't move out of the way, the image in the frame partially overlaps the text in the second and third lines. Text Wrap doesn't work with inline frames?

That's right, at least for InDesign CS — CS2 does support some text wrap for inline frames (more on that in a moment).

But since the inline is the *first* character in the paragraph, you can fake a frame text wrap in InDesign CS with the Drop Cap feature.

1. After cutting the drop cap frame to the clipboard, switch to the Type tool and paste it as an inline frame immediately in front of the first character of a paragraph.

2. Make sure your cursor is blinking in the paragraph containing the inline frame. In the Control palette (in Paragraph mode) or Paragraph palette, set a 1 character drop for as many lines as the frame is high.

InDesign drops the inline frame down the proper number of lines without changing its dimensions. You can adjust the size and baseline of the inline frame with the Selection tool as usual, if necessary.

Fortunately, InDesign CS2 is smarter and can wrap paragraphs around inline frames... but only text *after* the inline frame — it won't wrap text in previous paragraphs. (Of course, this isn't a concern with Drop Caps.)

To customize the wrap around a Drop Cap, such as making the body text follow the slant of the right side of a Drop Cap "W," see "Wrapping Drop Caps" later in this chapter.

TIP: If you find the inline frame wrapping text you don't want, but the Text Wrap palette already says that the text wrap on that side is zero, don't fret. Remember that you can type negative numbers into the Text Wrap palette. That allows the surrounding text to get closer to the object.

Character and Paragraph Formatting

Use the Keyboard to Jump to Text Format Fields

? **One of the things I do most often in InDesign—choose a typeface from the Control palette popup menu—has no keyboard shortcut.**

☑ Oh yes it does! Press Command-6/Ctrl-6 to select the first field in the Control palette. If the palette is currently showing Character formats—as it likely will be if you're editing text in a frame—that means you'll be highlighting the Font field.

Then, type the first few characters of the font's name, or use the up and down arrow keys to browse through the active fonts, or do a combination of both. Press Tab to jump to the next field (font style) and use the same keyboard tricks to choose Bold, Compressed, etc. Finally, press the Return or Enter key to put the focus back on your text frame, and continue typing (in your new typeface, of course).

To access the Paragraph formatting commands in the Control palette when it's currently showing the Character format fields (or vice versa), press Command-Option-7/Ctrl-Alt-7, which toggles the two modes. When the Paragraph mode is active, Command-6/Ctrl-6 selects *its* first field, which is Left Indent.

You can use these shortcuts even if you've selected a frame (or multiple frames) with the Selection tool. After they're selected, just tap the "T" key (to switch to the Type tool) so the Control palette shows Character or Paragraph fields. Your frames will still be selected and any changes you make to the formatting fields (via the keyboard or mouse) will be applied to *all* the text in the selected frame(s). Très cool!

Here's a second way to skin the cat, which you might find a little faster, depending on the circumstances. Press Command/Ctrl-T and the Character palette will open with the Typeface field highlighted. Choose a face and style using the keyboard as described above. To close the Character palette, press Command/Ctrl-T again.

TIP: The keyboard shortcuts we describe above (Command-6/Ctrl-6 and Command-Option-7/Ctrl-Alt-7) can be changed, if you think they're too hard to remember. Open Edit > Keyboard Shortcuts, choose "Views, Navigation" from the Product Area popup menu, and scroll down the list of commands until you reach the ones that begin with the word "Toggle."

Consistent Leading, Including the Last Lines

? If I'm reading a publication and notice that the leading changes from line to line in a single paragraph—most often, the last line is different from the rest— I know immediately the publication was created with PageMaker or InDesign. (QuarkXPress never did this, though it had its own dead giveaways). Why does this sometimes happen?

☑ InDesign, like PageMaker, assigns leading on a character-by-character basis by default; while in QuarkXPress it's a paragraph setting. However, in actuality, InDesign has *line* leading: The character with the largest leading in a line of text sets the leading for the whole line. So, if a paragraph contains even a single character, space, or non-printing character that has a larger leading than the rest of the characters, the leading will be thrown off in the paragraph (**Figure 3-7**).

You can avoid the problem by doing three things:

1. Avoid the default autoleading. If the leading amount appears in parentheses, autoleading is in effect. Instead, set your own absolute leading for everything (except perhaps paragraphs that contain an inline frame and nothing else).

2. When you want to adjust leading, select the entire paragraph first. But *don't* select it by swiping all the characters; it's too easy to miss the trailing Paragraph marker (choose Type > Show Hidden Characters

to see it) which is the cause of the dreaded "last line leading looniness" problem. Instead, click four times in quick succession inside a paragraph. This selects the entire paragraph, including the paragraph marker, even if it's not visible. *Then* change the leading.

3. If you're tired of quadruple-clicking, turn on the "Apply Leading to Entire Paragraphs" option in the Type panel of the Preferences dialog box. Now you can apply leading to a single character (or even with the cursor just flashing between characters) and InDesign applies the leading to the whole paragraph. However, turning this on does not affect paragraphs that might already have mixed leading; just paragraphs you change from now on (well, until you turn it off again). And even with the option turned on, changing the size of selected characters in an autoleaded paragraph will result in mixed leading.

Stop Vertical Justification from Spacing Out

? I like to vertically justify my text frames by choosing Object > Text Frame Options and then setting the Vertical Justification popup to Justify. But sometimes InDesign adds a ton of white space between every line messing up my leading. All I want is for the first paragraph to start at the top, the last paragraph to end at the bottom, and the remaining paragraphs to be equally distributed between them.

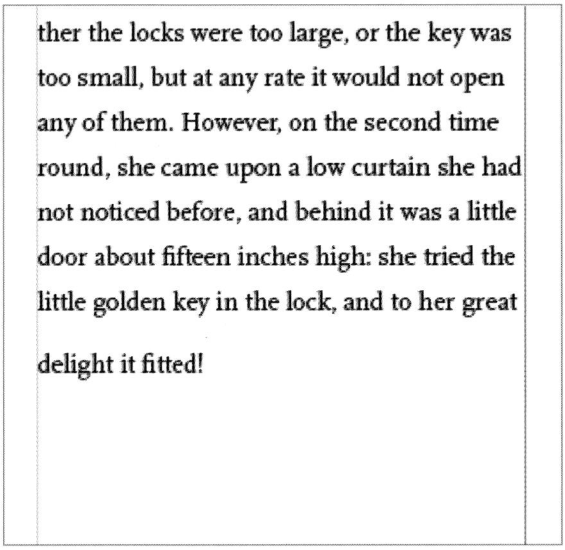

ther the locks were too large, or the key was too small, but at any rate it would not open any of them. However, on the second time round, she came upon a low curtain she had not noticed before, and behind it was a little door about fifteen inches high: she tried the little golden key in the lock, and to her great delight it fitted!

Figure 3-7: Dreaded last line leading problem

Did you notice the field next to the Vertical Alignment popup menu called Paragraph Spacing Limit? It's set to 0p0 by default. If you enter in a larger amount, InDesign will add space between the paragraphs in the frame (up to the amount you specify in the field) first, to see if that vertically justifies the text. If it hits the limit and still has empty space after the last paragraph, it also increases the leading — "the white space between the lines" — until the text is justified.

To prevent InDesign from adding *any* leading to vertically-justified text frames, set a huge measure in the Paragraph Spacing Limit. Try the height of the frame itself if you want to be sure.

> **TRIVIA:** The largest measure you can enter in the Paragraph Spacing Limit field is 720 picas (10 feet!).

Change the Default Font (and other formatting defaults)

? Our magazine uses Bauer Bodoni Book for its body face. I've created a paragraph style for "body" which changes the default Times face to Bodoni when I apply it, but it would be nice if I could just drag out a text frame, start typing, and the font used by default would be Bauer Bodoni Book.

You can make any active font the default font in the document by first making sure that's nothing's selected in your document (Command-Shift-A/Ctrl-Shift-A), then choosing the font you want from the Type > Font submenu or in the Character palette. All new text frames you create from then on in the document will use your new default font. If you change the default font without any documents open, that will be your new default font for all new InDesign documents you create.

Use the same method to customize other text formatting defaults in the active document or the application itself. For example, you could set your Body paragraph style to automatically be applied to text added to an empty frame by selecting it in the Paragraph Styles palette (instead of the default "No Paragraph Style" in CS or "Basic Paragraph" in CS2), you could turn off Hyphenation (normally on by default), change the leading to an absolute measure instead of auto, change kerning from Metrics to Optical, and so on. Even with nothing selected in your document (or no documents open at all), InDesign lets you access almost every text-related menu, palette or dialog box setting.

For more information about setting application defaults in InDesign, see the sidebar on page 9.

WARNING: Even though you can change the default font, InDesign has the Times typeface hard-wired into itself as the "real" default font. You'll see it eerily rise from the dead if you ever need to completely strip paragraph and character style sheet formatting from text by Option-Shift/ Alt-Shift-clicking on [No Paragraph Style]. Affected text reverts back to Times, even though your document's default font might be something else entirely.

Kerning Drop Caps

? **Some capital letters in certain fonts don't left-align properly when they're set as a drop cap, especially I and E. Their left edges don't touch the left edge of the frame; instead there's some white space on their left. They sort of look centered.**

☑ InDesign always aligns the left edge of drop caps to the left paragraph margin; but some fonts have overly-large side bearings (white space) built into the character design itself. To fix the problem visually, set the drop cap to two characters (in Paragraph settings) instead of the default single character. Insert a space in front of the first character so InDesign considers that space to be

the first of your two-character drop cap; then apply a negative kern between the space and the *real* drop cap so it moves to the left, crossing over the space, until it touches the left edge of the frame.

Wrapping Drop Caps

? **Why can't InDesign wrap text around a drop cap? For example, when the letter A or W is the drop cap, I want the adjacent body text to hug the right diagonal. InDesign always forces a square bounding box around the drop cap and I can't seem to adjust it.**

☑ The same issue of side bearings is the cause of InDesign not being able to wrap text along the right edge of character shapes; instead it wraps to the character's always-vertical right side bearing. Don't bother trying to embed the drop cap as an inline graphic to create a manual wrap in InDesign CS, because CS doesn't support text wraps around inline objects. (CS2 does, though; we'll get to that in a minute.)

The best you can do in InDesign CS is to place the drop cap on your page as a separate frame (**Figure 3-8**):

1. Place a text frame containing only the drop cap on top of the paragraph in the position you want.

2. Select this drop cap frame and turn on Wrap Around Bounding Box in the Text Wrap palette. The paragraph text will wrap around the drop cap's frame (but not the character itself).

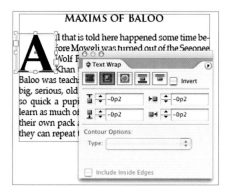

Figure 3-8: When you place a drop cap character in its own text frame, you can customize its text wrap to be any shape you want with the Direct Select tool. If you use InDesign CS2, you can anchor this frame into the text flow, too.

3. Set the wrap offset values to -2 pt (or some other small negative value) in the Text Wrap palette.

4. Now you can zoom in on the drop cap frame and use the Direct Select tool to reshape the text wrap boundary. Remember that you can add or remove points from the text wrap boundary with the Pen tool, including Bézier curves.

The only problem with this technique is that the drop cap won't flow with the text. So save this procedure until you don't expect any further copy changes.

However, if you're lucky enough to be using InDesign CS2, you can go one better and anchor the drop cap frame into the text flow.

1. Select the drop cap frame you just made and choose Edit > Cut.

2. Place the text cursor at the *end of the previous paragraph* and paste the frame in. Now it's an inline object, but it's in the wrong place. (If there is no "previous paragraph," then create a blank paragraph at the top of the text frame.)

3. Click on the inline drop cap frame with the Selection tool and choose Object > Anchored Object > Options.

4. In the Anchored Object Options dialog box, choose Custom from the Position popup menu. Click OK to close the dialog box without any further changes.

5. Use the Selection tool to drag the inline object (now technically called an "anchored object") to its

original position (where you want it to be sitting).

Since your custom-wrapped drop cap is an anchored frame, it will flow with the paragraph text, but the text after it will wrap around it.

Copy/Paste Text Formatting

? One feature I really miss from QuarkXPress is the ability to copy text formatting (not the text itself, just how it's styled) from one paragraph and apply it to other paragraphs in the same text box. I looked through InDesign's online help manual and keyboard shortcuts, but it's not mentioned anywhere. Oh well.

☑ The keyboard shortcut you're looking for is "I". That selects the Eyedropper tool (I... Eyedropper... get it?), InDesign's powerful tool for doing just what you ask and much more.

Click any paragraph with the Eyedropper tool to pick up its formatting. You'll know you've got it when the eyedropper cursor "fills up" with a mysterious black liquid. If any text was selected when you clicked with the Eyedropper tool, then whatever formatting you clicked on is applied to the selected text, even if it was in a different text frame.

You can also squeeze out drops from the tool — that is, apply the formatting to other text — by clicking on any other paragraph in any text frame (drag over text to also apply character formatting), even if it's a paragraph in another document in InDesign.

The Eyedropper tool can pick up and apply many more attributes than text for-

matting, or you can set it to just pick up certain aspects of text formatting (just character, and not paragraph formats, for example). To adjust what the eyedropper picks up and applies, double-click the Eyedropper tool to turn attribute check-boxes on and off before you use it.

Strip Formatting in Copied Text

? I copied some text from an email, and when I pasted it into my InDesign document it appeared in the same font and style as the existing text in the frame. Normally that's what I'd want, but for this text, I'd prefer that it remember its original formatting. How do I control whether formatting is applied or not?

☑ InDesign handles text slightly differently depending on whether the text came from another application or from within InDesign. When the text is coming from somewhere else, the relevant control is "Preserve Text Attributes When Pasting" in the General panel of InDesign's Preferences dialog box. This setting is off by default (text copied from other programs is stripped of formatting when it's pasted). Turn it on to keep the formatting around. In InDesign CS2, this preference is called When Pasting Text and Tables from Other Applications.

Note that InDesign can't retain formatting in text copied from some programs, (*e.g.*, it doesn't work with QuarkXPress text), but most work fine.

When it comes to text from another InDesign document, the Edit > Paste feature always retains the formatting. If you want to strip out the formatting (leaving the pasted text in the same style as the text where your cursor is), you'll be a lot happier if you use CS2 because it has a Paste Without Formatting feature in the Edit menu. However, if you use InDesign CS, you'll have to strip the formatting manually: Select the text in the source document that you want to copy, then hold down Shift-Option/Shift-Alt while clicking No Paragraph Style in the Paragraph Styles palette to completely strip the selection of all paragraph and character formatting other than the default. Copy the selection to the clipboard and then Undo (Command-Z/Ctrl-Z) to restore the formatting in the source document.

Now your clipboard contains unformatted text, ready for pasting in your current document without baggage.

> **TIP:** You may notice the Paste Without Formatting feature in InDesign CS2's Edit menu, but it will be inactive (grayed out) when your preferences are set to paste Text Only and the text is coming from another application (because InDesign is already going to paste without formatting).

Fix Leading Problems Due to Baseline Grid

? I get too much spacing between my body text and subheads when I turn on the Align to Baseline Grid paragraph format. Sometimes *all* the leading goes screwy, even if it's hard-coded into the paragraph style sheet.

Feature-not-a-bug alert! Think about it. The *purpose* of Align to Baseline Grid is to ignore any "hard coding" of leading and instead, to force all baselines to sit on the nearest baseline grid increment you set in Preferences > Grids. Nearest to what? To whatever "real" leading you've specified for that line of text.

So if your baseline grid increment is set to 14 pts., and the first line of body text after a subhead is supposed to fall 18 points below that (per the leading and space above/below paragraph settings you've applied to the text), InDesign will push the body text so it starts at 28 points (the next 14 pt. increment) below the subhead. Baseline grid allows text to skip increments, but never allows partial increments.

Solutions? You could turn off Align to Baseline Grid for the subhead and/or the body text. Or you could adjust your grid increment (try halving the amount) so InDesign has more increments to play with — though this affects the entire document, not just that paragraph or story, in InDesign CS.

If you only need the first line of the text to snap to the baseline grid, after you turn on Align to Baseline Grid, select Only Align First Line to Grid from the Control palette or Paragraph palette menu.

In InDesign CS2, you have another choice because each text frame can have its own baseline grid. You can change a frame's baseline grid setting by choosing Object > Text Frame Options. However, if each frame has its own grid, then it's pretty much the same as no frame having a grid. No?

Come Back to the Baseline, My Commas

? **For some reason, all the commas and numerals in my text are floating way above the baseline, even though the Baseline Offset field is set to 0.**

✓ Odds are you selected *all* the text and turned on the Fractions feature for your OpenType font (in the Character palette menu) or the same feature's being applied via a style sheet. Fix it by turning off the Fractions option in the OpenType submenu (in the Control or Character palette menu) for the text. Your commas and numerals will return to earth (**Figure 3-9**).

From now on, when you want to format a fraction using the OpenType feature, select *just* the unformatted fraction and apply the feature either from the Character palette menu or from a Character style.

Figure 3-9: Symptom: Mysteriously floating numbers and commas. Diagnosis: Someone doesn't know how to use the OpenType "Fractions" option.

Typographically Correct Underlines

? I don't like how underlines cross the descenders of text. It looks like the text was set on an IBM Selectric.

☑ Select the characters with descenders and apply a paper-colored stroke to them. Since underlines appear in back of characters, the thin white stroke makes the underline appear to "skip" the descenders (**Figure 3-10**).

Too tedious for you? You can use Find/Change for to speed it up:

1. Enter the same lowercase descender character in both the Find and Change fields.

2. Turn on Case Sensitive to restrict InDesign to using the lowercase character.

3. Turn on More Options and in the Find Format area, turn on Underline; in the Change Format area, turn on Underline *and* a Paper stroke.

4. Run the Find/Change All.

5. Do this for each character that's affected by your underline. (Cheat sheet for most typefaces: g, j, p, q, and y.) You can leave the Format area as is, just change the character it's searching and replacing.

Shade a Paragraph, Shade a Line

? It boggles the mind why InDesign can't apply a screened background behind a paragraph or a box around it

purgatory

purgatory

Figure 3-10: Adding a paper-colored stroke to characters with descenders (the p, g, and y in the word above) prevents an underline from marring their beauty.

or whatever, while MS Word has been able to do these sorts of things for eons. Putting a shape behind the text doesn't help because I have to keep adjusting its position as I edit the text.

☑ Select the text in the paragraph — but not the final invisible carriage return character — and convert it into a one-cell table (Table > Convert Text to Table). The table can be stroked and/or filled and flows along with the rest of the text.

You can put a screened background behind *any* text selection, by the way, by applying the Underline character format to it and then customizing the underline (**Figure 3-11**).

NOTE: Since the Strikethrough stroke is applied on *top* of the text, you can't use it to add shading behind text; it appears in front of the characters and obscures them if the line's too thick. Use the Underline format and Underline Options instead, which is applied *behind* the characters.

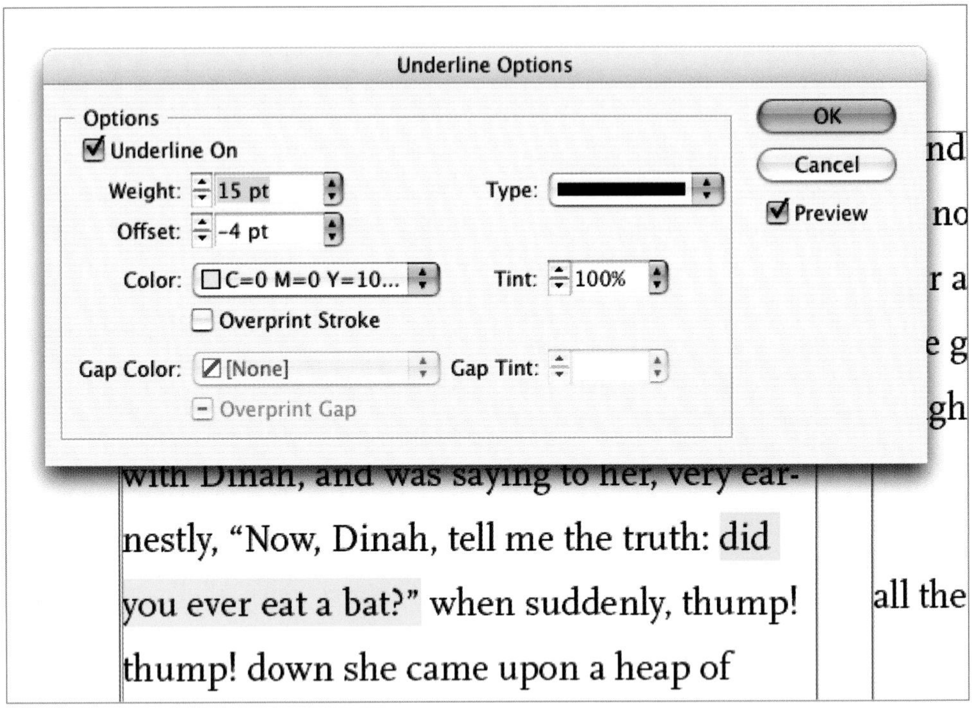

Figure 3-11: You can underline text and change the line's color, width and shade in Underline Options so it completely encompasses the characters. The modified underline is permanently attached to the text so as you edit, it sticks with the text, just as any normal underline would.

Prevent Runts (Too-Short Last Lines of Paragraphs)

? **I wish there were a setting in the Paragraph palette menu's Keep Options dialog box that would force a minimum number of words or even characters on the last line of a paragraph. Seeing a final line with a single short word, or worse, the second half of a hyphenated word, is just bad form, guv'ner.**

✓ Complete agreement here, bloke. If you're using InDesign CS2, head immediately for the Hyphenation dialog box (either in the paragraph style definition or from the Paragraph palette menu) and turn off the Hyphenate Last Word checkbox. That will avoid the worst offenders by refusing to break the last word of a paragraph.

If you're using CS (or if the offending runt spreads more than one word), select the last word or two in a "runting" paragraph and choose No Break from the Character palette menu. InDesign will recompose the paragraph so that the two unbreakable words are either sucked up into the penultimate line or appear together, by themselves, on the last line. We like to assign a keyboard shortcut to No Break to apply this faster.

TIP: Can't prevent runts the old fashioned way? You might be accustomed to fixing undesirable line breaks and "runts" by selecting some characters and slightly tracking them in or out, forcing a different wrap. That usually doesn't work in InDesign because the Paragraph Composer, which is on by default, will recompose the text after every edit. Use the No Break feature instead, or—if you must—turn off the Paragraph Composer (choose Single Line Composer in the Paragraph palette menu) and use the old-fashioned way.

Override Curly Quotes for Foot and Inch Marks

? I just got yelled at by the Art Director because the parts catalog I created in InDesign has "curly" inch and foot marks for all the product specs. I completely spaced on this. How can I prevent it from happening again?

☑ As you've found out, InDesign automatically substitutes typographically correct opening and closing apostrophes and quotes (the "curly" ones) when you enter the regular single and double quote keys from the keyboard. You can turn off the substitution with the "Use Typographer's Quotes" checkbox in the Type panel of the Preferences dialog box. Note that you can turn this preference on or off on the fly while you're typing by pressing Command-Option-Shift-"/Ctrl-Alt-Shift-".

But that only lets you enter *new* straight quotes, it doesn't change existing curly ones to straight. To do that, you'll have to run a couple Find/Changes (see the solution, "Find/Change Straight Quotes to Curly Ones" on page 96).

Understand How the Kern/Track Increments Work

? When I select some 12 pt. text and track it in by "-5" I expect to see the characters snuggle up to each other. But in InDesign (unlike QuarkXPress), -5 barely makes a dent.

☑ As you've discovered — as have ex-Quarkers around the globe — kern values and their default increments are not standardized across the board, like type size is. In general, you have to enter much higher values in InDesign to achieve the same effect in QuarkXPress (or MS Word for that matter). That's partly why the default kern increment used by the keyboard shortcut in InDesign is "20" (Option/Alt-Left or Right Arrow) instead of Quark's "10" (Command-Shift/Ctrl-Shift-Left or Right Bracket).

But since the two programs define the smallest kerning increment differently, InDesign's "20" is technically *not* twice the amount of Quark's "10." In InDesign, one increment is .001 of an em space; in Quark, one increment is .02 of an em, or twenty times more than InDesign's. And *that's* probably why InDesign's default kern increment is "20." It's the same as QuarkXPress's "1." Sort of.

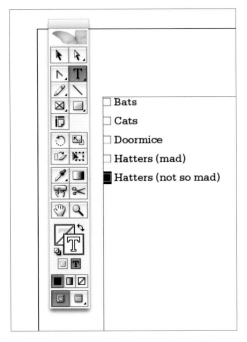

Figure 3-12: Add a stroke around a solid square dingbat and set the color of the character's fill to transparent and you've got a checkbox.

There's one more twist; and that is the two programs define an em space differently. No need to go into details; sufficeth it to say that after you take it into account, the ratio is reduced by half, roughly.

Thus a quick tip to help you make the transition from QuarkXPress to InDesign is to multiply the kerning amount you would normally apply in QuarkXPress by *ten* and use that number in InDesign. Example: To track in a selection by

Quark's −5, in InDesign you'd track it in by that amount times ten, or −50.

You might also find it helpful to reduce the default Kern increment from 20 (1000ths of an em) to 5 or 10 in InDesign's Preferences. That way you have much finer control over kerning and tracking from the default keyboard shortcut of Option/Alt-Left or Right Arrow. When you want to make larger adjustments (five times the default increment), add the Command/Ctrl key to the shortcut.

Fake a Missing Type Style

? **This document *needs* an italic box character, but no version of any of my dingbat fonts has an italic style.**

You didn't hear it from us, but to fake an italic or oblique character (one that will actually print), set the character in its normal upright face, select it, and apply a 20- to 25-degree Skew in the Character palette.

To fake a bold font, apply a thin stroke to the character in the Swatches palette. To fake an outline font, fill the character with Paper (from the Swatches palette) and apply a colored stroke (quite handy for creating hollow checkboxes from ZapfDingbats; **Figure 3-12**).

Style Sheets

Get Rid of the Plus Sign (Local Formatting)

? **I applied a style sheet to some text, but some or all of the text didn't change to match the paragraph style. And there's a "plus" symbol after the style sheet name.**

✔️ The plus symbol means that the text has local formatting (manual formatting) "on top" of the formatting applied by the style sheet. (Note: The plus symbol only appears when such locally-formatted text is part of a text selection, or your insertion point is blinking within it.) InDesign retains local formatting even when text is linked to a style sheet because it thinks that's what you want.

To clear local formatting from a selected paragraph, returning the paragraph to its base style sheet, Option/Alt-click on the Paragraph Style name. It's an all-or-nothing proposition, though. You can't use this method to clear out local formatting you don't want, but retain local formatting such as occasional bolded or italicized type that you *do* want.

In InDesign CS2 you have a bit more control: To remove all local formatting, click once on the Clear Overrides in Selection button in the Paragraph Styles or Control palette. To remove just the local character formatting (leaving any local paragraph formatting), Command/Ctrl-click on the Clear Overrides button. To remove just the local paragraph formatting (leaving the character formatting), Command-Shift-click/Ctrl-Shift-click on this button.

By the way, the same thing applies to Character Styles, if you see a plus symbol next to a Character Style name. To return selected text to its base Character Style, Option/Alt-click on the Character Style name. That will only "clear out" the local formatting applied to that selected text. Your paragraph may have other instances of text linked to a Character Style, with local formatting also applied to it, that you'll have to hunt down.

Really Remove All Formatting

? **Okay. Following the instructions above, I Option/Alt-clicked on the paragraph style name, but I'm *still* seeing some instances of text in the paragraph with different formatting! And there is *no* plus sign next to the style sheet name.**

✔️ Elementary, my dear Watson: Some characters in the paragraph have Character Style sheets applied. (Even if you didn't create Character Styles, they might have been applied in the word processor and imported with the text when you placed it. Microsoft Word is notorious for this.) InDesign doesn't define character styles as local formatting, so the paragraph style name has no plus sign after it.

To clear just Character Style links — but not local formatting — from a paragraph, select all the text in the paragraph and Option-Shift/Alt-Shift-click on [No Character Style] in the Character Styles palette (or click once on "[None]" in CS2). To clear all local formatting *and* any character style formatting from a selection, returning it to its base paragraph style formatting, Option-Shift/Alt-Shift-click on the paragraph style sheet name.

TIP: If you suspect that some characters in a paragraph may be linked to a Character Style (as opposed to carrying just local formatting), try selecting the entire paragraph. If one or more characters uses a Character Style, *no* Character Style sheet name will be highlighted in the Character Styles palette, because you have a mixed selection. If *none* of the characters is linked to a character style, the default [No Character Style] — or [None] in CS2 — is highlighted.

However, even if [No Character Style] or [None] is highlighted, some text could still be affected by a character style *nested* in a paragraph style. Click inside a word that you suspect is being styled because of this. If it is, the character style name appears in the lower-left corner of the Character Style palette.

TIP: When a paragraph style definition uses Nested Styles to assign a character style to some portion of a paragraph, Option-Shift/Alt-Shift clicking on [No Character Style] (or [None] in CS2) has no effect on that formatting. The only way to "turn off" these nested styles is to change the paragraph style definition or choose Drop Caps and Nested Styles from the Paragraph or Control palette menu and remove the nested style.

Reformat Text to [No Paragraph Style]

? **To start fresh, I'd like to strip out any and all formatting that's been applied to my text; whether by style sheets or local formatting. With the text selected I click on [No Paragraph Style] in the Paragraph Styles palette, expecting to see the text revert to InDesign's default formatting. But that's not what happens, is it. The text doesn't change at all!**

☑ All that happens when you click on [No Paragraph Style] in InDesign CS is that the paragraph style definition gets turned into local formatting. Text tagged with character styles maintain its link. Very often that's exactly what you want to do. Okay, not so often, but it's nice to know you can do it.

In InDesign CS2, Adobe took away the [No Paragraph Style] option in the palette. However, they added a feature called Break Link to Style in the Paragraph Styles palette menu which does the same thing.

To break the link to all user-defined style sheets — Paragraph and Character ones — *and* remove all local formatting from the text in one swoop, select the text and hold down Option-Shift/Alt-Shift as you click on [No Paragraph Style] (or [Basic Paragraph Style] in CS2). There you go, your text is as fresh and innocent as a newborn babe (**Figure 3-13**).

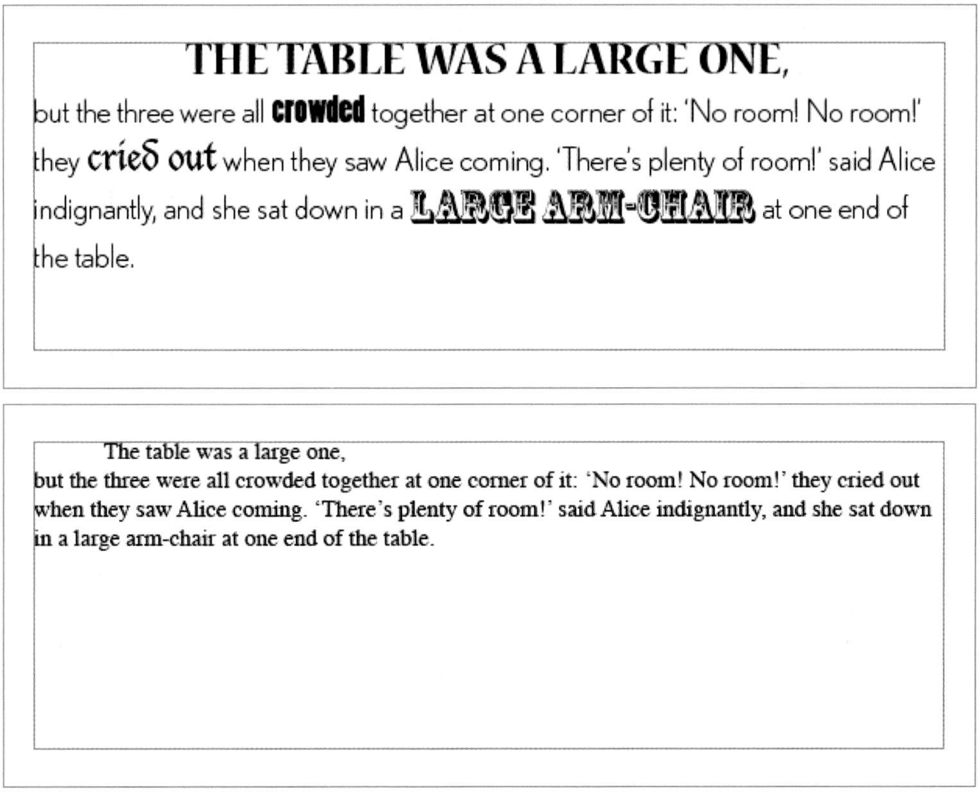

> **THE TABLE WAS A LARGE ONE,**
> but the three were all **crowded** together at one corner of it: 'No room! No room!'
> they **cried out** when they saw Alice coming. 'There's plenty of room!' said Alice
> indignantly, and she sat down in a **LARGE ARM-CHAIR** at one end of
> the table.

> The table was a large one,
> but the three were all crowded together at one corner of it: 'No room! No room!' they cried out
> when they saw Alice coming. 'There's plenty of room!' said Alice indignantly, and she sat down
> in a large arm-chair at one end of the table.

Figure 3-13: You can return crazy formatting to normalcy by selecting the sickly paragraphs and holding down Option-Shift/Alt-Shift while clicking on [No Paragraph Style] (or [Basic Paragraph Style] in CS2).

Dreaded Pink in Imported Files

❓ Our publication gets Microsoft Word files from various authors that we have to place into our layout. On occasion, chunks of text appear "pinked out" and in the wrong font. What's going on?

✅ Pink is InDesign's way of telling the designer that it can't find the font specified and is using a substitute font instead. Perhaps the writer applied a font that you don't have, or applied a character style that calls for a font you don't have or that doesn't really exist (like Symbol Italic). You could turn off the Highlight Substituted Fonts checkbox in the Composition panel of the Preferences dialog box, but that doesn't help fix the problem.

Place the text cursor in the pink text and check the Character Style palette to see if there's a character style applied. If so, change the style definition to reflect the proper font. If no character style is applied, then use Type > Find Font to change the font.

Plus Signs on All Imported Text

❓ I've imported a Word DOC or RTF file, but the formatting is all wrong and

when I try to apply one of my paragraph styles, the wrong formatting doesn't go away.

☑ If you place the cursor in the text and look at the Paragraph Styles palette, you'll probably see a plus sign next to the style name. That means there's local formatting on top of the underlying style definition. The most common reason for this is that the writer or editor selected a bunch of text in Word and applied local formatting (like changing the font and size to something more pleasing to them) rather than redefine the underlying style definitions in Word (which is what they should have done).

Unfortunately, this kind of massive "plus-symbol infestation" can be complicated to get rid of. One solution is to place the cursor in the offending paragraph (or select a string of similarly-styled paragraphs) and Option/Alt-click on the style name in the Paragraph Styles palette. This strips away all local formatting but leaves applied character styles. If you use Option-Shift/Alt-Shift-click, it strips away both local formatting *and* character styles.

Yes, you have to do this once each time the style changes in your document. And yes, you lose the italic or bold formatting that you were hoping to keep. Sigh.

Here's a better option: Figure out what local formatting the Word-user applied and get rid of it — either in Word or in InDesign.

1. To see what local formatting has been applied in InDesign CS2, hover the cursor over a style in the Paragraph Styles palette that sports a plus sign. The "tool tip" that appears after a moment shows the local formatting the plus sign refers to.

   If you're using CS, Option/Alt-click on the New Paragraph Style button in the Paragraph Styles palette. Then look at the Style Settings section of the New Paragraph Style dialog box; the stuff after the plus sign is the local formatting. Click Cancel to close the dialog box without saving this style.

2. Now select the text and apply the "proper" local formatting. For example, if the writer had applied Courier to all the text but InDesign's style definition calls for Palatino, then apply Palatino on top of the Courier.

As soon as the text formatting equals the style definition, the plus sign goes away.

Then, go shake some sense into the writer or editor, explaining carefully that local formatting is a no-no except in case of national emergency. Bold and italic local formatting is fine, but *only* when there is no other local formatting on the text. They should change style definitions instead.

TIP: Go to *www.editorium.com* or *www.bitmix.de/english/* for a great selection of cross-platform, cross-version Word macros designed to fix formatting problems in Word files *before* you flow them into a page layout program. They're not that expensive and they can save you a huge amount of time.

Save Your Bold and Italic Text

? Sadly, I've been reduced to the Option-Shift/Alt-Shift-click method of removing an author's unwanted formatting. But I'm losing all the italic text showing emphasis, and the editors are yelling at me. I hate it when they yell.

InDesign CS2 has a clever little feature that lets you remove all the paragraph formatting from text while leaving the character formatting. So if you're trying to get rid of paragraph formatting such as indents, you can Command-Shift/Ctrl-Shift-click on the Clear Overrides button at the bottom of the Paragraph Styles palette. Unfortunately, the chances that the author only applying local paragraph formatting to text is about the same as pigs flying to the moon.

Which leaves us with the problem of being able to retain the author's correct use of local bold, italic and bold/italic text.

Here's one solution:

1. Create a character style for each kind of local formatting you want to hold on to. For example, one character style that makes text italic, another for bold, and so on.

2. While you're looking at your Character Styles palette, select and delete any unwanted styles that were imported from the Word file that you didn't already have in your InDesign template (you can identify them by their disk icon). When you delete a Style Sheet, text that is formatted because of it retains the same formatting, but it's now defined as local formatting. (InDesign CS2 asks you if you want to replace the deleted style with another one; in this case, you want to replace it with "No Paragraph Style" and leave the "Preserve Formatting" option on.)

3. Open the Find/Change window from the Edit menu. Click the More Options button to reveal the Find Format and Change Format areas.

4. In Find Format Settings, click the Format button and specify the local formatting that matches one of the author's local formats you want to keep (that you created a character style for). For example, choose Times Bold in the Basic Character Formats section.

5. In Change Format Settings, click the Format button and choose the name of the Character Style that you created for this instance.

6. Run the Find/Change so that all instances of the author's local formatting gets the appropriate character style applied. Do this for each character style you created in Step 1, then close the Find/Change window.

7. Now apply your paragraph styles to each paragraph in your document, but hold down the Option/Alt key held down as you click on the style name.

Result: All stupid local formatting is stripped except for the stuff you want (the stuff that had character styles applied).

Plus Signs in Word Files Revisited

? I've tried removing the local formatting from imported Word documents; I've tried redefining my styles. I only have a few strands of hair left and I've emptied my bottle of aspirin. The plus sign won't go away.

Okay, try this one on for size. Unfortunately, InDesign sometimes chokes if Word's paragraph styles are based on the Normal style, or character styles are based on Underlying Paragraph Properties. Redefining Word's style definitions before importing the file into InDesign can often help:

1. Open the original Word document in Microsoft Word.

2. Choose Format > Style, and in the resulting Style dialog box, change the List popup menu to "Styles in Use."

3. Click each style in turn and look at the Description area in the dialog box. If you select a paragraph style and see the phrase "Normal +" in there, or if you select a character style and see "Default Paragraph Font +", click the Modify button.

4. If it's a paragraph style, the Based On Style popup menu in the Modify Style dialog box will read "Normal." Change "Normal" to "(no style)" (it's at the very top of the popup menu; **Figure 3-14**).

   If it's a character style, the Based On Style popup menu will read "Default Paragraph Font." Change it to "(underlying properties)."

5. When you've updated all the style definitions, close the Style dialog box and save the file under a different name.

   Now when you place this Word doc into your layout, see if the plus signs go away.

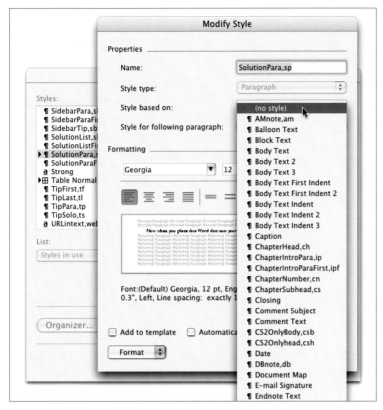

Figure 3-14: Changing a Word document's based-on styles to "no style" (in Word's Format > Styles dialog box) before placing the file in InDesign often fixes "plus sign" woes.

TIP: You can avoid a lot of problems with badly styled Word files by supplying your publication's contributors with a Word template containing the actual styles used in your InDesign document.

A fast way to create such a template is to start with a properly formatted story in InDesign, one that uses most of the paragraph and character style sheets your authors will need.

Click inside the story with the Type tool and choose File > Export. In the Export dialog box, choose Rich Text Format for the file format, and click Save. Then open this RTF file in Word.

You can make this file even more friendly to your authors by redefining the styles for them using fonts they're likely to have. For example, it's likely that your authors would prefer to write picture captions in black 12 pt. Helvetica instead of the purple 8 pt. Garamond Italic you're using.

As long as the names match up and they don't apply additional local formatting beyond basic bold and italic for emphasis, then everything will import fine.

Too Many Styles Are Imported

? When I import a Word document into InDesign, I get a bunch of unwanted paragraph and character styles—all kinds of stuff that isn't actually applied to any text but appears in the palette anyway.

☑ Often these paragraph styles appear because some other paragraph style references them. For example, if you have a "Ahead" style in Word that is based on "Heading 1," then when you import a file that has an "Ahead" paragraph, the "Heading 1" style will appear, too, even though it's not applied to any paragraphs. The best thing you can do is go back to Word and redefine those styles so that they're based on "No Style."

If you're using InDesign CS2, you should check to make sure that the Import Unused Styles checkbox is *not* turned on in the Microsoft Word Import Options dialog box. When this feature is on, you'll always get all those unused styles.

If you have a lot of unused styles in your Styles palettes that you want to get rid of, choose Select All Unused from the Paragraph Styles palette and click the Delete Selected Styles button at the bottom of the palette. Now repeat with the Character Styles palette.

Base a Paragraph Style on a Character Style

? Before we moved to InDesign, we usually based most of a publication's paragraph styles on one or another "root"

character style. To quickly change the text specs of a related group of paragraph styles, all we had to do was edit the single Character Style they were based on.

However, in InDesign's Paragraph Style Options dialog box, I can't find a place to specify the Character Style sheet.

☑ Sorry, but you might as well stop looking. It's not there. Character specs are always individually spelled out in each and every paragraph style. The only thing you can base a paragraph style on is another paragraph style.

There is a sneaky way to get what you want, though. Add a Nested Style to your paragraph style that applies the Character Style you want. For a stop character, enter something that doesn't exist in the normal text flow of any story, such as "Section Marker" or a single bizarre character like the infinity symbol.

Since InDesign never encounters the stop character, the Character Style is applied throughout the entire paragraph.

Adding the same sort of Nested Style to a group of related paragraph styles results in the "Based on Character Style" function that you're looking for. That is, editing the single Character Style sheet results in all the paragraphs which "nest it" to be updated with the new character specs.

If you ever need a particular paragraph or two to use its "real" character formatting instead of the nested one, just insert the special character "End Nested Style Here" (Type > Insert Special Character) before the first character of the paragraph.

Import a Subset of Style Sheets

? **The "Load Paragraph Styles" command in the Paragraph Styles palette doesn't give me the opportunity to choose which paragraph styles to import from another InDesign document. All of them come over, even if I need just a couple.**

☑ To bring over just a few style sheets from another InDesign document, try one of the following:

- In the source document, select some text that's styled with the style(s) you want to import; copy it to the clipboard, and paste it into the target document, perhaps in a text frame on the pasteboard. Any styles applied to that text are added to the current document's Styles palettes. You can delete the text you pasted; the style sheets remain.

- In the source document, drag a text frame containing styled text to an InDesign library (File > New > Library). To "import" those styles to any other document, just drag the library item into the layout, wait a second while the Styles palettes update, then delete the frame from the layout.

- Use InDesign CS2. The Load Paragraph Styles from the Paragraph Styles palette menu (or Load Character Styles from the Character Styles palette menu if you want character styles) lets you choose which styles you want. In CS2, if you want all the styles, then you have to choose Load All Styles from the palette menu.

Quickest Style Sync in the West

Want a fast way to add all the style sheets from one doc to a bunch of other ones? Or to make sure that each document belonging to a given client, publication or project shares the same style sheets (or defines same-named style sheets exactly the same)?

Book 'em, Dano!

Create a new Book file (File > New > Book) and add the documents to it. Select the document containing the "correct" style sheets and make it the Style Source by clicking the box to the left of the document name.

From the Book palette menu, choose Synchronize Options and check off the items you'd like to synchronize — Paragraph and Character Styles, for example. Turn off other options.

Then choose Synchronize from the palette menu or click the Synchronize icon at the bottom of the palette itself. That's it!

When you're done, you can remove the documents from the book (select them and click the Remove Documents button in the palette). Then close the Book palette and toss the file if you like, and open and work with each InDesign file as before.

Edit a Style Sheet Without Applying It

? When I'm working in a text frame and want to modify a style sheet that's not the active one—for example, I'm working in some body text and decide I need to tweak the subhead style—I always forget that double-clicking that style sheet in the palette will apply it to my paragraph. Very annoying!

✓ Deselect All first (Edit > Deselect All; or Command/Ctrl-Shift-A). Since nothing is active, there's nothing InDesign can affect. Unfortunately, because nothing is selected, this also sets the document's default style to the one you edited, so every new text frame you create from now on will get that style applied to it (if you forget to click on the default style when you're done). Dang.

Here are two better ways to edit styles: Hold down Command-Shift-Option/Ctrl-Shift-Alt while you double-click the style sheet. Or right-click (Control-click with a one-button mouse) on the style sheet name and choose Edit "[name of style sheet]". Neither of these methods will apply the edited style to the active selection or change the default style for that document.

Get What You Expect When Placing Text

? Sometimes when I place a text file into an existing frame, it takes on a very strange formatting. For example, the whole story might get one of my character styles applied to it.

✓ The problem has to do with default styles. Text frames can have a default style (such as if a style was applied to the master page text frame). Try clicking inside the empty frame with the Type tool and take a gander at the Paragraph Styles and Character Styles palettes. Both should have [No Style] selected by default. (In InDesign CS2, the Paragraph Styles palette should have [Basic Paragraph] selected and the Character Style palette should have [None] selected.)

If some other style is chosen, click on No Style/Basic Paragraph/None, and try placing the file again.

If you still have the problem, your *document* might have default styles. Deselect everything (Command-Shift/Ctrl-Shift-A) and look at the two style palettes. Make sure No Style/Basic Paragraph/None are chosen here, too.

Of course, the weird formatting may be appearing because that's how the text was formatted in the originating application, and you've elected to retain the formatting. If you want to strip out all formatting, choose that setting in the Import Options dialog box when you place the file.

Re-Sort Style Sheet List into Alpha Order

? I just noticed that the paragraph style names in my Paragraph Styles palette aren't in alphabetical order. InDesign has no "Sort" command for style sheets, nor will it let me rearrange them myself by dragging, like I can in the Swatches palette. I have a ton of styles here and it's really cramping my style!

☑ This is a known bug with some InDesign 2 files converted to InDesign CS. The fix is simple: Double-click any of the style sheets, make a single change to any of its settings (even the name), and click Okay to save your edits. The list of style sheets re-sorts into alphabetical order. You can go back and reverse your change now if you want.

Add a Keyboard Shortcut to a Style Sheet

❓ None of the keys I press in the Shortcut field (the one in the Style Options dialog box for style sheets) will "take." No matter what combination I try, all I get is my computer's error beep.

☑ InDesign is fanatically picky about which keys you can use in this field. It has to be any combina-

tion of your modifier keys (Shift, Option or Command on a Mac — the Control key won't work; or Shift, Alt or Ctrl on Windows) and one number from your keypad — the numbers running across the top of the regular keys won't work.

If you're using these keys and it's still not working, check your Num Lock key on your keyboard and make sure it's turned on. That should do the trick.

Then, if you really want your shortcut to be something like Command-Option-Shift-R, you can use a macro program like QuicKeys to map this shortcut to the keypad shortcut.

Note that the Quick Apply feature in InDesign CS2 has radically reduced the need for applying shortcuts to styles. Just press Command-Return/Ctrl-Enter and type a few characters from the style name. For example, Quick Apply is smart enough to know that if you type the number 2, it should display styles named "2Head", "Head2", "Body2List" and anything else with 2 in it. Use the Up and Down Arrow keys on your keyboard to select the one you want and press Return/Enter to select it. Very fast, very efficient.

Fonts

Find That Wascally Missing Font

? InDesign says a font is missing, but I don't see any telltale pink highlighting in my document. Now what?

☑ Go to the Type menu and choose Find Font, which opens a dialog box listing all the fonts used in the active document. Entries for missing fonts carry a yellow warning icon and appear at the top of the list. Select one of these MIAs and click the Find First button. InDesign jumps to the first character or character run using that font in the document and highlights them.

To replace missing fonts with ones you have, choose a font at the bottom of the dialog box. Don't forget to click the Change or Change All buttons; if you choose a replacement font and just click the Okay button to close the dialog box, InDesign doesn't change anything.

Sometimes, though, when you click the Find button, InDesign appears to do *something* in the layout, yet you can't see any highlighted text.

In this case, the bad boy is probably a difficult-to-spot space or non-printing special character (like a paragraph return), it's hiding in a frame's overset text, or it's the character "assigned" to an inline table or graphic. In all these cases, InDesign has difficulty showing you the location of the problem.

Our colleague Dave Saunders came up with a good tip for this: After you click the Find button, you can assume your text cursor is at the right place. Close the Find Font dialog box. Don't click anywhere — immediately choose Edit > Edit in Story Editor, and the blinking cursor will be at the location of the missing font.

WARNING: A missing font could be in a style sheet. InDesign's internal font checking also counts fonts called for in Paragraph or Character Styles, even if they're not used in the document. If you suspect this is the case, try deleting all your unused style sheets (choose Select Unused from the Styles palettes menus and then delete the selection) and checking Find Font again. If the dialog box reports no missing fonts, that was your culprit.

If you think you might need to use one of those unused style sheets at some point, choose Edit > Undo to resurrect them. Unfortunately, replacing fonts via Find Font doesn't do diddlysquat to style sheet definitions, so you'll have to do check each style manually for the missing font and choose a replacement.

Find the Font that Appears in Other Program's Font Menus

? As far as I know, the font I want to use is loaded and active; and indeed I can choose it from other programs' font menus. But it doesn't appear in InDesign's font list.

✓ InDesign's font menu doesn't simply list all fonts alphabetically; some are grouped separately toward the bottom of the list because they're a different class of fonts (foreign language fonts for example), and often the type foundry's name is ignored in the alpha sort (ITC Oficina is listed in the O's, not

the I's). So if at first you don't see a font, keep looking.

If you still don't see it, then go looking on your hard drive. Some programs install their own private fonts folder and set of fonts when the program itself is installed. Microsoft does this, so do some individual Adobe applications. Check your program's documentation or search your hard drive to see where the font is located. Unless it's in a special "required" folder, you can usually move it to a common fonts folder that all programs can access without a problem.

Unbold Bold-Looking Type

? I don't know what I did, but suddenly some of the text in the frame I was working in became very chunky, as though I had applied "Bold Ugly" style. According to the Typeface style field, though, it's a regular Book font.

✓ You accidentally applied a stroke to the type. Select the characters and look at the Stroke icon at the bottom of the Tools palette, or the Stroke icon at the top of the Swatches palette. If the "T" there has an outline, there's your problem. Click the Stroke icon to bring it to the front if necessary, and click the [None] color to fix it (**Figure 3-15**, next page).

Smooth Font Display

? Why does the type look jaggy in this particular document? All of it looks bad, regardless of the typeface. InDesign isn't reporting any missing fonts.

✓ Go to View > Display Performance and make sure it's set to Typical or High Quality. If it's set to Optimized (in CS) or Fast Display (in CS2), that means that text anti-aliasing (smoothing) is turned off.

Alternately, go to the Display Performance panel of the Preferences dialog box, and make sure that the Enable Anti-Aliasing checkbox is checked for your current View setting.

Figure 3-15: Type looking globby? Check the Stroke icon in the Tools palette. If the T is outlined (top), you've accidentally applied a stroke color. Change it to None (bottom) and the globbiness should be gone.

A Mad Tea-Party

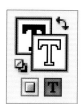

A Mad Tea-Party

Glyph Palette

Save Your Favorite Glyphs

❓ The number of individual character an OpenType font can contain boggles the mind, and it sure boggles my eyeballs when I'm scrolling through one in the Glyphs palette. There doesn't seem to be a way to "bookmark" places in the palette so I can quickly locate the ones I use over and over again.

✓ The Glyph palette contains an easy-to-overlook palette "flyout" menu. Open that menu and choose New

Glyph Set, then name the set. When you select a glyph that you think you'd like to use again, choose Add to Glyph Set from the palette menu, or right-click/Control-click right on the glyph and choose the command there. You can mix glyphs from different fonts in the same set.

The next time you need to use that glyph, open the Glyph palette and choose the name of your custom Glyph Set from the Show popup menu at the top of the palette. All the individual glyphs belonging to the set, and only those glyphs, appear for easy access (**Figure 3-16**).

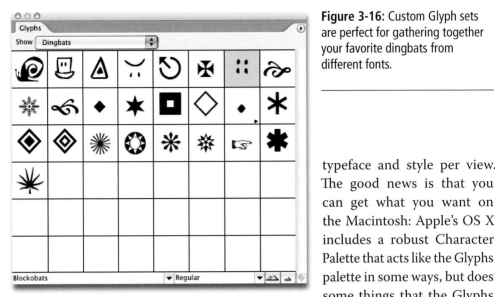

Figure 3-16: Custom Glyph sets are perfect for gathering together your favorite dingbats from different fonts.

TIP: Save your glyph sets! When you rebuild InDesign's preferences files — something some folks do routinely — all your custom glyph sets disappear. Truly annoying! The only way to save them from destruction is to back up your preferences files when they're in a healthy state. The next time you need to rebuild your prefs, don't do it, instead just drag a copy of your backup files into the InDesign preferences folder to overwrite them. Since custom glyph sets are part of InDesign's preference files, they'll come along for the ride.

View the Same Glyph in Different Fonts

? I'd like to use the Glyphs palette to view how a particular character looks in various fonts, all in the same window.

 The bad news is that the Glyphs palette is restricted to a single typeface and style per view. The good news is that you can get what you want on the Macintosh: Apple's OS X includes a robust Character Palette that acts like the Glyphs palette in some ways, but does some things that the Glyphs palette does not. One of its unique features is the ability to choose a glyph and see that same glyph as drawn by every active font, all in the same window. Fortunately, it works right within InDesign.

You can access the palette from within any program by choosing it from a menu. It's not in your menubar by default, though; you have to enable it. You only have to run through these steps once:

1. Open System Preferences and click on the International icon.

2. In the International preferences, click the Input Menu button.

3. Turn on the Character palette checkbox. While you're here, you might also want to turn on Keyboard Viewer (OS X's KeyCaps equivalent) and Unicode Hex Input, if you ever want to enter a glyph from the keyboard. Make sure the the Show Input Menu in Menu Bar option is also turned on.

Figure 3-17: Macintosh OS X's Character palette has a feature any designer would love. You can select a character in the top area, and see how that character looks in all active fonts on your system at the same time.

4. Close System Preferences, and return to InDesign.

5. To open the Character palette, click on the flag icon on the right side of your menu bar, and choose Show Character Palette. This is a

persistent palette and will appear on top of every window in every OS X program until you close it.

Now you're ready to enjoy the Character Palette's cool feature mentioned above.

1. From the Character Palette's View popup menu, choose Roman.

2. Make sure that "by Category" is the highlighted pane.

3. In the category list on the left pane, choose Latin (if the glyph is one of the 26 letters) or another relevant category. For example, if you want to see what an ampersand looks like in different fonts, choose the Punctuation category.

4. The right-hand panel shows generic glyphs for members of the selected category. Click the glyph you're interested in.

5. Below these panels you'll see a popup menu labeled Collections. Click on the menu and choose "Containing selected character."

6. In the bottom scrolling panel, OS X shows you the selected glyph as drawn by every font you have active in your system, with the name of the typeface and style below each one (**Figure 3-17**).

7. In this same panel, select the glyph you want to use, and click the Insert button (or just double-click the glyph). The character is inserted at your cursor location. If you think you'd like to use particular glyph/font combo again, click the Add to Favorites button. You'll be able to see and select glyphs added to Favorites by choosing that pane instead of "by Category."

Find/Change Dialog

Reset Character Color to "Any" in Find Format/ Change Format

? After spending ten minutes setting up Find Format and Change Format to do a complex operation, I realize that I shouldn't have specified a character color in either one. But in the Character Color section of the palette, there doesn't appear to be a way to empty the fill or stroke color so that InDesign will ignore it. Any way, that is, other than clicking the Clear

Format button in the main Find/Change dialog box, wiping out *all* my settings!

☑ In either Find Format or Change Format's Character Color area, Command/Ctrl-click on the swatch name (not the fill or stroke icon) of the color you mistakenly specified. The color icon will go back to its "Riddler" look (full of question marks, indicating "any color").

This trick also works when editing a character style: Command/Ctrl-click on the color swatch to remove it from the character style's definition (**Figure 3-18**).

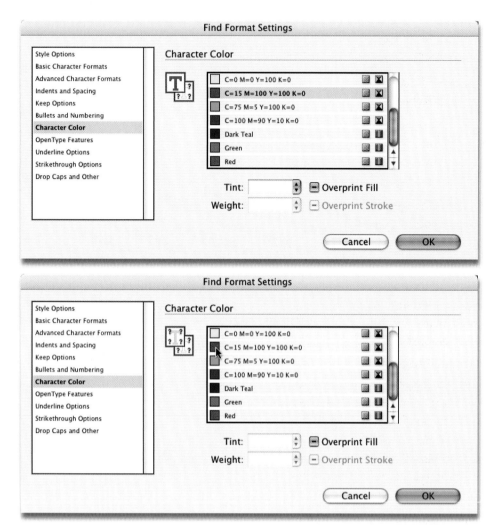

Figure 3-18: To clear out any Character Color you've specified in Find Format/Change Format, (top) hold down the Command/Ctrl key when clicking the Swatch's name. The question marks that now appear in the Fill icon (bottom) mean "any color."

Find/Change Straight Quotes to Curly Ones

 Remember me? I'm the one who got yelled at by my Art Director for using typographic quotes (the "curly" ones) instead of straight quotes for the item specs in a parts catalog. I need to know how to change them, hopefully in a way that's just a teensy bit faster than doing them one-by-one.

☑ To fix your catalog you'll have to run two separate Find/Changes, once for the inch mark and again for the foot mark. (Note that if there are some curly quotes in the regular text you'd like to retain, sharing the same formatting as the "bad" quotes, you can't do a document-wide Find/Change. You'll have to do it one selection at a time.)

1. Turn off Use Typographer's Quotes in Preferences.

2. Choose Edit > Find/Change (**Figure 3-19**).

3. From the popup menu to the right of the Find What field, choose Double Right Quotation Mark.

4. In the Change To field, enter a double straight quote mark from the keyboard.

5. In the Search popup menu, choose Document, Story, or Selection (depending on what needs changing).

6. If you're able isolate the quotes you want to change (versus the ones you want to leave curly) based on different text formatting, click the More Options button. You can use the Find Format command to select unique characteristics of the quotes you want to change.

7. Click Find First, then Change, at least a few times to make sure it's working properly. Then, when you feel confident, click Change All.

8. To Find/Change for the foot marks, replace the contents of the Find What field with the code for "Single Right Quotation Mark" from the popup menu; and replace the double quote in the Change To field to a single quote from the keyboard.

When you're done, re-enable the Use Typographer's Quotes preference.

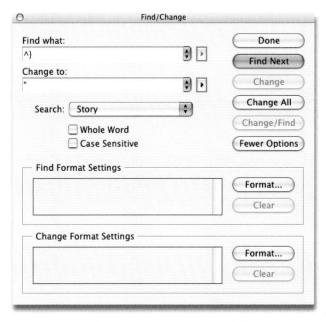

Figure 3-19: You can use Find/Change to turn curly quotes into straight quotes.

TIP: We know you're sitting there thinking, "Okay, so I have a document full of straight quotes that I need to make curly. What do I do now?" The answer is simple, but not necessarily obvious: Save the story as InDesign Tagged Text (using File > Export). Now, when you re-Place the story, turn on Show Import Options and make sure the Use Typographers Quotes option is enabled. All your quotes (single and double) will be converted.

Tabs

Clear All the Tabs At Once

? Is there anything more tedious than clearing out a mess of misplaced tab stops by dragging them off the tab ruler one by one, paragraph by paragraph? No, there isn't. QuarkXPress lets you do this really easily.

☑ It's easy here, too, though many people overlook it: the Tabs palette has a flyout menu. Choose "Clear All" from that menu (**Figure 3-20**). Bang, zoom, all custom tabs are cleared. In fact, you could shift-click multiple text frames with the Type tool, open the Tabs palette and choose that command to clear out *all* the custom tabs in *all* those selected text frames. Even better, if you need to do this a lot, you can assign a keyboard shortcut to this command using Edit > Keyboard Shortcuts.

Align the Tabs Palette to the Top of the Frame

? Sometimes the Tabs palette aligns perfectly with the top of the text frame containing the paragraph I'm setting tab stops for; sometimes it doesn't. What am I doing wrong?

☑ Scroll the page down or reduce the view scale until there's at least a half-inch or so of room between the top edge of the text frame and the horizontal ruler. If the Tabs palette is open but sitting elsewhere on the screen, click the little picture of the Magnet (no, it's not a horse shoe) in the right corner of the palette, and it will reposition itself to snap to the top of the frame.

Remember it's not that critical to keep the Tabs palette aligned with the frame in InDesign. Regardless of where the palette happens to be located, dragging a tab stop within it will still produce a vertical tab guide in the active frame, even if the frame's on the other side of the spread.

TIP: Did you know that you don't need to set a tab stop to create hanging indents? You still need to enter a tab character between a bullet and the first line of text, but you don't need to open the Tabs palette to set the stop. InDesign assumes you want the tab stop to equal the left paragraph indent, and inserts a "ghost" tab stop there for you automatically. It adjusts the spectral tab stop dynamically as you adjust the indents, too! Of course, if you use InDesign CS2's automatic numbering and bullets feature, then you don't have to worry about tabs or tab stops.

Giving Right-Aligned Tabs a Leader

? I love the right indent tab (Shift-Tab)! It's like a tab stop is placed at the paragraph's right margin and when the margin changes (such as when the text frame gets wider), the tab adjusts auto-

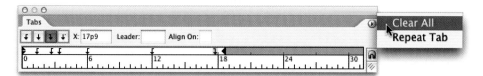

Figure 3-20: A fast way to get rid of all the tab stops in a paragraph is to choose the Clear All command from the Tabs palette menu.

matically. But there's one problem: I can't figure out how to get a tab leader (like dots) to fill the tab space.

✓ Unfortunately, InDesign CS cannot apply tab leaders to right indent tabs. But InDesign CS2 can! The trick is that the right indent tab always uses the tab leader from the last tab stop in the paragraph. Just add a tab stop with a leader character and the leader appears in the space created by the Shift-tab.

Tagged Text

InDesign Tags versus XPress Tags

? For years we've relied on tagged text documents to ensure that outside files imported properly into QuarkXPress using XPress's style sheets. We gave our writers cheat sheets listing which tags to insert to indicate a headline, subhead, and so on.

Now that we've moved to InDesign, these tagged documents no longer work; they don't import with InDesign styles applied even though the style names are the same as they were in Quark. Isn't tagged mark-up in a text file a generic sort of thing for all page layout programs? I tried searching InDesign's Online Help, but all the information on tags apparently is about XML tagging, which is a different beast altogether.

 The *concept* of tagged text documents is the same for all page lay-

out programs that support it, as is the general procedure, but the actual *tags* are different, program to program. Luckily, InDesign's tags aren't all that different from QuarkXPress's. The documentation you're looking for is in a PDF file on the InDesign CS installation CD. Look in the Adobe Technical Info folder for a file called Tagged Text.pdf.

However, if you're already using an XPress Tags workflow, you might consider just sticking with it because Em Software's XTags for InDesign plug-in lets you import XPress Tags into your favorite page-layout program. See *www.emsoftware.com* for more information.

> **TIP:** Contrary to examples shown in InDesign's documentation, where tags with inner caps are used, all tags for paragraph and character styles should be lowercase.

Include Inline Graphics in Tagged Text

? Our artists supply charts and graphs as Adobe Illustrator files that we need to embed in the copy flow as inline frames. I read through the documentation but apparently there's no tag available that means "insert X image file as inline frame." That really cramps our style!

✓ If you're on a Mac, there's a freeware scripted solution available. Include the image filename in the text, then run a script called Place Images 1.1, which you can download from the Adobe Studio here: *share.studio.adobe.com*

The Place Image script scans through a story's text, replacing any image filename with an inline image. Note that XTags for InDesign from Em Software can also handle this on-the-fly when you import the file.

Text on a Path

Set a Start Point for the Text

? Sometimes, InDesign ignores the position of my cursor when I click a path with the Text on a Path tool, and starts the text in an entirely different place. Argh!

✓ Text on a path is basically a one-line paragraph in a text "frame" that is the length of the path. So, when you click an insertion point with the Type on a Path tool, InDesign uses the current paragraph alignment to figure out where to start the text, just as it would with a normal text frame.

For example, if the current horizontal alignment for text is set to be left-aligned, InDesign will start the text at the left edge of the "frame" — the leftmost end of the path. You can change the paragraph alignment to centered or right and the text will shift accordingly.

Clicking on closed path is slightly different. The point where you click defines the left edge of the "frame," and the width of the frame extends around the entire perimeter of the shape, ending right before your insertion point. As soon as you click an insertion point you can change the paragraph alignment to suit your purposes, and the cursor and any text will reposition themselves within the bounds of the path text's frame.

Change the Starting Point of Text

? There has to be an easier way to change the starting position of the text other than what I've been doing, which is using the space bar, editing the path itself, or starting over with a new path.

✓ Use the Selection tool to click the text on a path. You'll see two I-beams appear, each with a text-threading port (a little box), one at the left edge of the path text's frame, the other on the right edge. Hover your cursor over either of these and drag to redefine the left and/or right boundaries of the frame, forcing the text to shift accordingly.

Don't forget that text on a path is the same as a single-line paragraph; so you could use a tab or a first-line indent to adjust the starting point as well.

TIP: Yes, they're thread-able! Those text-threading ports you see when you click on text on a path with the Selection tool aren't just for decoration; they're working In and Out ports. Thread one instance of text on a path to another, include them with normal text frames in a long threaded story, go crazy, man!

Center Text on Top of a Circular Path Quickly

? **Regardless of where I click on a circle with the Type on a Path tool, I can never get the text I enter to center perfectly on top.**

✓ Select the circle with the Selection tool so you can see its bounding box handles, and then switch to the Type on a Path tool (press Shift-T). Click an insertion point directly on the bottom handle at the 6:00 mark of the circle. Change the paragraph alignment to centered (**Figure 3-21**). Enter your text. Voilà.

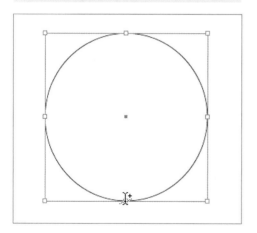

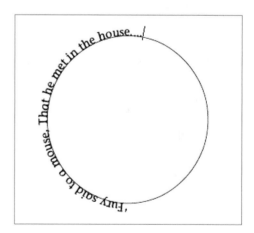

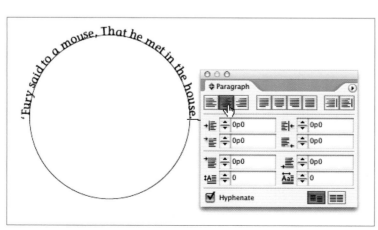

Figure 3-21: To center text on a path at the top of a circle, click your insertion point at the very bottom, enter your text, then change the paragraph alignment to Centered.

What if you want to put the text along the bottom of the circle instead of the top?

1. Start by putting the text along the top.
2. Choose Type > Type on a Path > Options.
3. Click the Flip checkbox.
4. Choose Ascender from the Align popup menu and Top from the To Path popup menu.
5. Click OK.

Now you can say voilà again.

TIP: Here's one more way to flip text on a path: When you select the path with the Selection tool you'll see a little perpendicular line sticking out in the middle of the path. If you drag that line to the other side of the path, the text follows and flips over, too.

TIP: You can also put the text inside a circle or under the path. Enter your text on a path normally, then change the position of the text in the Type on a Path Options dialog box. Try aligning the Ascender to the Top of the Path if you want the text to move downwards; or align the Baseline to the Bottom of the Path if you want the text to move upwards.

Text Wrap

Wrap Text Around a Table

? I need to get text to wrap around a table, but when I select the table, the Text Wrap icons are grayed out.

☑ The trick to making text wrap around a table is to place the table in a separate text frame:

1. Create the table in its own text frame, or cut an already-existing table to the clipboard and then paste it while nothing is selected on the page to put it into its own frame.

2. Select the table's text frame and choose Object > Fitting > Fit Frame to Content. (Or press Command-Option-C/Ctrl-Alt-C.) The frame snaps to the table's outer boundaries.

3. With the table's frame still selected, turn on the kind of wrap you want in the Text Wrap palette and set the offsets as you like.

4. Since InDesign CS does not support text wrap around inline objects, you'll need to place the frame containing the table on top of or underneath the main text frame (the one with the text) and the text will wrap around the table/frame. In this case, the table

will not change position if the text reflows.

However, InDesign CS2 *can* wrap text around an inline frame (as long as the wrapping text comes after the position where the frame is embedded). To anchor your table to a position in the text flow, cut the table's text frame to the clipboard, place the text cursor where you want to embed the table, and then choose Edit > Paste. Now you can select this inline frame and choose Object > Anchored Object > Options to adjust the position of the table.

TIP: To wrap text around the transparent area of a placed Photoshop image, place the image (saved in PSD format) in the layout, partially overlapping a text frame. Select the image with the Selection Tool and turn on the Wrap Around Object Shape option in the Text Wrap palette. If you don't see a Contour Options popup menu at the bottom of the Text Wrap palette, choose Show Options from the palette menu. Now, in the palette's Contour Options menu, select Alpha Channel. The text will use the image's transparency to define a wrap boundary. Use the Top Offset field to adjust how close the text comes to the 100% opaque pixels in the image.

Where Did My Caption Go?

? Whenever we place a photograph in an article, we turn on Text Wrap so the article text flows around. That's InDesign 101. But then when we put a caption immediately beneath the photo, or any text overlapping the image, the text disappears. It's like it gets pushed right out of the box by the photo's text wrap, even though the text is on top of the image.

QuarkXPress will only wrap text around an object when the text wrap object is above the text, but InDesign has no such limitation — the text can be above or below the image. So how do you get some text to wrap around the object and some text not to? One option is to select the text frame that has the text you don't want to wrap, choose Object > Text Frame Options, and turn on the Ignore Text Wrap checkbox at the bottom of the Text Frame Options dialog box.

If you'd rather InDesign act like XPress and ignore objects higher in the stacking order, as other programs do, you can set that in the Composition panel of the Preferences dialog box.

Make a Custom Wrap Border

? The four Text Wrap Offset fields (Top, Bottom, Left and Right) don't give me enough control. I wish I could tweak the text wrap in finer increments.

 Many people don't realize that you can see *and* finesse the text

'Well, there was Mystery,' the Mock Turtle replied, counting off the subjects on his flappers, '—Mystery, ancient and modern, with Seaography: then Drawling—the Drawling-master was an old conger-eel, that used to come once a week: he taught us Drawling, Stretching, and Fainting in Coils.'

'What was that like?' said Alice.

'Well, I can't show it you myself,' the Mock Turtle said: 'I'm too stiff. And the Gryphon never learnt it.'

'Hadn't time,' said the Gryphon: 'I went to the Classics master, though. He was an old crab, HE was.'

'I never went to him,' the Mock Turtle said with a sigh: 'he taught Laughing and Grief, they used to say.'

'So he did, so he did,' said the Gryphon, sighing in his turn: and

Figure 3-22: The Direct Select tool lets you see and edit a text wrap. You can use the Pen tool to add or remove points along the text wrap line.

wrap outline in InDesign. The trick is to select the object with the Direct Select tool rather than the Selection tool. As long as you can see the text wrap boundary when the wrapped object is selected, you can adjust it. Just drag on any of the corners or subpaths in the wrap boundary with either Selection tool to customize it (**Figure 3-22**). You can even switch to the Pen tool to add or remove points in the text wrap outline, too, just as though you were editing any other path!

Tables

Easy Selections

? **No matter where I click on a table with either Selection tool, InDesign refuses to recognize my "clicks" and doesn't select anything. But Selection tool-clicking works fine with everything else in InDesign, so I know the tool is working.**

 The Selection tool doesn't let you select a single paragraph in a text frame, does it? Tables act the same way: You have to use the Type tool to select them or edit them. Once you understand that simple requirement, InDesign makes it very easy to select exactly what you want in a table.

Here's one example: Click an insertion point inside a cell, and from there you can select the cell itself, the cell's row, the cell's column or the entire table via:

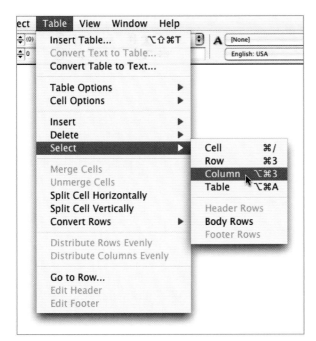

Figure 3-23: If you click inside a table cell with the Type tool, you can use the Table > Select submenu options to easily make a variety of table-related selections.

- The Table > Select submenu (which offers: Select Cell, Select Row, Select Column, and Select Table; **Figure 3-23**)

- The contextual menu (right-click, or Control-click with a one-button mouse), which also has a Select submenu;

- The keyboard shortcuts for Select Cell, Select Row, Select Column, and Select Table; which are listed next to the menu items.

If you hover with the Type tool over the top or left-edge table border, you'll see the icon turn into an arrow. Click to select an entire row or column, or click and drag to select multiple rows and columns. Hover over the top left corner of a table and the arrow points down and to the right, if you click when you see that arrow, the entire table is selected.

Scale a Table and its Contents

I know how to *resize* a table— I just hover over the lower right corner with the Type tool to see the double-headed arrow, then drag—but that maneuver doesn't also resize the *contents* of the table, which is what I really want. I can scale inline frames, why not an inline table?

 Ah, one of the great mysteries of life.

While you can't scale an inline table, you *can* scale the text frame that contains it, which will also scale the table and its contents. To prevent scaling everything else in the text frame, you should isolate it in its own frame first. Select the table, cut it, paste it into an empty text frame, and choose Fit Frame to Content (from Object > Fitting) so the new frame hugs the border of the table.

Then select that frame with the Selection tool, switch to the Scale tool, and drag to scale it just as you would for any other object. The contents of the table will scale along for the ride.

You can copy or cut the scaled frame and paste it back into the original text frame (with the Type tool) as an inline frame if you want the table to be part of the text flow again.

Freely Rotate Cell Contents

? Like Ford Motors in its early days (the Model T was available in any color, as long as it was black), InDesign lets me rotate text in a cell at any angle, as long as it's 90, 180, or 270 degrees. But need my column labels to be rotated at 30 or 45 degrees; 90 degrees is too hard to read.

☑ The tedious but do-able workaround is to put a cell's contents into its own frame, then cut and paste the frame as an inline frame into a cell. Now you can select the inline frame with the Selection tool and use any Transform command, including Rotate, freely.

Add a Tab Inside a Cell

? Whenever I click the Tab key inside a cell, InDesign moves my cursor to the next cell. I have set up custom tab stops for the text in this cell, all I want is for InDesign to honor them.

☑ That's a feature-not-a-bug for cell navigation. Use Option/Alt-tab

to insert a tab within a cell. It will move the cursor to the next default or custom tab stop it encounters, just as it works outside of a table.

Extend the Left Edge of a Table Outside its Frame

? I'm trying to create a table that extends beyond the width of its enclosing text frame on both sides, evenly. I notice that I can drag the right edge of a table outside of the text frame with no problem. But the same isn't true of the left edge of a table—in fact, I can't drag the left border *anywhere*, I get the right-arrow cursor for selecting the row instead.

☑ Click an insertion point next to the table (not inside the table, but to the left or right of it) and change the horizontal alignment to Centered from the Paragraph or Control palette.

That doesn't magically allow you to drag on the left border of the table, but when you increase the width of the table by dragging its right edge, the amount the table extends beyond the text frame will now be evenly split between the left and right edges (**Figure 3-24**).

Widen a Cell Without Widening its Column

? One of the cells in my table is a little too narrow to hold the content that has to be there. If I widen the cell by dragging or Shift-dragging on its right-hand border, I change the layout of the rest of the table, which I don't want to do. I could

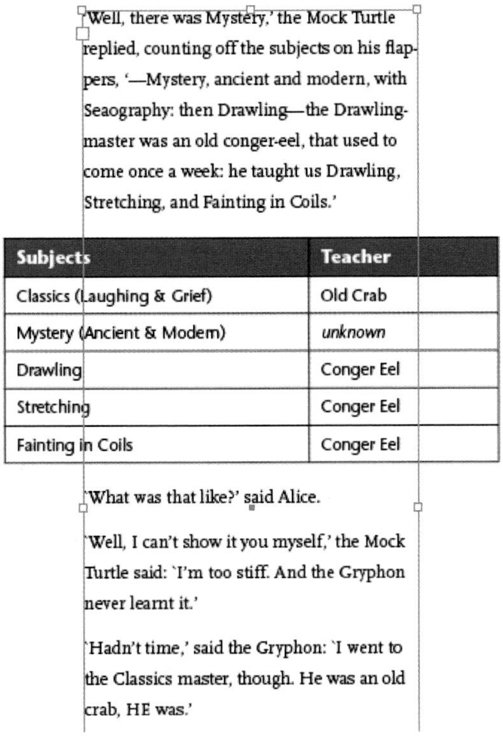

'Well, there was Mystery,' the Mock Turtle replied, counting off the subjects on his flappers, '—Mystery, ancient and modern, with Seaography: then Drawling—the Drawling-master was an old conger-eel, that used to come once a week: he taught us Drawling, Stretching, and Fainting in Coils.'

Subjects	Teacher
Classics (Laughing & Grief)	Old Crab
Mystery (Ancient & Modern)	*unknown*
Drawling	Conger Eel
Stretching	Conger Eel
Fainting in Coils	Conger Eel

'What was that like?' said Alice.

'Well, I can't show it you myself,' the Mock Turtle said: 'I'm too stiff. And the Gryphon never learnt it.'

'Hadn't time,' said the Gryphon: 'I went to the Classics master, though. He was an old crab, HE was.'

Figure 3-24: You can't drag the left edge of a table past the left side of its enclosing text frame, but if you make the table wider than the frame and then center it, InDesign will do it for you.

---

select the cell and the one to its right and choose "Merge Cells," but I don't really want to merge them into one cell—I need to keep the cell to the right as its own cell.

Select both the cell that you need to widen and the one to its right (drag across to select both of them) and choose Split Cell Vertically from the Table or contextual menu. You now have four cells where before there were two. We'll call them Cell 1, 2, 3 and 4.

1. Select any text in Cell 1 and cut it to the clipboard. Set the cell's left and right insets to 0.

2. Shift-drag the line between Cells 1 and 2 all the way to the left, as far as you can go. Cell 1 has now

virtually disappeared, and Cell 2 is wide.

3. Select Cells 2 and 3 by dragging across them, and choose Merge Cells (**Figure 3-25**).

4. Click inside the merged cell and paste the text in your clipboard into it.

5. Shift-drag the line between the merged cell and Cell 4 and drag to the left as far as possible without causing an overset in the merged cell. There's your wide cell.

Cell 4 should now be wide enough to hold the text that it originally held (when it was the one to the right of cell you needed to widen). If you run into minor alignment problems with the text in the merged cells, reduce the cells' left inset amounts.

NOTE: You can't click on a table with the Selection tool to delete it; you'll end up deleting the entire text frame. Instead, select the table with the Type tool and choose Delete Table from the Table or contextual menu; or click an insertion point to the right of the table (outside of it but next to it) and press the Delete key.

Color	Description	Quantity	Code
Red	Sweater	45	AB332
Green	18-wheeler	27	FF229
Blue	Suede Shoes	18	GA991

Figure 3-25: Following the step-by-step instructions in the "Widen a Cell" solution on the previous page, you can adjust a single cell's width without adjusting the width of the other cells in the column.

Color	Description	Quantity	Code
Red	Sweater	45	AB332
Green	18-wheeler	27	FF229
Blue		18	GA991

Color	Description	Quantity	Code
Red	Sweater	45	AB332
Green	18-wheeler	27	FF229
Blue	Suede Shoes	18	GA991

Color	Description	Quantity	Code
Red	Sweater	45	AB332
Green	18-wheeler	27	FF229
Blue	Suede Shoes	18	GA991

Paste Pictures in Cells Perfectly

? **When I paste an image inside a table cell, I seldom get what I want right off the bat. I'll end up with a blank cell showing an overset, or a huge cell that ruins the formatting of the rest of the table.**

✓ If you keep in mind that InDesign table cells are actually individual text frames, you'll be able to prepare the cell properly for accepting an image and avoid unpleasant surprises. When you paste an image into a table cell, it's the same as pasting an image into a text frame as an inline frame. All images in InDesign tables are, in fact, inline image frames.

That means that you can move the image up and down in the cell with the Selection tool, but you can't move it left or right, just like regular inline frames. (In InDesign CS2, they can also be anchored objects, so they can sit outside the table cell or even outside the text frame.) It also means that the image is treated like a text character in some ways — it's subject to the text frame's (cell's) paragraph alignment, text insets, first line offset, vertical alignment, and so on.

Here are some general guidelines for working with images in tables. Before you paste:

- If you want the image to "kiss fit" the edges, select the cell and set its text inset to 0 from Table > Cell Options or from the Table palette text inset fields.

- If you don't want the cell to automatically grow to fit the image,

image will appear in the cell, overlapping surrounding cells and text if the image is larger than the cell. So you'll probably also want to turn on Clip Contents to Cell in the Cell Options dialog box. That way the cell boundaries act as a clipping path for the image if it's too large (**Figure 3-27**).

ruining the table geometry, select the cell or row and set the Row Height to "Exactly." (You don't have to worry about Column Width, that's permanently set to an exact amount.) Of course you should set a height for the row that makes sense at the same time.

- If you set the cell to an exact height, and you paste in an image that's taller than that amount, you'll end up with a blank cell with an overset icon, and no way to select the image and scale it. Blech! To prevent this, open the Cell Options dialog box and change the First Baseline Offset settings for the cell to Fixed (**Figure 3-26**). When you click OK, the overset frame will appear and you can click on it with the Selection tool to scale it or drag it into place.

- If you set the cell to an exact height, *and* you changed the First Baseline Offset as described, the entire

Then, after you paste the image in, you can select it with the Selection tool to drag it vertically, crop or scale it, apply transparency, and do other Object-related things to it. You can also select the image inside the inline frame with the Direct Select tool to adjust its position within the frame, or scale it without scaling its frame. Finally, you can drag over it with the Type tool and set text formatting commands like space above/below, indents (from the cell boundaries), horizontal alignment, and so on.

Update Table Data Without Losing Formatting

? Between the powerful table features and the ability to place linked Excel spreadsheets, I'm in hog heaven. Well I *thought* I was in hog heaven, until the first

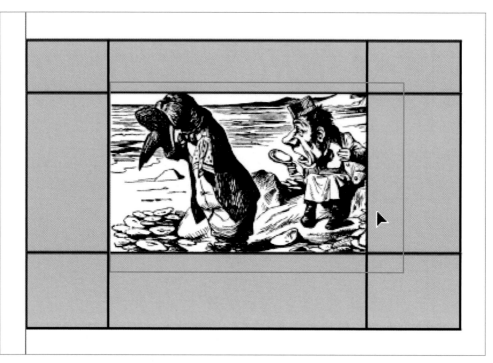

time I used the Links palette to update a linked spreadsheet. When the text repopulated the table I had spend so much time on, all the formatting was lost!

Figure 3-27: If you set a cell to an Exact Height, and you set its First Baseline Offset to Fixed (Figure 3-26), and you turn on Clip Contents to Cell, images that are too large for the cell are much easier to deal with.

Yup, you're in hog hell. The good news is that there are a few different solutions, the not-so-bad news is that they cost a few bucks.

First, Dave Saunders wrote a shareware cross-platform script called PopTabFmClp.js (Populate Table From Clipboard) which you can download, along with documentation, from his site: *www.pdsassoc.com*. After you've placed and formatted the original Excel or Word data into a table in InDesign, at any time you can go back to the Word or Excel file, select the updated data and copy it to your clipboard. Back in InDesign, you select the first cell of the formatted table and run the script from the Scripts palette (choose Windows > Automation >

Scripts). The script pastes the data into the cell and reapplies the formatting.

There are also two plug-in solutions for this problem. The first is Teacup Software's (*www.teacupsoftware.com*) TableStyles, which lets you — surprise! — create named styles for tables. After you have saved your table formatting as a style, you can update the linked spreadsheet (which wipes out the formatting) and simply reapply the table style. Another solution is the InDesign plug-in SmartStyles from Woodwing Software (*www.woodwing.com*) which does a similar thing but with a very different user interface.

Graphically Speaking

Graphically Speaking

*H*OW DO I PLACE THEE? LET ME COUNT THE WAYS.
I place thee from File > Place, and to the depth and
breadth and height
My OS can reach, by clipboard, or by drag and drop
From Finder, Explorer, or Photoshop's File Browser.
I place thee in the image format of my choice,
Or of my client's or stock photo company's, depending.
I place thee traditionally, as TIFF and EPS.
I place thee wantonly, as JPEG and GIF and BMP.
I place thee transparently, as PSD and AI and PDF.
And when placed on the page, thou patiently endures
Application of scale and crop, shadow and feather, until
Thine opacity is slid and mode blended till the end of being.
Old griefs may annoy, but they are few and easily fixed.
I place thee with a love I seemed to lose
With the software of my childhood. I place thee with the breath,
Smiles, tears, of all my life; and, if Adobe choose,
I shall but place thee better in the next version.
(Apologies to Elizabeth Barrett Browning)

Pesky Placing Problems

Place Multiple Images at Once

? I'm working on a parts catalog that has an average of twenty images per page. When I choose File > Place, I can only select one image at a time to import into my document. This is going to take forever!

✓ Open a Windows Explorer window or a Macintosh Finder window and navigate to one of the folders on your hard drive that contains some (or all) of the images you want to import. Make sure you can also see a part of your InDesign document window at the same time — you may need to resize and rearrange the windows a bit.

Now you can Shift-click (use Command-click/Ctrl-click for a discontiguous selection) or drag a selection rectangle around multiple image filenames in your Explorer/Finder window, and drag and drop the selection onto the InDesign window (**Figure 4-1**).

All the images you dragged over are placed onto the active page at the same location. Each is at 100% scale, has its own graphics frame that InDesign creates on the fly, and comes with its own link to the actual image in the Links palette. (In other words, exactly as if you had used the File > Place method and clicked on the page with your loaded graphics cursor, over and over.)

The images overlap each other, so you'll have to drag each one to its correct page position on your own. We're hoping that the next version of InDesign

will magically read your mind and position them for you.

What do you lose with this method? You can't access the Import Options dialog box (an optional screen in the Place dialog box) for any of the files. If you need to set up Import Options, turn it on when you place one image of the same type as the others. The next time you use drag-and-drop, InDesign uses those same Import Options.

> **TIP:** Mac and Windows users can use the same drag-and-drop technique from Adobe Photoshop's File Browser window or — if you're using CS2 — the Adobe Bridge application. Just Shift- (or Command/Ctrl-) click multiple image thumbnails in the Browser/Bridge, drag the selection out of the Browser/Bridge window and over any portion of your InDesign document window, and drop it.

> **TIP:** You can drag a single image directly from the Finder, Explorer, or Adobe Bridge into a frame that already exists on your page as long as the frame is empty.

Which Layer, Which Transparency?

? The guy down on the fifth floor is preparing the Photoshop files that I need to place in InDesign. He doesn't know exactly what we need, so he sets

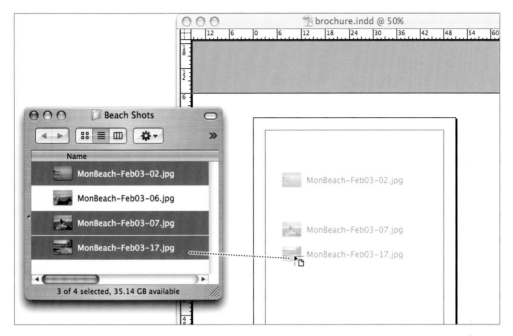

Figure 4-1: Drag the selection over any part of the InDesign document window that's visible. When you see a black outline appear, release the mouse button.

up a bunch of extraneous layers in his files for us to turn on or off. But we're getting mighty tired of opening these big files in Photoshop each time we need to make a change.

☑ If you're still using InDesign CS, we don't have a lot of good news for you other than a quick reminder that you can click the Edit Original button in the Links palette (or right-click/Control-click on the image and choose Edit Original from the contextual menu; in CS, this is in the Graphics submenu) to open those Photoshop files quickly. The good part about using Edit Original instead of opening the files from Photoshop or the desktop is that InDesign automatically updates the links as soon as you return to your document.

TIP: In InDesign CS2, the Edit Original feature moved to the Edit menu. But we eschew menus whenever possible. Instead, the fastest way to the Edit Original feature is to Option/Alt-double-click on the image with the Selection tool.

But the best solution for handling Photoshop layers is to get InDesign CS2, which lets you control which layers are visible at any time, right from within your InDesign layout. You can control layer visibility when you first import a Photoshop (PSD) or PDF file by turning on the Show Import Options checkbox in the Place dialog box. Or, you can change layer visibility for a selected image at any time by choosing Object > Object Layer Options (**Figure 4-2**). This feature is also available in the context menu by right-clicking — or Control-clicking on the Macintosh — on the image.

If you and your Photoshop guy haven't explored Photoshop's Layer Comp fea-

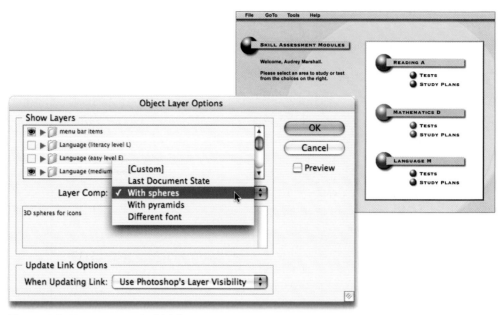

Figure 4-2: You can control which layers are visible in PSD and PDF files from within InDesign CS2.

ture, we encourage you to do that, too. At its most basic, a layer comp is a named set that remembers which layers are visible and which are not. But a layer comp can also remember where objects are positioned on a layer and which layer effects are applied. That means the guy on the fifth floor can create a bunch of different options — moving text around to different places, turning on the drop shadow effect or turning it off, and so on — and save each one as a layer comp in the same PSD file. Then you can pick the one you like best from within InDesign CS2, because the Object Layer Options can read layer comps as easily as it can read layers. Very slick.

Bring in Microsoft Charts and Graphs

? I've got a pie graph embedded in Microsoft Excel worksheet that I want to place in my InDesign document. I can import the Excel data, but the graph doesn't come along for the ride. The same thing happens — err, doesn't happen — with Word files that have charts or graphs. Very frustrating.

You're right, when you place a Word or Excel document, InDesign doesn't include — in fact, it doesn't even recognize — embedded artwork. Even if it did, though, you probably wouldn't want to use the artwork in a professionally printed piece. Microsoft-generated charts and graphs are RGB and low-res, which is fine for on-screen viewing and printing to your local inkjet. It's *not* fine for high-end, separated process- or spot-color printing.

The key is to isolate the artwork and get it into a "real" graphics program where it stays intact but editable, so you can tweak the paths, fonts and colors as necessary. Then you can save the file in any of the image formats InDesign can deal with and place it in your document.

Select the chart or graph in Excel by clicking on it. Hold down the Shift key and go to Excel's Edit menu. You'll see that the command "Copy" changes to "Copy Picture" when the Shift key is held down. When you select Copy Picture, Excel displays a dialog box asking which *appearance* and *size* you want to copy—"as shown on screen" or "as shown when printed." Choose the latter for both.

Open up Adobe Illustrator (or the vector drawing program of your choice) and choose Edit > Paste. The chart comes in as editable vector shapes—woo-hoo! From there, you can copy it again as paths (with AICB turned on; see "Paste Paths from Illustrator" on page 118) and paste it into InDesign as an editable chart. You can also paste it into Adobe Photoshop, but it comes in as a flattened raster layer, quite difficult to edit. Or, stay in your drawing program and modify the chart there. Save the file and use InDesign's File > Place to import it just like any other image.

TIP: Want a quick-and-dirty way to get your chart into InDesign? Copy it as a Picture as described above, but skip the "paste into a drawing program" step. Just paste it right into InDesign as an embedded, low-res RGB graphic. We don't really recommend this method, but it does work—usually.

Place Slides from Microsoft PowerPoint

? We're working on our company brochure and need to include some examples of PowerPoint slide presentations we've created for clients. But InDesign's Place dialog box grays out all PowerPoint filenames (the ones that end in .ppt), making them inaccessible.

☑ Convert your presentation to a file format that InDesign understands. From within PowerPoint, you can choose File > Save As and choose the TIFF format. In the same dialog box, click the Options button and choose a higher resolution for the file (the default is 72 ppi) so the TIFFs won't get all pixelated upon output. Microsoft creates one RGB TIFF file for every slide in the presentation and puts them neatly in a folder you specify.

To maintain crisp text outlines and vector shapes, you might consider making a PDF of the presentation, and

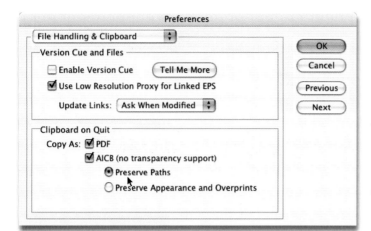

Figure 4-3: Set up Illustrator's Clipboard handling preferences as shown if you want to copy and paste editable paths between it and InDesign.

Turn on "AICB (no transparency support)" and the "Preserve Paths" radio buttons (**Figure 4-3**). Now you can copy Illy's paths and paste them in editable form in InDesign.

> **TIP:** This works in reverse, too, as long as AICB is selected in Illustrator's Clipboard preferences. You can copy InDesign paths and frames and paste them into Illustrator for editing. That's what we call "Suite!"

placing selected PDF pages/slides into InDesign. PowerPoint has no built-in PDF capabilities, so you'll have to do this "the old fashioned way": Print the file to PostScript and run it through Distiller, or print directly to "Adobe PDF" which appears as a virtual printer if you've installed Acrobat 6 or 7.

Paste Paths from Illustrator

? A couple months ago I went to a seminar on InDesign. The presenter did this one cool trick that for the life of me I can't replicate: He selected a vector path in Adobe Illustrator, copied it to the clipboard, switched to his InDesign document and pasted it. The path came in completely editable. Every time I try the same thing, the path I paste comes in as an uneditable graphic. Lame.

✓ Maybe you were busy at the snack table while the presenter talked about setting Illustrator preferences? That's the key to getting this technique to work.

In Illustrator, open Preferences and go to the File Handling & Clipboard panel.

Place Multiple Pages from PDFs

? We have a 64-page PDF that needs to be imported into our InDesign document. The Place dialog box only lets us choose one page at a time, but we need to get all 64 pages in here, one per page.

✓ Importing a multi-page PDF file into InDesign is a major hassle in InDesign CS, but now CS2 speeds up the process. It's still not fully automatic, though: You have to click once for each page in the PDF that you're importing. (You can Option/Alt click to automatically import all the pages at once, but they all end up on the same page of your document.) Here's another option, if you're on a Macintosh running CS: try the free script by Martin Sretr available for downloading in the InDesign scripts section of the Adobe Studio Exchange site, *http://share.studio.adobe.com*

Previews that Don't

Fixing Preview-less Illustrator Images

? What's all the hoo-hah about InDesign being able to place native Illustrator files? It seems half-baked to me. Some Illustrator files come in just fine, but others show an error message (something about "missing PDF compatibility") in the frame instead of a preview of the image. I'm back to using EPS's, which import and preview just fine, every time. But I'm still scratching my head about the whole .ai thing.

✓ Those preview-less images are probably native Illustrator files from a much older version of the program. (Perhaps from an old clip art collection?) Open one of these in a more recent version of Illustrator and choose File > Save As. From the Format popup menu, make sure it's set to Adobe Illustrator Document (.ai) — it should be chosen by default — and click the Save button. You'll get one more dialog box called Illustrator Options. Turn on "Create Compatible PDF" and click OK. Now try placing it again, and see if the "hoo-hah" makes sense to you.

Highest-Quality Previews, Automatically

? The screen previews of images that I place into InDesign are sometimes so pixelated they're almost worthless. (Especially vector EPS's. They're the worst!) Scaling them down in InDesign doesn't help, and zooming in just makes it worse. When I'm trying to create a tight text wrap to the image's contour, I have to make printouts to see how I'm doing.

✓ You can fix this on an image-by-image basis, or if you have a fast computer, you can fix it for all images.

InDesign's default settings for image previews are controlled by the options in Preferences > Display Performance, which assume your computer isn't fast enough to create high-quality previews for every image. And this may well be true, especially if you're working on an image-intensive document.

To override the default preview setting ("Typical") for a particular image, and force InDesign to create a High Quality preview for it, select the image and choose Object > Display Performance > High Quality Display. (Or choose the command from the context menu.)

To make it so that *all* images get a high-quality preview from the get-go, change the Preferences defaults themselves. In Preferences > Display Performance > Default View, change the setting from Typical to High Quality.

Alternatively, you can leave the Default View at Typical, and change what "Typical" means by moving the sliders in the lower part of the dialog box. A good suggestion would be to leave Raster Images at the "Proxy" setting (so it doesn't slow down InDesign too much), but slide Vector Images and Transparency all the way to their highest settings (no more chunky EPS's).

Scaling Insanity

View the Scale Percentage

? I scaled my image down to about 50% with the Scale tool. I can see that the image is much smaller than before, but the Scale X Percentage and Scale Y Percentage fields in the Control palette and Transform palette still say "100%."

☑ Yes, this is crazy-making. To see the actual scaling percentage of the image, switch to the Direct Select tool, and click on the image inside the frame. Now take another look at the fields. Ta-da! You see the percentage your image is scaled to (**Figure 4-4**).

It's a pain to switch tools all the time, so if you need to scale an image to an exact percentage, the fastest way is to select it with the Selection tool (which selects the frame and its contents), enter the scale amount in the Scale X/Scale Y fields, and press Return/Enter.

The "100%" technically refers to the scaling of the *frame*. And the reason it says the frame is still 100 percent even though you just scaled it down? Artwork created inside the program — including frames that InDesign creates on its own when placing images — is always considered at 100 percent scale, regardless of how much you manipulate it.

Scale the Stroke Along With It

? My book catalog has tons of images of book covers, each with a 1-point black frame (stroke). When I scale one of these images, I get unpredictable and confusing results regarding the stroke weight. It seems that when I want the stroke to scale the same percentage as the image, it won't, and when I want it to stay at the original 1 pt. weight, it scales in tandem with the image. And even then, when it's obvious the stroke weight is far more than 1 pt. (because I scaled the book image up a great deal and the stroke got thicker), the Stroke Weight field still says 1 pt. What's going on here?

☑ There are three factors that influence what you describe — two menu items and the tool you use to scale — and different combinations of these factors have different results. Let's take it step-by-step.

Figure 4-4: Use the Direct Select tool to see a selected image's current scaling percentage.

other than dragging on its corner with the Command-Shift/Ctrl-Shift keys held down.

So what about the other problem — that the Stroke Weight field doesn't change, even after scaling a frame? InDesign is trying to be helpful by remembering your original stroke

You may have noticed there's a Scale Strokes command in the Control palette and Transform palette menus. When it's turned on (choose it so it gets a checkmark), stroke weights are scaled as you scale a graphic frame; when it's off, stroke weights stay the same regardless of frame scaling (**Figure 4-5**).

However, even if Scale Strokes is turned on, InDesign won't scale the strokes of frames you're scaling via the Command-Shift-drag/Ctrl-Shift-drag method. It only kicks in when you scale via entering numbers in the Scale X/Scale Y fields, or by using the Scale or Free Transform tool.

Thus, if you want the stroke to be scaled along with the image frame and its contents, you have to 1) Turn on the Scale Strokes command; and 2) Use any method to scale the image

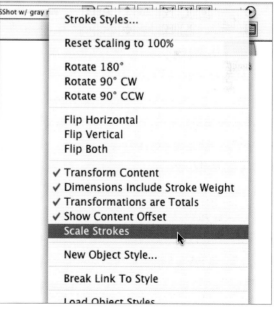

Figure 4-5: The Scale Strokes command is found in either the Transform or Control palette menus.

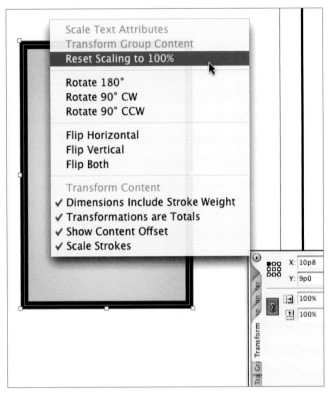

Figure 4-6: The Reset Scaling
to 100% command can also
be found in the Transform or
Control palette.

one for scaling *up* by 1%,
Command-[period], replaces
all my images with gray
boxes, and I can't Undo it.
Weird! The keyboard shortcuts for scaling images by
5% increments in either
direction work fine. It's only
the "scale up by 1%" one
that's wonky.

✓ You need to buy a
new computer. Just
kidding! That's a definite
bug in InDesign CS for the
Macintosh. The gray boxes you're seeing are the images' Optimized previews.
Normally you'd get this effect by choosing
View > Display Performance > Optimized
Display ("Fast Display" in CS2). You can
fix what's happened to your previews by
going to that same menu and resetting
it to Typical or High Quality Display (or
pressing Command-Option-Z/Ctrl-Alt-
Z). Fortunately, Adobe fixed this short-
coming in InDesign CS2.

While you're still using CS, you can
fix the keyboard shortcut itself: Just add
Command-. (period) as the keyboard
shortcut to the "Increase size/scale by
1%" feature (choose Edit > Keyboard
Shortcuts, then choose Product Area:
Object Editing). That fix appears to
goose InDesign into remembering what
Command-. (period) is for.

weight. Or maybe it got the munch-
ies and went out to the kitchen to look
for some Fritos, figuring you wouldn't
notice. Whatever the case, you can
pour a bucket of cold water on its head
by choosing "Reset Scaling to 100%" in
the Transform or Control palette menu
(**Figure 4-6**). Magically, the stroke weight
field shows you the actual weight currently in effect.

Broken Mac
Keyboard Shortcut
for Scale Up 1%

? I'm on a Macintosh. When I use the
default keyboard shortcuts for scaling an image by 1%, scaling down works
okay—Command-[comma]—but the

Manipulating Madness

Take the Image, Leave the Frame

? Okay, I admit it, I'm a recovering Quark-aholic. As such, I'm having a grand old time with the cool advanced features in InDesign, but it's the little, simple things trip me up, because I'm so accustomed to how I used to do it. Case in point: Moving an image around inside the frame. I can't. There's no Content tool. It's not the Hand tool, even though it looks like it should work.

The closest equivalent to Quark's Content Tool in InDesign CS is the Direct Select tool (press A when not editing text), the hollow arrow (or white-filled arrow, for you optimists out there). With nothing selected, click on the *image* (not the frame) with the Direct Select tool. Now you can drag it around with abandon, and the frame will stay put. If you press and hold for a few seconds before you start dragging, you'll get a nice surprise: You can see the image move, and areas outside the image frame are ghosted back.

The Direct Select tool lets you do even more, though: You can move the frame and leave the image in place by Option/Alt-clicking on the edge of the frame first. Then drag the frame (or its center point) around.

In InDesign CS2, you have one more option: The Position tool (press Shift-A) is more similar to QuarkXPress's Content tool or PageMaker's Position tool. It lets you move an image inside a frame (you

even get your coveted hand icon), crop the frame differently by dragging side or corner handles, or move the whole frame by dragging on the side of the frame (not a handle) or the centerpoint handle.

Find the Offset

? Did Adobe forget to include the fields for X and Y image offsets? I've looked in every nook and cranny but I just can't find them.

You missed a cranny. Look in the Control palette menu (or Transform palette menu) for "Show Content Offset" and turn it on by choosing it. To see how much an image is offset from its frame, click on the image with the Direct Select tool. The X Position and Y Position fields in the Control and Transform palettes will show the X and Y offsets, respectively (**Figure 4-7**). With Show Content Offset turned off, the same selection would show the image's offset from the 0/0 mark on the *page*.

Swap Images in Frames Without the Place Command

? I've got a couple of bad images in perfect frames. The frames are sized, shaped and stroked just right. So I'd like to replace these images with different ones, leaving the frames untouched. Since the new images are already in my document, I thought I could just copy and paste them

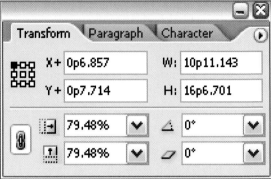

Figure 4-7: By turning on the Show Content Offset command and selecting an image with the Direct Select tool, you can see how much the image is offset from its frame.

in, instead of rooting around my hard drive again in the Place dialog box.

I took care to use the Direct Select tool to select one of these new images before I copied it to my clipboard via Edit > Copy. But when I click on the image that I want to replace and choose Edit > Paste, InDesign ignores the selection and puts my pasted image in its own frame in the center of the page. Argh! Is there no pleasing this program?

☑ Chill, dude, everything was copasetic until the pasting part. To replace one image with another in your clipboard, leaving its frame untouched, select the target *frame* (not the image) with the Direct Select tool, and choose Edit > Paste *Into* (not Edit > Paste).

Colorize a Grayscale

? I need to place the same grayscale image several times in InDesign and colorize it using different swatches. However, when I select one of these placed grayscales and click on a color only the frame background fills with a color. The black pixels are still there, unaltered.

☑ To get the effect you're after — that monotone look — use the Direct Select tool (instead of the Selection tool) to select the image, and then apply your color. Now the color affects the pixels in the frame instead of the frame (background) itself. This works with TIFF and PSD grayscale images as well as bi-level (black-and-white, no shades of gray) bitmap images.

You can achieve a fake duotone of sorts by applying a different color to the frame background, using the regular Selection tool.

WARNING: If your grayscale image has transparency, you won't be able to colorize it in InDesign.

Set an Illustrator File to Overprint

? When a placed Illustrator image is selected, the Overprint Fill and Overprint Stroke options in the Attributes palette are grayed out. I need them on!

✓ InDesign can only overprint its own strokes and fills, not those of imported graphics. To make sure an Illustrator vector image will overprint everything underneath it in InDesign, set the overprints in Illustrator's own Attributes palette. InDesign will honor those settings saved with the image.

Quickly Apply Graphic Styles

? There's no way in InDesign CS to save all the attributes of an object as a "style," similar to how you can save all the text formatting commands affecting some type as a paragraph or character style. So if I decide that I like the look of a particular image frame in my publication — its stroke (weight, color and style) and maybe even

Mastering the Eyedropper

Suppose you want to make sure that all the shadows you applied to objects in your document carry the same settings (color, blend mode, blur amount, and so on).

If you use the Eyedropper to do this without changing its default settings, you'll apply not just the source frame's Shadow, but also its stroke weight, color, transparency, and more.

Before you use the Eyedropper, always double-click its icon in the toolbox to set its options. Attributes that are checked in the Eyedropper Options dialog are settings that the tool will pick up and apply. If you want it to ignore something, click the checkbox next to the attribute to turn it off. Be sure to twirl open the category triangles to review and set subcategory attributes.

In our "Make consistent shadows" example, you would open the Eyedropper Options dialog and uncheck all the main categories: Stroke, Fill, Paragraph, Character and Transparency. Checking/unchecking a main category also checks/unchecks all its subcategories. Then you'd twirl open the Transparency category and click a checkmark next to the Shadow setting.

After you've set the Options, click OK to close dialog. When you click with the Eyedropper on a shadowed object, it only picks up the Shadow settings and ignores all other attributes of the object. And when you click with the loaded Eyedropper cursor on other objects in your document, it applies only the Shadow and leaves all other attributes untouched. If the object already had a shadow, the Eyedropper changes it to the Shadow settings of the source object if necessary.

its background tint—I have to memorize all its settings and then tediously apply them, palette by palette, to the other image frames in my document.

☑ You have hit on one of the best reasons to upgrade to InDesign CS2: Object Styles. But until your boss wakes up, smells the coffee, and orders you the upgrade, you may need to settle for the Eyedropper tool (the keyboard shortcut is, of course, "I") to eliminate a lot of the tedium. Click on the "source" frame (not the image or text inside the frame) with the Eyedropper to pick up all the settings the Eyedropper is capable of. You'll see the Eyedropper cursor "fill up" (turn black and flip direction) with the information. Now you can click on the other frames in your document with the loaded Eyedropper to apply those settings.

The Eyedropper is cool (even if you are using CS2) because you don't have to bother selecting objects before you click on them, and it "remembers" what it's loaded with if you switch to another spread or even another document! However, this powerful tool in your arsenal warrants a bit of study; see the sidebar "Mastering the Eyedropper" on page 125.

For all its glory, the Eyedropper can't pick up *everything* (it ignores image scale and offset, rotation, corner effects and table settings, among other attributes) nor does it create anything close to your yearning for a "graphic style sheet." For that kind of power you'll have to pay for the upgrade or check out Woodwing's Smart Styles plug-in (*www.woodwing.com*) or Teacup Software's TableStyles (*www.teacupsoftware.com*).

> **TIP:** To "empty" the Eyedropper on the fly so you can load it up with another object's attributes, hold down the Option/Alt key, and keep it held down while you click on the new source object.

Then, when you do get CS2, check out Object Styles. The fastest way to make an object style is to format a single object (like the frame you described above) and then Option/Alt-click on the New Object Style button in the Object Styles palette.

The Links That Bind

Tracking Down Picture Usage

❓ After all these years using XPress, I miss a "Picture Usage" dialog box in InDesign. Where is it?

☑ Welcome to InDesign, freshie. The information you're looking for is in the oddly named "Links" palette: Window > Links. It's not called the "Picture Links" palette because it also tracks any linked text files. (Fortunately, InDesign doesn't link placed text files by default, like it did in version 2. You have to turn on that option in Preferences > General.)

You may have assumed the Links palette was for embedded hyperlinks, a common assumption with new users. *That* palette is found in Window > Interactive > Hyperlinks.

Point "Edit Original" to the Right Program

? Something is screwy with InDesign's innards, I think. I selected a placed Photoshop image that I wanted to modify and clicked on the Links palette's Edit Original button. Instead of it opening in Photoshop, though, it opened in Adobe Reader! It doesn't happen all the time, but enough so that I've resorted to using Windows Explorer to open images I've placed, right-clicking on them to get the "Open With" option so I can select Adobe Photoshop. I wish I could right-click in InDesign and get an "Open With" menu.

☑ Yeah, that would be great! It's a commonly-requested feature for both platforms, you can be sure.

In the meantime, though, InDesign is subject to the file associations set up by your computer's operating system. Normally these work fine. However, in the case you mention, you probably saved your Photoshop file as a Photoshop PDF with a .pdf file extension. When you went to Open Original, InDesign queried your Windows operating system: "Hey, the kid wants to open a PDF file. Which program goes with that?" The OS replied, "Let me look this up… okay, here you go, PDF files open in Adobe Reader. Want me to open it up?" "Yes, please."

You can modify which files are associated with which applications. See the step-by-step instructions for both Windows and Macintosh operating systems in the sidebar, "Roll Your Own Edit Original Settings" on the next page.

TIP: Photoshop PDFs are a special case. On the Macintosh, Photoshop PDFs are *always* associated with Adobe Photoshop, even if all other "normal" PDF files are associated with Reader, Acrobat or Preview.

On Windows, you should use the optional .PDP extension when saving an image as a Photoshop PDF. That tells the OS (and, in turn, InDesign), that 'forest_scene.pdp' is a Photoshop PDF file and thus should be opened in Photoshop, not Reader or Acrobat or whatever.

Update Multiple Entries at Once

? The same image (logo.tiff) appears ten times in my InDesign document, and so it appears ten times in the Links palette. If I make a change to the artwork, save the file and return to InDesign, each of the ten entries in Links shows the yellow triangle icon, meaning the art has been modified. If I update one of the entries, the other ones still show the yellow triangle. I don't understand why I have to update each entry individually. Shouldn't InDesign update all of them as soon as I update one of them?

Roll Your Own Edit Original Settings

As explained in the "Edit Original" solution, InDesign uses your computer system's internal file extension mappings to decide which program should open a given placed image. If InDesign is opening images in the "wrong" program, you need to modify your system's settings manually. Luckily, it's pretty easy.

As an example, let's say that you want to change which program InDesign uses for JPEG images when you choose Edit Original.

Windows (XP)

1. Select a JPEG file in Windows Explorer. Make sure the filename ends with .jpg.

2. Right-click on the file and choose Properties. The first panel, General, shows which program will open that JPEG image by default. Let's say it currently says "Paint" and you want JPEGs to open in Adobe Photoshop CS2. Click the "Change" button to the right to open the Open With dialog.

3. In Open With, select Adobe Photoshop CS2 from the scrolling list of installed programs. Make sure that the checkbox underneath the list, "Always use the selected program to open this kind of file" is checked on (it is, by default).

4. Click OK in both dialog boxes to close them and apply your new setting.

Macintosh (OS X)

1. Select a JPEG file in a Finder Window. Make sure the filename ends with .jpeg.

2. Choose File > Get Info, and click on the triangle next to the "Open With" panel to twirl open its contents. You'll see the name of the program the Mac currently associates with that file extension. Let's say it currently says, "Preview" and you want JPEGs to open in Adobe Photoshop CS2.

3. Press and hold on the application popup menu (which currently shows Preview) and choose Adobe Photoshop CS2 from the list of suggested alternates.

4. In this same section of the Get Info window, click the "Change All" button. Click "OK" in the resulting "Are you sure?" warning dialog box to apply your new setting. Close the Get Info dialog box.

On either platform, you may want to repeat these steps for filename variations such as .jpg and .jpeg or .tif and .tiff. Open With settings are quite literal!

It's a feature-not-a-bug, because you may want to inspect each of those instances (Go to Link) to see if you really do want to update the artwork — perhaps you'd prefer to replace it (re-link it) with something else. Seems kind of lame, though. InDesign should at least give you the option of updating all the instances at once with a dialog box or preference setting or something.

Meanwhile, here's what you do. Open the Links palette menu and change the sort to "Sort by Name" so all the logo.tiff entries appear together. Click on the first one in the palette and Shift-click on the last one so all ten are selected. Now when you choose Update Link, all the entries will be updated at once. Change the sort back to "Status" (if that's how you had it) when you're done.

Or, if you have a lot of modified images to update all at once, make sure *no* images are selected in the Links palette by clicking in the blank area at the bottom of the list of links. Now when you click the Update button, InDesign updates them all. Much faster.

TIP: Selecting multiple entries in the Links palette (by Shift-clicking or Command/Ctrl-clicking) works with the Relink command too. As you relink each image, InDesign keeps the Relink dialog box open, updating the "current path" field with the next image in the selection.

Force a "Scroll to Top" in the Links Palette

Most of the projects my co-workers and I produce are dense, image-laden parts catalogs for our company. The Links palette for one of these catalogs, which we update quarterly, typically contains hundreds of entries for all the parts artwork. It's sorted by Status (the default sorting) so that "problem" links appear at the top of the palette. No problem. But as soon as I fix one of the links — re-link or update it — InDesign scrolls the palette all the way down to the last entry, which is the link I just fixed. I have to scroll and scroll to get to the top of the palette to fix the next link. It's not a big deal until you're doing it for the 35th time that morning.

Close the Links palette and then open it again with its keyboard shortcut, Command-Shift-D/Ctrl-Shift-D (press the combo twice, once to close it, once to open it). When it's freshly opened, the Links palette is scrolled to the top by default.

Drop Shadow Shenanigans

Change the Angle of a Drop Shadow

? There's no angle setting for shadows in Object > Drop Shadow. The images I've placed in my movie poster all have a light source coming from the lower right, so shadows that I want to apply should appear on top and to the left. InDesign seems locked into a light source that is up and to the left.

☑ Use a negative number in the Shadow Offset fields to move the shadow to the left and/or top of your selection. Is this as good as an "angle" feature? No. But it's all we've got. In InDesign CS2 you can save the negative offsets as part of an object style, which helps. For more drop shadow power, check out InEffects at *www.alap.com*

Apply a Drop Shadow to Just Some of the Words

? I selected the two words in my six-word headline that I want shadowed, but the Object > Drop Shadow command is grayed out.

☑ The only way to shadow live, editable text is to select its frame with the Selection tool and choose Object > Drop Shadow. All the text in the frame gets shadowed; it's all or nothing.

So you have two options: First, you can cut the two words and paste them into their own frame, apply a shadow to

it, press Command-Option-C/Ctrl-Alt-C to shrink the frame down to the size of the text, then cut/copy that frame, and paste it back into the headline as an inline frame. The second method is to select the two words with the Type tool and convert them to outlines (Type > Create Outlines) which automatically inserts them in the same location as an inline frame, then select that inline frame with the Selection tool and apply the shadow to it (**Figure 4-8**).

The first method is the better one if you think you'll need to edit the words at some point, because it's still live text. Outlined type is a bunch of paths and not editable with the Type tool. But the second method is much faster.

Fix Drop Shadows on EPS Images

? For some reason, I can't get the Drop Shadow to apply to the contents of placed vector EPS images, they appear on the image's frame instead. I know the EPS has a transparent background because I checked it in Illustrator. InDesign says the frame is transparent too (it has a fill color of None). The weird thing is that the drop shadow looks correct when I turn on High Quality Display, but it still prints or exports as a PDF incorrectly.

☑ You've stumbled on a major bug in InDesign, and one that was not entirely squashed in CS2. Here are some ways you can avoid being bitten by it:

- Open the EPS in the illustration program and resave it as a PDF file

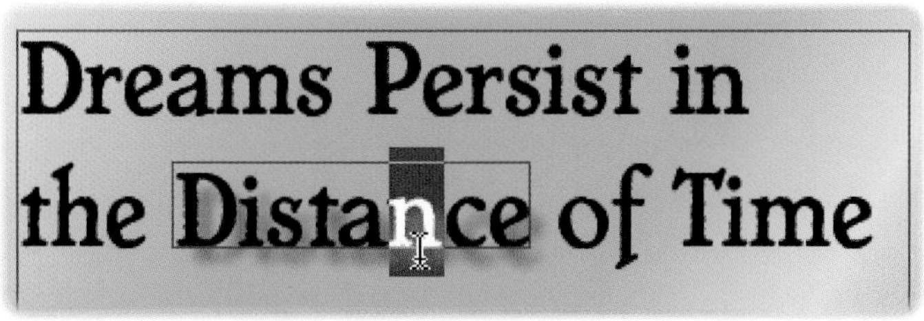

Figure 4-8: If you isolate words in their own frame and paste it into the text flow as an inline frame, you can apply a drop shadow and retain the ability to edit the text.

instead of an EPS. Or, if you need to use EPS for some reason, use a TIFF preview instead of PICT (or just use no preview at all, in which case InDesign will just make one for you). Since you're using Illustrator, you can also save as a native .AI file.

- If you don't want to resave all your EPS files, you can force InDesign to use a TIFF preview on the fly by opening the Display Performance panel of the Preferences dialog box and changing the Vector Graphics slider to the right until it reads "High Quality" (**Figure 4-9**).

- Another option is to change how you import vector EPS files: Turn on the Show Import Options checkbox in InDesign's Place dialog box (or hold down the Shift key while you double-click on the filename to force the Import Options dialog box to appear). In the Import Options dialog box, change the Proxy Generation from the default "Use TIFF or PICT Preview"

to "Rasterize the PostScript" and click OK. This forces the image to be placed with a high-resolution preview instead of its ordinary preview, if it had one. Note that this choice is "sticky"—InDesign remembers your Proxy Generation choice and uses it for all vector EPS's you place in that document or any others from then on, even if you don't open the Import Options dialog box for them. (But it reverts to "Use TIFF or Pict Preview" if you rebuild your InDesign preferences.)

- If that didn't fix it, open up the image in Illustrator and see if there's an old, superfluous bounding box around the image. (If there is, InDesign considers that to be part of the contents and is putting the shadow around it.) You may need to view the file in Illustrator's Outline mode to see it. If it's there, select the bounding box and delete it, then save the file and update the link in InDesign.

- Final fix: Select the image frame, remove the drop shadow (Object > Drop Shadow), and deselect it (Edit > Deselect All). Now grab the Direct Select tool and click on the *image* (inside the frame) and re-apply the drop shadow. This shouldn't be necessary with vector EPS's, but sometimes it's the fix that finally works.

Figure 4-9: A placed Illustrator EPS file to which a Drop Shadow has been applied in InDesign may give you an inaccurate preview (left). On the right: the same graphic after its Display Performance was changed from Typical to High Quality.

Increase the Shadow Resolution

? **The service bureau kicked back the PDF I gave them (which I had exported from my InDesign file with the Print preset) because their preflight check said the resolution of my shadows was too low — 150 ppi. They want at least 225 ppi. I can't find a place in InDesign where I can specify the resolution of the shadows, so I have to recreate them in Photoshop.**

☑ We're going to ignore the fact that your output provider is obviously clueless; no one needs a drop shadow to have that high a resolution because there are no fine details in drop shadows. However, since you asked: The resolution of any raster artwork created as a result of InDesign's transparency features — and

Drop Shadow is one of these — is governed by the Transparency Flattener setting. If you choose Medium Resolution in the Flattener popup menu when you export a PDF or print, InDesign creates 150 ppi shadows (and other rasterized elements).

While there's probably nothing wrong with that, we generally recommend choosing High Resolution flattening whenever we print to anything other than a desktop laser printer (**Figure 4-10**). The High Resolution setting creates 300 ppi shadows (and much higher resolution — 1,200 ppi — for rasterized text and other detailed elements).

Next time, before you export a PDF to give to a service bureau or printer, ask them to send you a list of the settings they require for exporting PDFs from InDesign, especially those settings involving transparency and flattening.

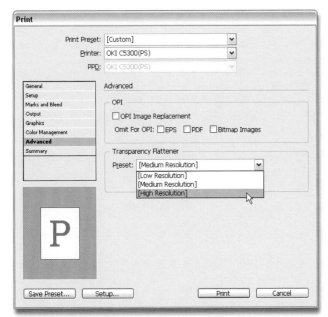

Figure 4-10: Change which Transparency Flattener Preset InDesign should use in the Print dialog box's Advanced panel.

Crop a Drop Shadow

? I need to crop out the bottom right corner of a rectangular image, to "bite a chunk out of it." When I do that (by editing the frame path with the Direct Select and the Pen tools), the shadow I applied to the image keeps redrawing on top of the crop. I need both the image *and* the shadow in that corner cropped out.

✓ Remove the shadow you applied and start again. This time, use the Direct Select tool to select just the image, and apply the shadow to that. Since your frame is presumably tightly-fit to the image, you won't see anything at first. Use either Selection tool to drag the frame sides away from the image so the shadow is revealed where you want it.

> **TIP:** You can use this method to apply a shadow to just one side of an image, too.

> **TIP:** If your image isn't square cut, you'll have to edit the frame edge (the one you're using to crop the shadow) to match the outlines of the image, similar to a clipping path.

Vendors should tell you this information as soon as you tell them they've got the job, but they hardly ever do. They're too busy complaining to each other about the files they get from designers.

> **TIP:** Want more realistic drop shadows? InDesign CS only creates mathematically perfect shadows. However, InDesign CS2 lets you add some noise to drop shadows, which makes them much more natural-looking. You typically only need 4 or 5 percent to make the difference.

Color My World

Color My World

COLOR HAS JUST ABOUT TAKEN OVER THE DESIGN AND PUBLISHing workflow. With the confluence of short-run digital color presses and high-end, affordable color printers in the office, black-and-white publications are quickly becoming an anachronism. It's even hard to find a section of a mainstream newspaper without a splash of color.

Luckily, designers armed with Adobe InDesign are at the top of their game as far as color is concerned. All the colors of the rainbow (and probably more) are available at the click of an icon. Would you like your color served as CMYK, RGB, Lab, Pantone, Toyo, or TruMatch, sir? They're always on the menu. And palette. And palette menu.

As you get deeper into InDesign, the choices multiply: process and spot colors? Okay, we get it. But then you also have mixed inks, tint colors, ink aliases, overprinting colors, transparent colors, not one but two color palettes, a Gradient tool that doesn't apply a gradient, oy!

With such an array of choices, you're bound to run into a problem or two along the way. Or three.

Follow along, and we'll see if we can clear up any of your chromatic conundrums.

Swatches Palette Quirks

Where's White?

? **The default Swatches palette doesn't contain the color White. Bizarre! I have to select it in the Color palette and then add it to the Swatches palette.**

✓ True, there's no "White" listed in the Swatches palette, but if you double-click the default swatch called "Paper" to open its Swatch options, you'll see its color mix: C0 M0 Y0 K0 — in other words, White. Use that when you want to color something white (**Figure 5-1a**).

It's called Paper because it matches the preview color of your document, which by default is white as well. If you're designing something that's going to be printed on colored (or unbleached) paper, such as a brown paper grocery sack, you can change the color mix for Paper and get a somewhat-accurate preview (enable color management and use View > Proof Colors if you really want a high-quality color match). Applied to objects, the brown paper color still "acts" like white, though — it knocks out colors beneath it to show the color of the paper (**Figure 5-1b**).

The only time you really need to add the color White (in addition to Paper) is if you're going to be using white ink, such as in a silk-screened T-shirt design. In that case, you'd change the Paper color to match the color of the T-shirt fabric, and use the White color — defined as a spot color — to make things white (**Figures 5-1c and 5-1d**).

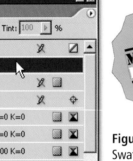

Figure 5-1a: The Swatches palette's "Paper" color serves as white for most documents.

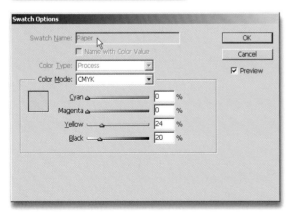

Figure 5-1b: If you're printing on colored stock, you could edit the Paper color to match.

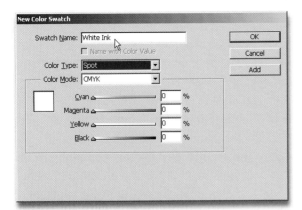

Figure 5-1c: Create a spot color called "White" and fill an object or text with it when you actually do plan on using white ink.

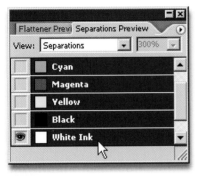

Figure 5-1d: This way, the White artwork will separate onto its own plate. Your silkscreen vendor will thank you.

Edit Swatches Without Applying Them

? It drives me crazy that when I just want to double-check a color mix of a Swatches palette color, or change its name, or do almost anything in the Swatches palette, I end up applying that color to something in my document. I didn't tell InDesign to apply the color, so why does it insist on doing so? And can I make it stop?

☑ The problem is that to open a swatch's Options dialog box (to check its color mix, to rename it, to change it from process to spot, or whatever) you have to double-click on the

swatch, and InDesign "reads" the first click of that double-click as: Apply the color to any selected objects. We've been telling the folks at Adobe that "double-click" should *not* be the same as "click once and then click again" but they're stubborn on this one.

Anyway, the first fix that comes to mind is the ever-useful Edit > Deselect All command (Command-Shift-A/Ctrl-Shift-A). If you use that first before futzing with the Swatches palette, InDesign has nothing to apply the color to. (*Except* the default fill or stroke colors—those will update to the most recently-clicked color swatch, regardless. It may not matter to you, though.)

If you'd rather not lose your selection, and/or you don't want the current default fill/stroke color to change, hold down Command-Shift-Option/Ctrl-Shift-Alt while double-clicking the color swatch. That tells InDesign "ignore what I'm doing with this color, I don't want to apply it to anything right now." You can release the keys as soon as the Swatch Options dialog box is open.

> **WARNING:** The "ignore" keyboard shortcut will only work if a color swatch — any swatch other than None — is selected in the Swatches palette when you want to use the shortcut. If you click in the blank area under the list of swatches to deselect them or choose the None swatch, and then use this shortcut on a swatch, the "ignore" workaround is, um, ignored.

> **TIP:** You can also use either of these same two strategies (Deselect All first, or use the "Ignore" keyboard combination) to edit Paragraph and Character Styles without applying the style sheet to selected text.

Customize the Default Swatches

? The default CMYK swatches aren't bad, but I never use them, so I always delete them. I just want the basics: White, Black, None, and Registration. It would be great to add my company's identity colors — the spot color we use in our logo and its CMYK equivalent — to the default palette, but that would be too much to ask, I guess.

☑ There's no such thing as "too much too ask" with InDesign — okay, maybe there is, but in this case, you're covered.

The Swatches palette is one of the many palettes that are editable in InDesign even when no documents are open. Any changes you make to it in this state are saved as the new Swatches palette defaults. (See the sidebar "Application Defaults" on page 9 for more details.)

So: Close all documents and open the Swatches palette. Choose "Select All Unused" from the Swatches palette menu, then delete the colors it selects. You're left with Paper (white, by default), Black, None (transparent) and Registration, none of which can be deleted. Paper, however, can be edited to match the color of the paper you print on.

Go back to the Swatches palette menu and use any of the New Swatch commands to add colors to your default palette. In your case, you'd choose New Color Swatch and add your spot and CMYK colors. You might want to add tint swatches for each of these while you're at it, and what the heck, a couple new gradient swatches that use your corporate colors.

Quit InDesign to save your new defaults. The next time you open a new document in InDesign, the Swatches palette will list your customized colors.

Change the Swatch Order

? What a pain that there's no Sort command in the Swatches palette! The magazine we produce uses over fifty custom swatch colors, and of course the

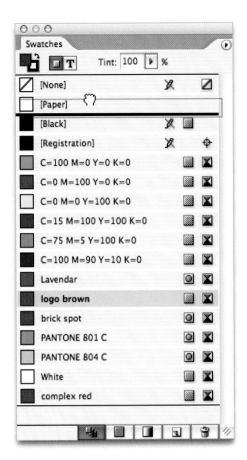

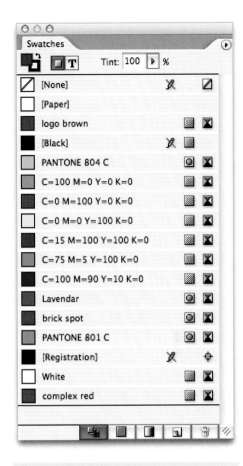

Figure 5-2: Drag and drop swatches in the Swatches palette to move your favorites to the top.

ones we use most often are in the most inconvenient locations on the list. Half our production time is spent scrolling through the palette looking for a color.

☑ Until Adobe adds the command you're looking for, you can drag and drop swatches to different locations in the palette and they'll stick there (**Figure 5-2**). Drag your favorite ones to the top and your scrolling time will be reduced significantly.

TIP: Drag the default Registration color to the bottom of the Swatches palette. It's probably the least-used color in your documents, why allow it to hog top billing? Do this while all documents are closed, and it'll stay there for future files you create.

Also, you can quickly jump to a swatch by Command-Option/Ctrl-Alt-clicking in the Swatches palette to activate it (you'll see a thin black frame surround the swatches list), then type the first few letters of the swatch name. You can also use the Up and Down Arrows on your keyboard to navigate the list. If you've added a Pantone, TruMatch or other library color that uses a numbering system to the palette, you only need

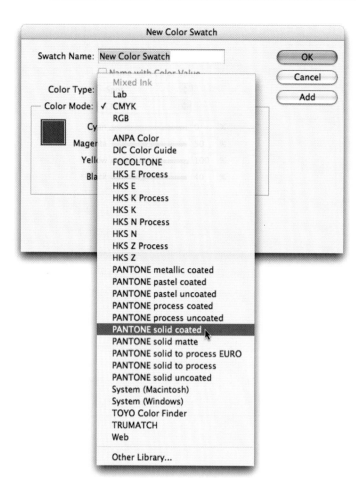

Figure 5-3: The secret lair of the third-party Swatch Libraries.

Hey, you're getting warmer… warmer… you're so close! Choose New Color Swatch from the Swatches palette menu, then look in the Color Mode popup menu. When you click the Color Mode popup menu (**Figure 5-3**), all the Swatch Libraries appear. Choose a library to view its swatch collection. Select a swatch and click the Add button to copy that color to your Swatches palette.

to type the number to jump to it. When you're done, press Enter or Esc to move the "focus" out of the palette and back to your page.

Find the Hidden Swatch Libraries

? Where are the Swatch libraries for Pantone, Trumatch and Toyo? In Illustrator I can open them from Window > Swatch Libraries > [name of Swatch Library]. I've searched all the menus in InDesign and they're nowhere to be found, not even in the menu for the Swatches palette itself.

Add Metallic and Pastel Swatch Libraries

? I want to use a Pantone Metallic color in the über-cool presentation folder I'm designing for a client in InDesign CS, but that library doesn't appear in the Swatch Library list. It *does* appear in Illustrator's list of Swatch libraries, though. Does that mean if I want to use Pantone Metallics, I have to design the folder in Illustrator?

No, but it does mean you'll have to either upgrade to InDesign CS2 (which does ship with these libraries — see **Figure 5-3** above) or grumble at

Figure 5-4a: Open one of these swatch libraries in Illustrator.

3. After the Swatch library document opens, choose File > Export. Don't worry about messing up the file for Illustrator's purposes; exporting always exports a copy of the file, and you won't be saving any changes to the original.

Adobe while you convert a copy of the Illustrator swatch library you want to a format InDesign CS can read.

Both programs store their default Swatch libraries here: [Name of Application] > Presets > Swatches. The libraries themselves are stand-alone native Illustrator documents.

You can't just copy and paste the swatch libraries over, though. The ones in the Adobe Illustrator CS folder are in Illustrator CS format (.ai files), and for some reason InDesign can only access them if they're in Illustrator version 8 format.

No problemo! Just follow this step-by-steppo:

1. Open Adobe Illustrator CS.

2. Choose File > Open, navigate to Adobe Illustrator CS > Presets > Swatches (**Figure 5-4a**) and double-click the Swatch library you want to convert.

4. In the Export dialog box:

   a. Navigate to the Swatches folder in *InDesign's* Presets folder so the exported file is saved to that location. That way, the "new" Swatch Library will appear as just another library in InDesign's Color Mode: popup menu (**Figure 5-4b**).

   b. Rename the Swatch Library if you like.

   c. In the Format popup menu, choose Illustrator Legacy (.ai), and click the Export button.

   d. In the Illustrator Legacy Options dialog box, open the Version popup menu and choose Illustrator 8. Click the OK button to complete the export of the converted file. (Don't worry about the alert

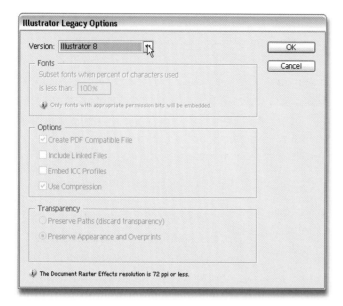

Figure 5-4b (left): Export it to InDesign's Swatches folder in Illustrator 8 format.

Figure 5-4c (below): The swatch library appears in InDesign.

Now you can switch to Adobe InDesign and check out the list of swatch libraries available: Choose New Color Swatch from the Swatches palette menu and then look at the Color Mode popup menu (**Figure 5-4c**). You don't even have to restart InDesign for the new libraries to appear.

If you saved the exported file to the correct folder (InDesign's Presets > Swatches folder), you'll see it listed along with the default libraries. If you saved it elsewhere, choose Other Library and navigate to the swatch library's location on your hard drive.

that pops up after you click OK — something about editing legacy files — you won't be opening this file again.)

e. Close the library document (don't save any changes) and quit out of Illustrator.

Load Just the Swatches You Want

? I want to use a few of the colors I used for another client's project (done in InDesign) in the one I'm working on now. According to the manual, to add swatches from another InDesign document, I should choose Load Swatches from the Swatches palette menu, and then double-click the name of the InDesign document that has the swatches I want. When I do that, though, *all* the colors come over. I just want two, not thirty! It's annoying to have to delete all the swatches I never wanted InDesign to add.

✓ Ah, you can always tell the folks who haven't upgraded yet! InDesign CS2 offers what you want: the options to import just a few swatches out of many. But while you're stuck in the last version, you can try one of two methods.

Method 1: Open the "source" InDesign document (the older one that has the swatches you want) on top of your "target" InDesign document (the project you're working on now). Resize the source document window a little smaller so you can see a bit of the target document in back. With the source document in front, open its Swatches palette, select the color swatches you want (you can Shift- or Command/Ctrl- click to select more than one), and drag and drop them anywhere on the target document window. They immediately get added to the target document's Swatches palette.

Method 2: Don't bother opening the source document; we're going to sneak in its back door. In your current (target) InDesign file, open the Swatches palette and choose New Color Swatch from its menu. Don't worry about the Color Type (spot or process) popup menu. In the Color Mode menu, choose Other Library and double-click the name of the source InDesign document. Its swatches open

as a "library" just like any other Swatch Library. Select a swatch and click the Add button to add it to your Swatches palette. (If it's a spot color, it gets added as a spot; if it's a process color, it gets added as a process color.) Repeat the procedure as many times as necessary to bring in your desired colors, then click the Done button.

> **TIP:** You can use Method 2 to roll your own custom Swatch Library! Create a new InDesign document and add your favorite swatches to it using any method you like. Save the blank document (with a name like "My swatches.indd") in the same folder as the other InDesign Swatch Libraries: Adobe InDesign > Presets > Swatch Libraries. That way, your custom library appears in the list along with the other ones — you won't have to choose Other Library to find it.
>
> You could get quite creative with this and create custom libraries for each of your larger/ongoing client projects: Acme Inc. colors.indd, New Print Ad Campaign swatches. indd, and so on.

Identify Mystery Colors

❓ Just by scrolling through my document I can tell at a glance that it uses a ton of colors that aren't in the Swatches palette. Are they process? RGB? Spot colors? I have no idea. Where did they come from?

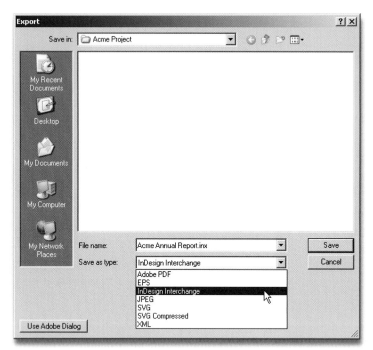

Figure 5-5: Be glad Adobe left the Adobe Interchange format as an export option, it can fix a lot of problems.

list before going on to something else. Or you can drag the little color icon from the Color palette into the Swatches palette. One way or another, it's just a good practice to make sure the colors are in the Swatches palette.

✓ Anyone could have snuck into your office in the middle of the night and used the Color palette to add these "unnamed" colors (colors with no equivalent in the Swatches palette). Unnamed colors are unpredictable, because it's hard to tell if they're RGB colors or not. Fortunately, InDesign has a quite useful safety net that will fix the situation. From the Swatches palette menu choose Add Unnamed Colors. This scans through the entire document and adds a new swatch for every mystery color. It just takes a second or two. When it's done, you can scroll through your new swatches and look at their icons to get an at-a-glance readout if they're spot, process, CMYK or RGB, and so on. (And of course you can double-click a swatch to change any of these settings.)

When you (or whomever is sneaking into your office) use the Color palette to mix a new color, try to remember to click the New Swatch icon at the bottom of the Swatches palette to add it to the

No-Surprise Swatch Merging

? I could learn to love the Merge Swatches feature if it would give me a chance. In theory, it would let me replace a group of similar swatches with a single one, changing the color of all affected objects to the new swatch in the process. But it's impossible to predict which of those selected swatches InDesign will designate as the replacement! Sometimes it's the top-most swatch in the selection that replaces the others, sometimes it's one somewhere in the middle . . . is my palette missing a checkbox or something?

✓ There *is* a method to its madness: Top dog status goes to the first swatch you select. Shift-click or Command/Ctrl-click the other swatches — the ones you want replaced by the first swatch you clicked on — to add them to the selection. Then choose Merge Swatches from the Swatches palette menu.

Banish Zombie Swatches

? **Somehow I've ended up with a color Swatch that refuses to die. It's not used in the document, nor in any placed image, but I can't delete the color nor merge it with another one.**

✓ No one has been able to explain to us why this sometimes happens. It's kind of scary. Fortunately, you can use this cure-all for flaky InDesign CS documents and the swatch will disappear:

1. Open the document in InDesign and choose File > Export.

2. In the Export dialog box, change the filename slightly (so you don't end up replacing the original) and then choose InDesign Interchange from the Format menu (**Figure 5-5**). The file's extension will change to .inx. Click the Export button.

3. Go to the File menu again and choose Open. Find the .inx file you just created and open it. InDesign converts .inx files back to .indd (InDesign format) files when they're opened.

Check your Swatches palette: Magic! The zombie color is gone.

What's an Adobe Interchange Format?

InDesign CS can export documents to a number of formats: JPEG, EPS, Tagged Text, and… Adobe Interchange. What's that about?

Apparently, during the development of CS, Adobe engineers were working on a way InDesign version 2.X users could open documents created in version 3 (CS). A document in the newer version would be exported to an intermediate state called "Adobe Interchange" with its own .inx extension to distinguish them from "normal" InDesign files. Then, Adobe would make a free InDesign 2.X plug-in available so users who hadn't upgraded to CS yet could open .inx files and convert them to InDesign version 2 files.

Unfortunately, by the time InDesign CS was released, only half of the plan was completed. Exporting to .inx format works in InDesign CS, but there is no InDesign 2.X plug-in to read them, and as of this writing no announced plans to do so.

Intrepid InDesign CS users have found that exporting a misbehaving InDesign document to .inx format and then reading it back in (opening the .inx file in InDesign CS), often clears up inexplicable problems, such as the "Zombie Swatch" solution described on this page.

The story has a happy ending: Adobe finally got this working for CS2. To open a CS2 file in CS, you can export it as .inx. InDesign CS has to have the free "April 2005" update for this to work, however.

Color Palette and Gradient Palette Weirdness

Show the Color Gamut Ramp

? Coming from Photoshop, I'm a big fan of the Color palette. I like using the rainbow-ish color ramp at the bottom to quickly pick out a color and then tweaking the sliders above the ramp to fine-tune it (and yes, I'm always careful to make a new Swatch out of the colors I create in the palette). What drives me crazy is how InDesign keeps replacing the CMYK or RGB color ramp and sliders in the Color palette with a single-color tint ramp and slider. If I wanted a tint of a color, I'd use the Tint field in the Swatches palette.

☑ It sounds like you want to change the Color palette's default view. With no documents open, open the Color palette. You'll see the default view is a tint ramp (**Figure 5-6a**). Use the Color palette menu to change it to the CMYK (**Figure 5-6b**) or RGB color spectrums, whichever you prefer. Quit InDesign to save your new application defaults and then launch it again.

Now, the only time you'll see a tint ramp in the Color palette is when you've selected an object linked to a Swatch color (other than None). Otherwise you'll see the default color gamut ramp you chose above.

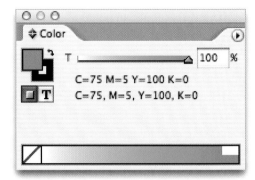

Figure 5-6a: The fairly useless tint ramp. (If you're going to make a tint, you might as well turn the color into a swatch and create a tint swatch.)

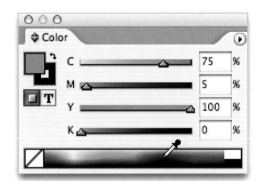

Figure 5-6b: Shift-doubleclick on the tint ramp to switch to the CMYK gamut ramp.

TIP: To quickly change from a tint ramp to a CMYK gamut ramp in the Color palette, Shift-double-click on the tint ramp. Each single Shift-click cycles through one color ramp, and it takes two clicks to get from a tint ramp to the CMYK one.

Figure 5-7: Click on the middle icon to invoke InDesign's hidden default gradient.

No Default Gradient Swatches

? When I click on the "Show Gradient Swatches" icon at the bottom of the Swatches palette, all I get is a None (transparent) swatch.

☑ There *is* a default gradient built into InDesign CS (black to white), but for some reason Adobe didn't add it to the Swatches palette. Look for the three little icons in a row near the bottom of your Tools palette, right above the bottom icons for Normal/Preview mode (**Figure 5-7**). In the row of three icons, click the middle one, "Apply Gradient." You'll see either your Fill or Stroke icon, whichever was active, fill with a black-to-white linear gradient.

Now open your Swatches palette and click the New Swatch icon at the bottom. The gradient gets added to your Swatches palette.

It's not much, but at least it's a start. If you want to add more default gradients, you'll have to create your own and add them to your default Swatches palette (see "Customize the Default Swatches" on page 140).

Use Swatch Colors in Your Gradients

? When I create my own gradients I often want to use one or more of my custom Swatch colors in it. But InDesign won't let me click a color in my Swatches palette when I'm building a gradient—I either get the "error" alert sound, or a selected object fills with the solid color I click on (instead of filling the gradient ramp I'm working on), or nothing happens at all.

☑ You *can* get a Swatch color in your gradient, but the way you get it depends on how you're creating the gradient. Just as InDesign offers two ways to create a solid color—from the Color palette or from the Swatches palette menu's New Color Swatch command—there are two different ways to create a gradient: The Gradient palette or the New Gradient Swatch command in the Swatches palette menu.

One thing the two methods share in common is what you've already discovered: You can't just click on a color in the Swatches palette to assign it to a selected gradient color stop. That would be too straightforward, son! Where's your head?

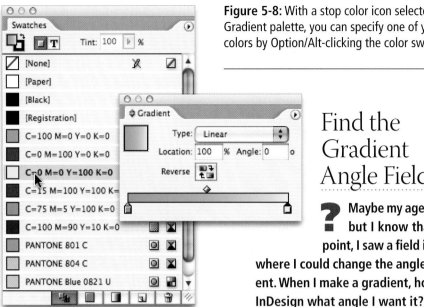

Figure 5-8: With a stop color icon selected in your Gradient palette, you can specify one of your swatch colors by Option/Alt-clicking the color swatch.

Find the Gradient Angle Field

? Maybe my age is showing, but I know that at some point, I saw a field in InDesign where I could change the angle of a gradient. When I make a gradient, how do I tell InDesign what angle I want it?

When you're using the Gradient palette, you need to hold down the Option/Alt key when you click on a color in your Swatches palette (**Figure 5-8**). That tells InDesign "I don't want this color to become the new Fill/Stroke color, I want to apply it to the stop color icon I've selected in this gradient I'm working on."

When you open the New Gradient Swatch dialog box from the Swatches palette menu, you can't get to the Swatches palette at all — your clicks are ignored. And there's no reason to, actually, because they're right there in front of your face: Click on the Stop Color popup menu and choose the Swatches option. All your solid color swatches appear in a scrolling list in the dialog box. Click on any of them to apply it to a selected stop color icon in your gradient ramp.

✓ You're not that old, dear. Select an object that's filled or stroked with a gradient and open the Gradient *palette* (**Figure 5-9a**). There it is! The angle you enter only affects how the gradient is applied to the selection, not to the gradient itself. Note that the Gradient palette also offers a "reverse gradient" icon so the gradient colors are applied in the opposite order of the stop colors.

Neither of these fields is really necessary, however. It's easier to use the Gradient tool from the Tools palette. Use a Selection tool to select an object with a gradient fill or stroke, then drag the Gradient tool over it. The gradient's angle changes to match the angle you dragged the tool. Drag the tool from right to left to "reverse" the colors of the gradient.

Unfortunately, with InDesign CS there is no way to globally set a particular angle for a gradient swatch. You have to apply the swatch and then change the angle each time you need it. You can work

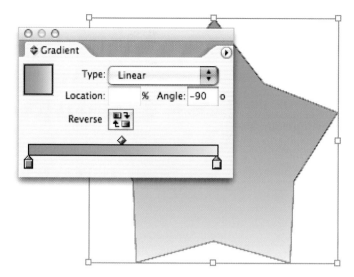

Figure 5-9a (left): The Gradient palette is the keeper of the Angle flame.

Figure 5-9b (below): You can specify an angle for a gradient fill in the Object Style Options dialog box (CS2 only).

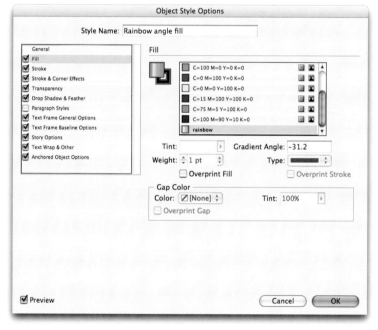

Add a "None" Stop Color to a Gradient

? A sidebar background for the newsletter I'm working on is supposed to be filled with a gradient going from a solid color to transparent ("None"). But I can't set a stop color to be transparent. It doesn't appear as a choice in the Gradient Options > Stop Color > Swatches list, even though the color "None" is a default swatch.

around the problem in CS2 by creating an Object Style for the angled gradient fill — the Object Style dialog box's Fill panel includes a field for Gradient Angle (**Figure 5-9b**). To fill another object with that same gradient at the same angle, just select the object and apply the Object Style.

☑ Use white (Paper) instead of None as your stop color (**Figure 5-10a**). Fill the object with the new gradient, then change the object's blending mode from

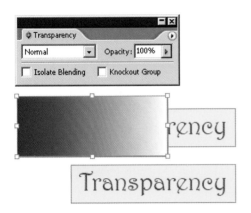

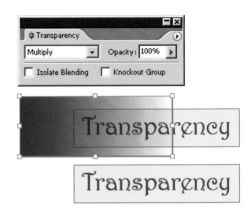

Normal to Multiply in the Transparency palette. The white color drops out to transparent (**Figure 5-10b**). This doesn't always give you the results you're looking for — the other colors in the gradient are also in Multiply mode — but it may do in a pinch.

Figure 5-10a (above left): A color-to-white gradient in Normal blending mode…

Figure 5-10b (above right): …and after changing its mode to Multiply.

Putting Colors to Work

Stop the Color Shifting

? When I place an image that I know contains the same color as one of my InDesign swatches, the images color doesn't match other objects that use the swatch color.

☑ Make sure InDesign's color management system is turned on (choose Edit > Color Settings) and make sure the settings are appropriate for the type of publication you're creating. Even if a placed image was created in a non-color managed program, InDesign will use its color settings to manage the screen preview. You may need to turn on View > Overprint Preview and View > Display Performance > High Quality Display for the best-looking EPS and PDF images. For more on color management, check out the book David wrote with Olav Martin Kvern, *Real World InDesign*, or Bruce Fraser's (*et al*) *Real World Color Management*.

Color the Text, not the Text Frame

? There is a secret password or incantation, I believe, that InDesign needs to hear before the action of selecting a text frame, then clicking a color swatch results in the *text* being colored — the letterforms themselves — and not the frame background. I know it can be done because I saw an Adobe magician perform the feat at a local seminar. But when I searched the

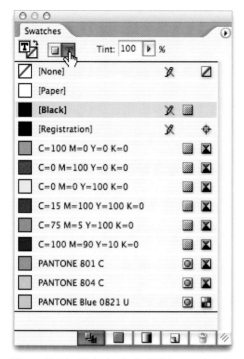

Figure 5-11: Click the little "T" icon to let InDesign know you want to change the text color, not the text frame color.

Book of Runes — InDesign's online help files — I came up empty.

☑ You'll need a rubber chicken, three candles and a newt's eyeball . . . oh wait, that's for the QuarkXPress Breakthroughs book. For you, it's simple. Select the text frame with either Selection tool, but before you click a color swatch, click the tiny T icon (below the Fill/Stroke icons) in the Tools, Color, or Swatches palette (**Figure 5-11**). That tells InDesign that any formatting commands you make, including color swatch selection, will format the Text — all the text in the frame — not the Frame itself. The icon to the left of the tiny T stands for "formatting affects frame" and is selected by default.

Accurately Preview Text Color Changes

? **When I select text with the Type tool and change its color, the color that gets applied is the opposite of the color I want. I choose a green color swatch, InDesign shows me purple text. I click on a red color, the text turns blue. It's not until I click elsewhere to *deselect* the text that I see the actual color applied to it. Often, it's not exactly the right shade, so I have to repeat the madness, all the while guessing what the final color is going to look like once I deselect the text.**

☑ Here are three fixes for you. First, you can click an insertion point right before the word(s) you want to color and open the Story Editor (Edit > Edit in Story Editor). Your cursor will be at the same point in the Story Editor's text flow, making it easy to find the text you're about to edit. Resize and/or reposition the Story Editor window if necessary so that you can see the about-to-be-colorized text in the Layout window in back. While still in the Story Editor, select the text you want to color and click a color swatch. Nothing will change in the Story Editor, but the Layout will update to show the new color applied (**Figure 5-12**). When you're satisfied with the text color, close the Story Editor window and return from whence you came.

Second, you can select Window > Arrange > New Window to create a second window of your document. Similar to the Story Editor fix, if you change the color in one window, you can see what it'll look like in the other window.

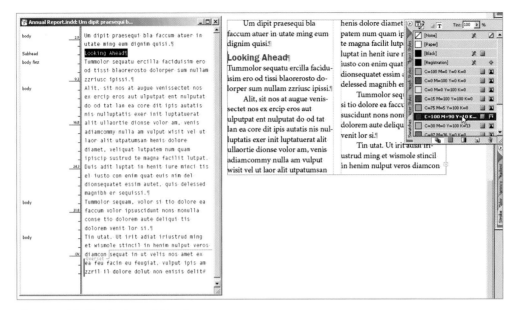

Figure 5-12: Use the Story Editor for previewing color changes to text. It doesn't mind.

Here's our favorite method, though: After applying a color to selected text, Command-click/Ctrl-click on the text frame and keep the mouse button held down. Don't move the mouse (or else you'll reposition the text frame). But while the mouse button is held down, the text appears deselected so you can see the color. When you let go of the mouse button, the selection comes back.

Preview Aliased Inks

? In the middle of a project, when I use the Ink Manager (from the Swatches palette menu) to alias one ink to another, nothing changes on my screen. I can only see if InDesign is actually going to alias it correctly if I print separations. (I have faith in InDesign, but not *that* much faith.)

To see the effects of ink aliasing, turn on Overprint Preview in your View menu. By the way, there's really no reason to print out separations if you're just checking what's going to end up on which plates. Use the Separations Preview palette instead (Window > Output > Separations Preview). It's faster and kinder to the environment.

Replace Color

? I need to search for certain colors in my document and replace them with another color, but InDesign has no find/change for colors. Do I have to search manually throughout my 300-page file? Ouch.

It all depends on what the color is applied to. If you need to replace every instance of the color throughout your file, you can either redefine the color swatch to what you need, or just delete the swatch. When you delete a swatch, InDesign asks what color you want to

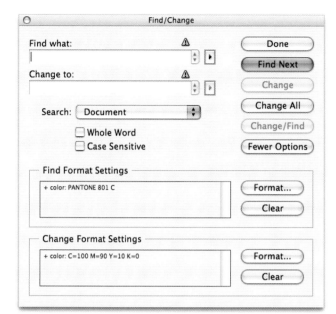

Figure 5-13: The Find/Change dialog box set up to do a document-wide text color change.

replace it with (as long as at least one object in your document is assigned that color).

If you have text and objects colored with a swatch and you only want to change the text color, you can use Edit > Find/Change. Don't enter anything into the Find What or Change To fields, because you're not going to change characters, just how those characters are formatted (their color, in this case). To do that, click the More Options button, revealing the Find Format and Change Format fields. Click on each of these buttons, in turn, to set up what color text should be found, and what color it should become (**Figure 5-13**).

If you want to change the objects' color but not the text, then take an extra couple of steps: Duplicate the color (drag its swatch on top of the New Color button) and perform the Find/Change to change the text color to this duplicate color. Finally, delete the original color, replacing it with some other color.

Clear Just the Text Color, Not Everything, in Find/Change

❓ I use the "More Options" fields in Find/Change a lot. I'm happy with most of the features, but one thing bugs me. If I choose a Character Color swatch in one of the Format Settings areas, and later decide that I don't want to include that setting in my format changes (that is, I don't care what color the character is), I can't get rid of just that setting. I have to click the Clear button for *all* the settings. Then I have to reconstruct everything else (Font Family, type size, indents, etc.) that used to be part of my Format Settings.

☑ Command-click/Ctrl-click the Fill or Stroke icon in the Character Color panel to clear just that setting. You'll see the icon revert back to its "Riddler" state (filled up with all those question marks, like The Riddler's costume on Batman), which means "any color" (**Figure 5-14**).

This works in the Edit Character Style dialog box, too. (It doesn't work for paragraph styles, though; there you always have to specify a color.)

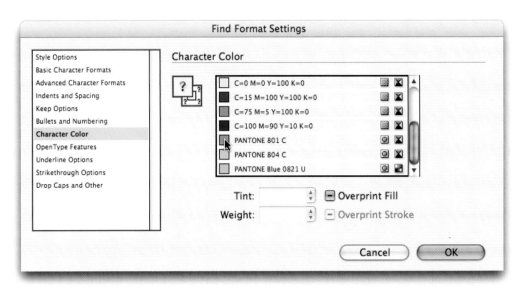

Figure 5-14: Riddle me this, Batman!

Track Down Mystery Spot Colors

? InDesign's Preflight dialog box (File > Preflight) is reporting that I'm using Pantone 286 somewhere in my 200-page document. I'm sure it got imported when I placed an image that uses it, but how am I supposed to tell which image? The Preflight dialog box doesn't have a "Show" button. (And of course, neither does the Swatches palette.)

✓ Open the Separations Preview palette (Window > Output > Separations Preview), turn on Separations from its popup menu, and hide all the plates except for the one belonging to the mystery spot color. Any instance of that color will appear to be colored Black in your document, since you're viewing a single separation plate."

Your document may look completely white, meaning that the spot color isn't used on the pages you're currently viewing. You'll have to scroll through all the pages to find the one(s) with the stowaway.

Since your document is 200 pages long, you might want to decrease the view scale drastically to something like 10% or 20% so you can see multiple spreads at a time as you scroll. When you see some black-colored artwork, click on it with the Selection tool. The graphic immediately becomes selected in the Links palette, so you know who the culprit is.

Drawing in InDesign:
Designers are from Mars;
Paths, Strokes and Scaling
are from the Orion Nebula

Drawing in InDesign:
Designers are from Mars; Paths, Strokes and Scaling are from the Orion Nebula

OVER HALF OF THE TOOLS IN InDESIGN'S TOOLS PALETTE ARE there to help you draw paths: The Pen tool and its three add-ons (Add, Delete and Convert Point), the Pencil tool and its two helpers (Smooth and Erase), the Scissors tool, the Line tool, and the simple Shape and Frame tools (each with Rectangle, Ellipse and Polygon variations). Obviously, those Adobe folks drew heavily (no pun intended) on ol' Grandpa Illustrator when creating baby InDesign.

But InDesign doesn't do nearly as much as Illustrator, and some of the things it does do work differently. Drawing paths and frames, and then transforming them (rotating, scaling, and so on) can be a royal pain in the *tuchus* at times. Fortunately, there are fixes for most of InDesign's annoying path and transformation problems.

Bent Out of Shape

No Rounded Rectangle Tool

? Every design software program I know of has a tool to create rounded-corner rectangles: CorelDraw, QuarkXPress, PageMaker, Freehand, Illustrator, even Photoshop has one. But not InDesign!

✓ Adobe's categorized the "roundedness" of a frame's corners as just another corner effect. So create (or select) a normal rectangle frame, then go to Object > Corner Effects and select "Rounded" from the Effect popup menu. Turn on the Preview checkbox so you can see the effect of changing the corners' diameter in the Size field. Click OK when you've achieved optimum roundosity.

If you're using InDesign CS2, you have one more option: You can convert any frame into a rounded-corner rectangle by selecting it and choosing Objects > Convert Shape > Rounded Rectangle. However, to change the default radius of the corner, you'll still have to go visit Corner Effects.

Edit A Shape's Frame

? I created a text frame, filled it with text, applied style sheets, added a custom stroke and background color to the frame, and positioned it just-so in my layout. In other words, it's perfect. Except that now, I'd like to make one side of the frame have an S-curve. Since there's no "convert to Bézier shape" command like there is in QuarkXPress, I have to start all

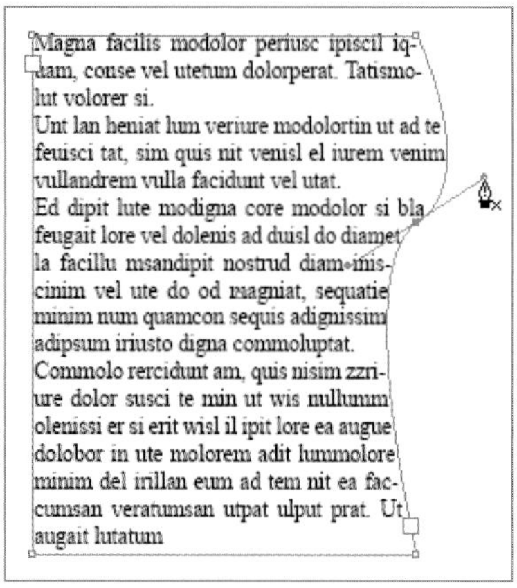

Figure 6-1: Every frame in InDesign is an editable shape.

over again and recreate the frame by hand with the Pen tool.

✓ InDesign doesn't have that command because *every* frame — text, graphics, and unassigned ones — *is* an "editable Bezier shape." Use the Direct Select tool to select and edit the individual points in your frame, and/or use the Pen tool to add, remove or modify existing points (**Figure 6-1**). No intermediate "conversion" command is required. You could even click on the frame with the Type on a Path tool (an alternate to the default Type tool) to get text both in *and* on the text frame.

Create a Triangle Tool

? I want to add a series of smallish triangles running across the bottom of my page for a kind of "arty" effect. I can make a triangle with the Pen tool by clicking once for each corner, but they always come out uneven, and I want the three sides to be the same length. If only InDesign had a Triangle Shape tool!

☑ You know what we're going to say: Yes, InDesign CS2 does this for you automatically. No, there's no Triangle tool *per se*; instead, just draw any rectangular frame and then choose Object > Convert Shape > Triangle. The triangle always "points up," but you can rotate it to whatever direction you want.

Here's a triangle trick that works in both CS and CS2: Use the Polygon tool. Press and hold the mouse button down on either the default Rectangle Frame or Rectangle Shape tool, then drag down the resulting pop-up menu of alternate tools to select the Polygon tool. Double-click the Polygon tool in the Tools palette to open its options dialog box. Set it to 3 sides and a Star Inset of 0% (**Figure 6-2**) and baby, you've got yourself a Triangle tool. Drag the cursor in your document and watch the triangle appear. Hold down the Shift key as you drag to create a perfectly equilateral triangle.

One Special Corner

❓ The commands in Object > Corner Effects apply to *all* corners of a selected frame. If I just want *one* corner of the frame to be rounded, or have an inset (or whatever) I have to edit the shape by hand . . . and edit and re-edit, because I never get it right the first time.

☑ Go to the InDesign scripts section in the Adobe Studio web site (*http://share.studio.adobe.com*) and

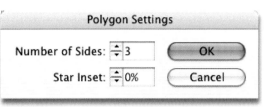

Figure 6-2: Set the options for the Polygon tool like this to create triangles.

download CornerEffects.js, a free cross-platform script that lets you apply corner effects to one or more corners of a selected frame. (See the "Using InDesign Scripts" sidebar on the next page if you need help installing and running InDesign scripts.)

This corner effects script offers another benefit over the normal Object > Corner Effects feature. In InDesign CS, the corners made with the normal Corner Effects feature are not subject to the Pathfinder features (like Add or Subtract). That is, these normal corner effects are simply stripped away or applied mindlessly to the final shape. The script, however, actually changes the path itself (it adds real Bézier points to the path), so these shapes work with the Pathfinder effects flawlessly. The Pathfinder effects in CS2 work the way you'd expect, so you don't have to worry about it as much.

> **TIP:** Keep your scripts elsewhere on your hard drive and just put aliases (shortcuts) to these files into the Scripts folder. That way, if you have to reinstall or upgrade InDesign, the installer software won't accidentally delete all your scripts.

Using InDesign Scripts

If you pine for a missing feature, there's a good chance that a script would solve your problem. A script is like a Microsoft Word macro, if you're familiar with that concept, or sort of like an Adobe Photoshop action (but actually much more powerful than an action).

InDesign scripts are plain text files written in AppleScript (Mac only), VBScript (Windows only) or JavaScript (cross-platform). You install scripts — these text files — by dropping them—or an alias of them—into your Scripts folder (Adobe InDesign > Presets > Scripts). You run a script by opening InDesign's Scripts palette (Window > Automation > Scripts) and double-clicking the script's name.

If you open *your* Scripts palette, chances are you'll find it's empty. For some reason, the default installation neglects to add the free scripts that come with InDesign. It's easy enough to install them yourself:

1. Open the InDesign installation CD-ROM and look for a folder called Scripting. It's probably in another folder called Adobe Technical Information, which may be inside yet another folder, depending if you have the full Creative Suite or just InDesign.

2. Inside the Scripting folder on the disc you'll find the InDesign Scripting Guide (a 1,600-page PDF) and a folder called Sample Scripts. Open the Sample Scripts folder to see a healthy list of useful JavaScript text files (cross-platform scripts). Copy the files over to your own Scripts folder on your hard drive: Adobe InDesign > Presets > Scripts. If you don't have a Scripts folder in your Presets folder, just make one yourself.

3. Eject the InDesign installation CD. You're done, the scripts are installed. Check your Scripts palette to see for yourself.

If these freebies don't do the trick, there are three ways to get a script that does: Search the Internet, especially *studio.adobe.com*, to see if someone has already written the script and is giving it away or selling it; ask or pay someone to write it for you (the Scripting Forum on Adobe's web site is a good place to do this); or write it yourself — the InDesign Scripting Guide is an excellent place to start.

Paths and Points
and Their Peculiarities

Uniting Paths

? Somehow, instead of creating a single, curving path, I created two paths. The second path begins about a quarter inch from where the first one ends. (I think I must have taken a phone call or something when I was drawing.) So I used the Direct Select tool to select the two end points, but now I can't find the Average or Join commands to combine the two paths. Illustrator has had these commands for years, explicitly for situations like mine. I can't believe InDesign doesn't.

✓ InDesign can be a real tease, can't it? Only *some* of Illustrator's drawing functions are in the program, just enough to make you complacent: "No need to boot up Illustrator for *this* little drawing." And then you run head-on into a dead end like this one. "Join" and "Average" are two of the many long-time Illustrator features not found in InDesign.

> **TIP:** In case you don't feel like reading the rest of this page, note that you can actually copy those paths and paste them into Illustrator to do your work. When you're done, you can copy them back into InDesign. This only works when the AICB feature is turned on in Illustrator's Preferences dialog box. (See "Paste Paths from Illustrator" in Chapter 4.)

You *can* join the two paths in InDesign, but you have to do it manually. With both paths selected, switch to the Pen tool, zoom in very closely, and hover over one of the selected points. When you see a little slash mark appear in the cursor (meaning it's over a point), click (for a corner point) or click and drag for a curve point. Now hover over the other selected point in the second path. When you're directly over that point, the cursor gains a "merge icon" — a small rectangle with a horizontal line through it — telling you you're about to join the two paths (**Figure 6-3**). Click or click and drag on that point. The two paths will become one, with a new path segment bridging the gap.

Instead of the Pen tool, you may find it easier to use the Pencil tool to unite the two paths. Drag from the endpoint of one path to the endpoint of the other (you don't need to select the paths in this case). Hold down the Command/Ctrl key after you start dragging so InDesign knows you want to merge the two paths when you hover over the second path's endpoint. You'll see the same merge icon when you're over the second endpoint. Release the mouse button before the Command/Ctrl key. Voila, one single path, where before there were two. You are omnipotent.

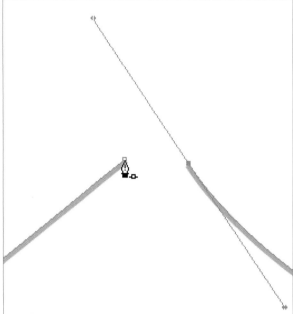

Figure 6-3: Both the Pen and Pencil tool show a merge icon when you hover over the endpoint of a path you're about to join to another.

to the path with the Pen or the Add Point tool to fine tune your work of art.

Force a Closed Path with the Pencil Tool

? The Pencil tool is convenient for freehand drawing of shapes, but no matter how careful I am to end my path where I started, it won't close the path. I have to manually join the two endpoints myself.

☑ You forgot to hold down the "make better" key: Hold down the Option/Alt key after you start drawing your shape, and don't release it until you're done (release the mouse button first). This forces InDesign to close the shape, even if you end the path far away from where you started.

Controlling the Control Handles

? I can't figure out how to create a point that's a combination of a curve and a corner with InDesign's Pen tool. For example, the bottom point in a simple Valentine's Day heart, which is pointy (a corner), but it has two curves that leave it, each going in a different direction. If I

Better Pencil Tool Results

? Does anyone actually use the Pencil tool to create anything? It adds far too many points on a path, making it difficult to edit. Or maybe it's just me.

☑ No, it's not just you. No one but a trained *mohel* with an extra-steady hand could draw anything reasonable with the Pencil tool's default settings. However, you can change these settings. Double-click the Pencil tool to open its settings dialog box. Move both the Fidelity and Smoothness sliders all the way to the right and click OK. Now the freehand paths and shapes you create with the tool will contain as few points as possible. The artwork will not exactly match the path your cursor took — especially any small jigs and jogs — but after too many coffees, that's probably a good thing. You can always add points

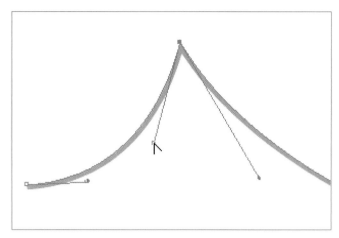

Figure 6-4: Drag one end of a control handle with the Convert Direction tool to point it in a different direction than its other end.

start by dragging out a curve point, I can't move the point's control handles independently of each other so that one points up/left and the other up/right. InDesign always moves one of the handles in the opposite direction that I'm moving the other handle.

What you want is called a "cusp" point, in which the control handles move independently. Select the point with the Direct Select tool so you can see both control handles. Now use the Convert Direction Point tool (in the Pen tool pop-up menu) to drag one of the handles (not the point itself) and it will leave its "mate" in place (**Figure 6-4**). If you have the Pen tool active, you could hold down Option/Alt to get a temporary Convert Direction Point tool. When you have the Direct Select tool, you can get this Convert tool temporarily by holding down Command-Option/Ctrl-Alt.

TIP: You can make control handles move independently of each other *while* you're drawing a shape, instead of editing the points afterward. When you're using the Pen tool to draw, and you're about to create a curve point that should have independent control handles, drag out the "normal" control handles as usual but don't release the mouse button. Hold down the Option/Alt key and you'll be able to drag the outgoing control handle (the one under your cursor that you're dragging away from the curve point) in a different direction without affecting its mate. Release the mouse button and go on to create your next point in the path. When the path is complete, use the Direct Select tool to adjust the "incoming" control handles for the curve points you did this to, if necessary.

Delete Just One of the Control Handles

? I want to create what I call a combination point: A curve comes into the point, but a corner (a straight line) leaves the point. That means the point should have only one control handle, the incoming one that defines the curve. I've tried everything, but I can't delete the outgoing control handle that defines the corner.

☑ It ain't easy, but it's possible. You have to "put away" one of the control handles by hand, and unlike Illustrator, InDesign doesn't give you any visual feedback when it's completely put away. But it does work.

Select the point with the Direct Select tool. Zoom in as close as you can so you can see the point and the control handle you want to put away. Use the Convert Direction Point tool (so you don't accidentally modify the other control handle) to drag the control handle "in" towards the point, and keep dragging until the handle itself is right on top of the point. Don't look for any visual clues in the cursor that you're at the right spot, because there are none. Release the mouse button and the handle should be gone for good.

Don't Have a Stroke

Begone, Default Stroke!

? The basic shape tools—Rectangle, Ellipse and Polygon—have a 1 point black stroke by default, which I hardly ever want. It's simple enough to change a shape's stroke weight to 0 points (in the Stroke or Control palettes), but it gets tiresome after a while. And it's easy to forget to do this, especially since the stroke is almost undetectable beneath InDesign's frame outline preview (in Normal View Mode).

☑ With no documents open, select a Shape tool—any one of the three—and change the stroke weight to 0 points in the Stroke or Control palette. Quit InDesign to save your new application defaults. The next time you start up the program and create a Rectangle, Ellipse or Polygon shape, its stroke will automatically be 0 points.

In InDesign CS2, you can also edit the Basic Graphics Frame object style (in the Object Styles palette). This is the default style for those shape objects—though not for graphic frames, which always have a fill and stroke of None.

Move the Border Inside the Frame

? Coming from QuarkXPress, I'm used to a preference setting for the placement of borders (strokes) in a box (frame): Inside or Outside. InDesign doesn't have a preference setting for this. In fact, it looks like InDesign splits the difference and places strokes halfway between "inside and outside" so they actually straddle the frame boundary. This is a real problem

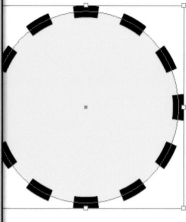

Figure 6-5a:
Because the default alignment for strokes is "centered on path," a stroke with a gap can look weird.

A quick fix to get rid of those uglies (**Figure 6-5a**) is to use the Stroke palette to set the stroke's gap color to the same color as the frame background. Of course, every time you change the frame's fill color, you have to remember to change the stroke's gap color as well.

A more permanent fix is to move the stroke completely inside or outside of the frame boundary. Select the frame with a Selection tool and open the Stroke palette. You'll see three small icons labeled "Align Stroke" towards the top the palette (**Figure 6-5b**). The first icon, Align Stroke to Center, is chosen by default. If you want to move the stroke outside the frame, click the third icon, Align Stroke to Outside (**Figure 6-5c**); to move it inside, click the second one, Align Stroke to Inside (**Figure 6-5d**).

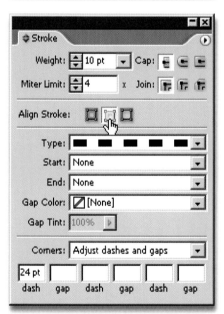

Figure 6-5b: Change the stroke alignment by clicking the second or third Align Stroke icon in the Stroke palette.

Stroke alignment is an application preference. If you want all your shape strokes to start out as "Inside" or "Outside" borders, close all your documents, choose any Shape tool and click the appropriate Align Stroke icon in the Stroke palette. Quit InDesign to save your new defaults.

because when I apply a stroke that has a gap to a colored frame, I get ugly white areas in the "outer half" of the stroke.

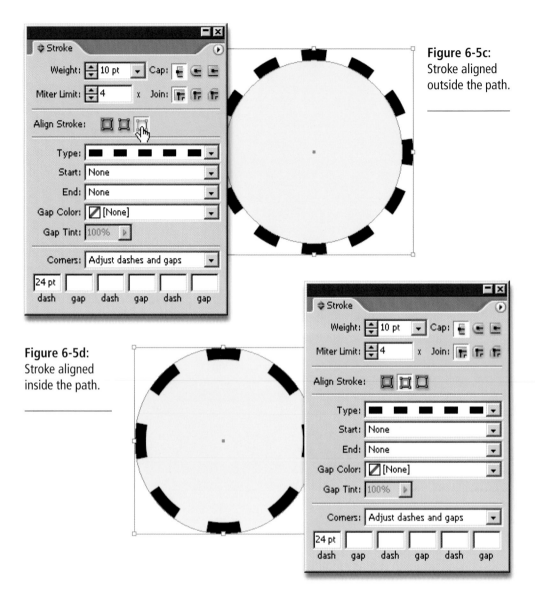

Figure 6-5c:
Stroke aligned
outside the path.

Figure 6-5d:
Stroke aligned
inside the path.

Change Arrow Direction

? The page I'm working on has a diagram overlaid with numerous boxed call-outs that I created in InDesign. Currently, the call-outs have a single line leading to the parts of the diagram they refer to. The client took a look at the page and wants me to add arrowheads to each of these paths. When I select a path and choose an arrowhead for an End style in the Stroke palette, sometimes the arrowhead ends up pointing the wrong way.

☑ InDesign applies the End style to the part of the path that was drawn last. You're supposed to remember which end of the path this was. What? You didn't keep a detailed record listing which direction you drew every path? And you call yourself a professional . . . tsk tsk.

Don't sweat the small stuff. When you end up with a path "pointing" the wrong way, just select it with the Direct Select tool and choose Object > Path > Reverse Path. The arrowhead will flip over to the other side. In InDesign CS2, there is also a Reverse Path button in the Pathfinder palette. Note that both the palette button and the menu item are grayed out if you try this with the Selection tool... it has to be the Direct Select tool.

Overprint the Stroke

? **The Stroke palette has no Overprint Stroke checkbox. It's not in the Stroke palette menu either. How annoying!**

✓ Those wacky folks at Adobe have hidden InDesign's overprinting features in the Attributes palette (Window > Attributes). Note that this only works on objects you create in InDesign, and not placed images. For those files, set overprint attributes in the authoring program before placing them in your layout.

> **TIP:** The Attributes palette can't control overprinting for strokes and gaps created with paragraph rules, underlines, strikethroughs, or table and cell borders. Instead, look for the Overprint Stroke and Overprint Gap checkboxes in those features' own dialog boxes.

Set Your Own Dashes and Gaps On The Fly

? **While I appreciate InDesign offering me two different Dashed stroke styles—"3 and 2" and "4 and 4"—I want "9 and 2." That is, a 9-point dash followed by a tiny 2-point gap. Where are the Stroke palette's dash and gap fields?**

✓ Force your eyeballs further down the menu of default Stroke styles in the Strokes palette—past the two default Dashed stroke styles, all the way to the end, to plain old "Dashed." When you select that style, a magic genie opens up a new section of the Stroke palette where you can set your own numbers for an alternating pattern of dash fills and gaps (**Figure 6-6**).

Of course, if you're going to use this style a lot, you're probably better off creating it as a special custom dashed stroke style (Stroke palette menu > Stroke Styles > New). That way you can call it up any time you want, and even save the style to disk to use in other InDesign documents.

> **TIP:** We rarely use the Transform palette (we just use the Control palette instead), so we thought Adobe actually removed it when InDesign CS2 was released. After all, it doesn't seem to show up in the Window menu. We were wrong: It's hiding in the Window > Object & Layout submenu—along with some other palettes, like Align and Navigator.

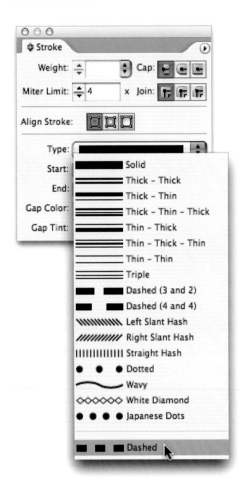

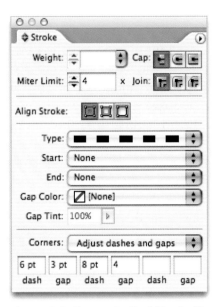

Figure 6-6: Choose the final "Dashed" stroke style to reveal its editing interface.

Quickly Apply Complex Strokes

? **Stroke styles only contain the very basic underpinnings of a stroke. I can't save the weight, colors, tints, or overprint settings I want along with it. I have to virtually reinvent the wheel every time I want to apply the same "look" to a complicated stroke I'm applying to a new object.**

✓ You're absolutely right, but fortunately there are at least four workarounds available:

Method 1: Use the Selection tool to select all the frames to which you want to apply the same sort of stroke, including all those settings you listed. That way you only need to apply your stroke style, color, gap color, and so on, once. All selected objects get that same stroke applied.

EASTER EGGS: There are several "Easter Eggs" (just-for-giggles functions created and hidden in the software by its programmers) in InDesign's Stroke Styles > New dialog box. For example, create a new Stripe stroke and name it "Rainbow." Now create a new Dash stroke and name it "Feet." Try "Woof" or "Happy". Don't bother editing the actual strokes in the styles. Save your new styles and apply them to objects to reveal the Easter Eggs. (Make sure the stroke weight is thick — like 20 points — to get the full effect.)

Method 2: If you've got a tricked-out stroke applied to an object already, and you want to "copy and paste" the same stroke to another object, use the Eyedropper tool. Double-click the Eyedropper tool first to turn off everything other than Stroke settings in its Options dialog box and click OK. Then, while nothing is selected on your page, click once on the frame that has the cool stroke so the Eyedropper picks up its settings. Click on any other frames with the loaded Eyedropper to give them the same stroke. It works even if the frames are in different spreads or different documents. (For more info, see the sidebar "Mastering the Eyedropper," on page 125.)

Method 3: Purchase Woodwing Software's Smart Styles plug-in (*http://www.woodwing.com/smartstyles.htm*). Powerful stroke styles that are easy to apply and are linked to a "source" style are just one of its many features.

Method 4: If you use InDesign CS2, skip all the above and just create an object style using the Object Styles palette. The object style can include all the stroke properties you want so you can apply them all with a single click. The only downside is that you can't apply more than one object style to an object at the same time.

Scaling: Super Solutions

Scale Multiple Objects at Once

? I dragged a selection rectangle over a bunch of items on my page, then Ctrl-dragged on the corner of one of them. Shouldn't that scale everything in the selection? Only the item I happened to be dragging on scaled.

☑ Oddly, the keyboard shortcut (Command/Ctrl) for drag-scaling only works if the items are grouped (Object > Group) first — or if you drag a corner handle of any text frame inside the multiple selection. (Don't forget to add the Shift key to scale proportionally.) If you don't want to group the objects or the selection doesn't include a text frame, the Scale tool or the Scale X/Scale Y fields in the Control or Transform palettes will do the job.

Scale From the Center

? Even though the center point of the proxy icon (on the left side of the Control palette and Transform palette) is selected, I can't get a selected object to scale from its center when I press Command/Ctrl to drag-scale it.

☑ Yup, it's a quirky keyboard shortcut. The only way to scale something from the center by dragging on it is to use the Scale tool (make sure the center proxy point is selected) by itself. You can also scale from the center with the Free Transform tool by dragging any handle while holding down the Option/

Alt key. (The Free Transform tool ignores the proxy; that's why it's free, baby.)

Scale the Text as Well as the Text Frame

? I scaled a text frame and the text inside didn't scale.

☑ Scaling in InDesign can be so confusing that we wouldn't blame you if you just gave up and never scaled anything again. As you probably know, if you just drag a corner of a text frame, it won't change the size of the text inside; the text just rewraps to the new frame boundaries. That's a feature-not-a-bug. Instead, you have to hold down the Command/Ctrl key while you click-and-drag on a corner or side handle to scale the frame and the text inside it. (Add the Shift key and drag on a corner handle to keep the scaling proportional.)

The same is true if the text frame is part of a selection of multiple, ungrouped objects: Use a handle of any text frame in the selection to do your Command/Ctrl click-and-dragging. All objects in the selection scale, including the text inside the selected text frames. (If you try to Command/Ctrl-drag something other than a text frame in the selection, only that one object scales.)

As long as you're working with a single text frame, or text frames that are part of a multiple, ungrouped selection, the Scale and Free Transform tools always scale the text inside the frame(s), as does adjusting the percentages in the Scale X/Scale Y fields of the Control or Transform palettes. (If the text frame is part of a grouped selection, see the next solution.)

Rarely, you may be doing everything right but the text just refuses to scale. We've found that you can sometimes remind InDesign who's boss by selecting all the text with the Type tool and entering the same or slightly different point size and leading amounts in the appropriate fields of the Control or Character palettes. Subsequent text scaling actions are usually successful.

Scale the Text in a Grouped Selection

? An advertiser gave us their InDesign file for a display ad, but it's a little too large. I selected all the objects, grouped them, and entered 90% in the Scale X/Scale Y fields in the Control palette. Everything scaled down appropriately except for the text. The text *frames* scaled just fine, but the text *inside* the frames remained the same size, and now I'm seeing a bunch of overset icons.

☑ Curiously, when using a scaling tool (or the scaling fields in the Control or Transform palette), whether or not text will scale depends on two things: Whether the text frame is part of a *group* (Object > Group), and the state of the Scale Strokes setting (**Figure 6-7**). If Scale Strokes is "off" (its default state) — that is, it's turned off in the Transform or Control palette menus — using the Scale or Free Transform tools or the ScaleX/Scale Y fields of the Control or Transform palettes *won't* scale the text inside the frame. If Scale Strokes is turned on, the text

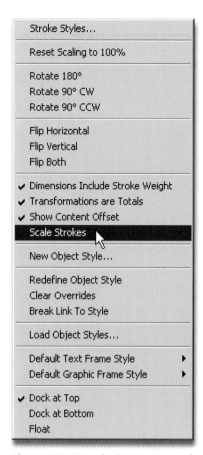

Figure 6-7: To scale the text in text frames along with everything else in a group, turn on the Scale Strokes option in the Control or Transform palette menu before you scale. Of course, scaling text size has nothing to do with scaling stroke weight, but that's beside the point.

will scale, but of course, all the strokes applied to the objects scale as well.

InDesign doesn't care about the Scale Strokes setting if you use the Command/Ctrl click-and-drag-on-a-handle method to scale a grouped selection by eye. In this case, text and strokes are always scaled along with everything else in the group.

When you need to use one of the scaling tools or fields to scale a group, and you want *everything* to scale except for the strokes, you'll have ungroup the group (Object > Ungroup), then scale using one of these tools, then group them again. Try to think happy thoughts while banging your head against the wall.

Scale the Text Frame But Don't Scale the Text

? I need to scale a text frame precisely, so I use the Scale tool or the scale features in the Control or Transform palettes. Unfortunately, the text inside scaled along with it, and I don't want it to.

✓ You can just drag on a text frame handle to resize it without scaling the text, but if you need to precisely scale the text frame to a certain percentage amount, you can't use any of the normal scaling methods. Instead, do this:

1. Click on the frame with the Selection tool (**Figure 6-8a**).

2. Choose a point of reference (from which the frame will grow/shrink) on the Proxy icon in the Control or Transform palette.

3. If you want the scale to be proportional, turn on the Constrain Proportions icon (the little chain) next to the Width and Height fields in the Transform or Control palette.

4. Click an insertion point after either of the Width or Height measures,

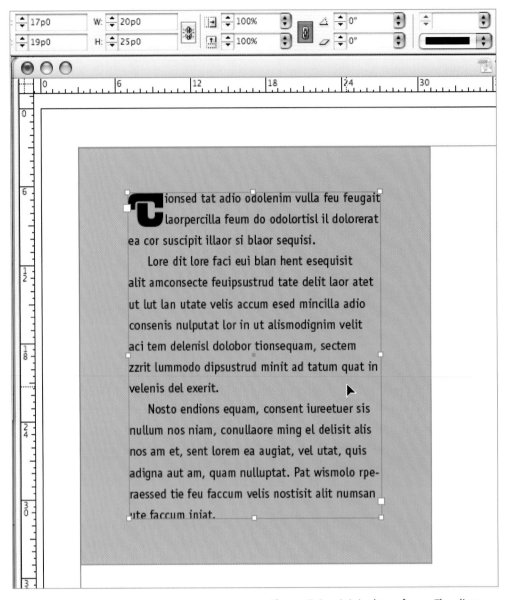

Figure 6-8a: Original text frame. The client says they want it exactly 125% larger, but to keep the text inside it the same size. In this example the text frame is set to Vertically Justify, so when the frame is enlarged, additional leading will automatically be added to keep the vertical space filled.

enter "+ [your scaling percent-age]" and tap the Return/Enter key (**Figure 6-8b**). For example, if the current width of your text frame is 20 picas and you want to scale it up to 125-percent of its size, click after the "20p" in the Width field and enter "+ 25%" (so it says "20p + 25%") and hit Return/Enter.

The text frame scales appropriately, the Width and Height fields do the math and show the new measures, and the text inside the frame doesn't scale, it just

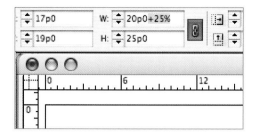

Figure 6-8b: Tell InDesign to increase the size of the text frame by 125% by entering a math calculation in the Width and Height fields, and then press Return/Enter.

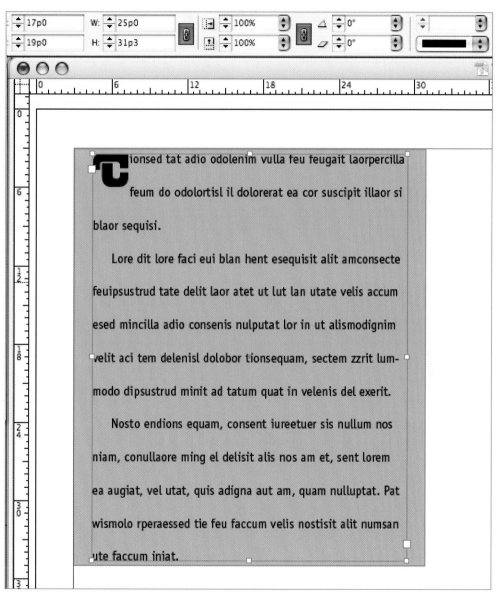

Figure 6-8c: The width and height fields show the new measures, 125% of the original ones, and the frame reflects the new size. The text size doesn't change, but it does rewrap to its new boundaries (and the leading changes due to the vertical justification).

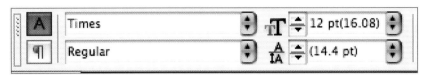

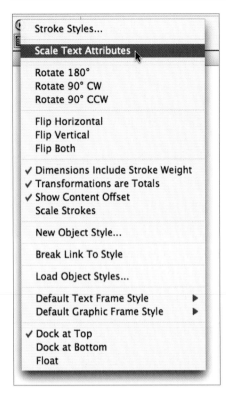

Figure 6-9a (above): Look familiar? Some people actually like that InDesign shows both original and "post-scaling" text sizes by default.

Figure 6-9b (left): If you're not one of those people, turn on the Scale Text Attributes command in the Control palette menu or Transform palette menu.

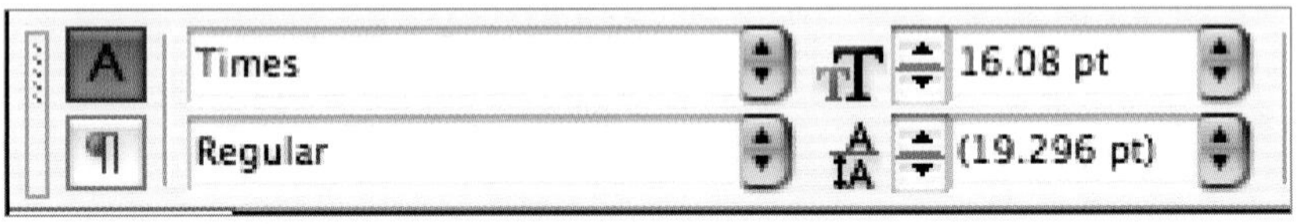

Figure 6-9c: Ah, sweet, sweet normalcy.

rewraps to the new frame boundaries (**Figure 6-8c**).

Reveal the True Size of Scaled Text

? I scaled a text frame to 200% and the text inside it scaled as well, just as I wanted it to. But I can't figure out the size of the text. According to the Character and the Control palette, it's "12 pt(16.08 pt)." Well . . . which is it?

This craziness (**Figure 6-9a**) occurs in two situations. First, InDeisgn behaves like this when someone sneaks onto your computer and turns off the Adjust Text Attributes When Scaling feature in the Type panel of the Preferences dialog box. This makes InDesign act like it did back in version 1.x. Fortunately, there's a solution: Select the text frame with the Selection tool and choose Scale Text Attributes from the Control or Transform palette menus (**Figure 6-9b**). The size, leading, and other text attribute fields will recalculate to show the actual, current measure (in this case, the size will update to read "16.08 pt"; **Figure 6-9c**).

The dual measures you saw in the Text Size field were the text's original size (12 pt) and what it was after you scaled it 134 percent (16.08 pt). While you were getting this readout, you may have also noticed that the Scale X/Scale Y fields in the Transform and Control palettes showed 134 percent whenever the frame was selected with the Selection tool. Choosing "Scale Text Attributes" not only recalculates before/after text attribute measures to show the single current measure, but it also resets the Scale X/Scale Y fields to 100 percent.

To force InDesign to always show a single, current measure for scaled text attributes (and keep the Scale X/Scale Y field at 100 percent), turn *on* "Adjust Text Attributes When Scaling" in the Type panel of the Preferences dialog box. This will only affect text frames you scale afterwards. To "fix" existing ones, you'll have to use the Scale Text Attributes method described above.

The second situation where this happens is when the text frame is part of a group, and you scale the group. In this case, the preference doesn't have any effect. Why? Because life isn't fair. In this case, you have to ungroup the objects, then choose Scale Text Attributes from the Control or Transform palette menu, and then group the objects again.

Reveal the True Scaling of a Placed Graphic

? When I scale a placed graphic, the Scale X/Scale Y fields in the Control and Transform palettes always display "100%." Even if I scale the graphic by using those fields—entering 50% in both—after I hit Return/Enter, the fields revert back to 100%!

☑ Gee, this sounds familiar. Oh yeah, we dealt with this back in Chapter 4, *Graphically Speaking*. But it bears repeating: To see the actual scaling applied to a placed image, click on the image with the *Direct Select* tool.

Transform Just the Graphic Frame (or Just the Image)

? The Transform tools—Scale, Rotate and Shear—always transform both the graphic frame and the image it contains. I can't transform just the image, leaving the frame alone; or vice versa.

☑ InDesign is very picky about making you select exactly what you want to transform. To rotate or scale just the image, click on it with the Direct Select tool first. To transform the frame without the image, Option/Alt-click on the frame itself with the Direct Select tool. (You need the Option/Alt modifier to select all the points on the path; otherwise, it probably won't transform properly.)

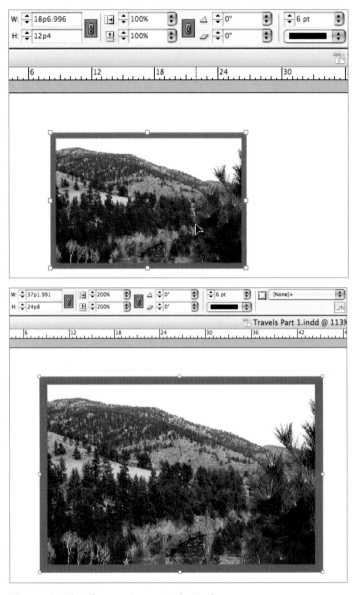

Figure 6-10a: This frame has a 6 pt stroke. Note the Scale X/Scale Y field in the Control palette says 100% and the Stroke weight says 6 pt.

Figure 6-10b: After turning on Scale Strokes in the Control palette menu and scaling the frame to 200%, the Scale X/Scale Y fields confirm the scaling applied, and the stroke is obviously thicker, but the Stroke weight field still says 6 pt.

Alternatively, you can also transform just the frame by selecting the object with the Selection tool and turning off the Transform Content option in the Transform or Control palette menu. Any transforms you then apply within the palette will only affect the frame, not the content. If you want to use a tool instead, double-click the transform tool you're going to use and turn off the Transform Content feature in its Options dialog box. Note that the Transform Content feature inexplicably won't work for text frames; just graphic frames or frames with other objects pasted into (nested in) them.

Reveal the True Weight of a Scaled Stroke

? InDesign is testing me, I know it. And I'm not sure how much more I can take. Here we go: I turn on Scale Stroke in the Control or Transform palette menu. I'm careful to use the Transform tools or palette fields to scale a stroked object so the stroke scales as well. I do the scaling

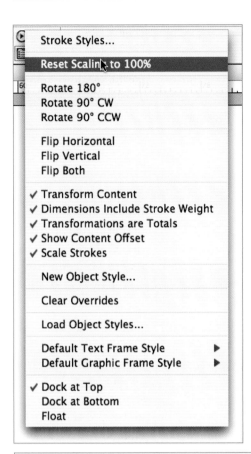

Stroke Styles...

Reset Scaling to 100%

Rotate 180°
Rotate 90° CW
Rotate 90° CCW

Flip Horizontal
Flip Vertical
Flip Both

✓ Transform Content
✓ Dimensions Include Stroke Weight
✓ Transformations are Totals
✓ Show Content Offset
✓ Scale Strokes

New Object Style...

Clear Overrides

Load Object Styles...

Default Text Frame Style   ▶
Default Graphic Frame Style ▶

✓ Dock at Top
Dock at Bottom
Float

Figure 6-10c: Choose Reset Scaling to 100% in the Control or Transform palette menu (left) to see the "true" weight of the stroke. Note that the Scale X/Scale Y fields change back to 100% but the frame size remains the same (below).

and the stroke is obviously scaled. But the Stroke weight field shows the same weight as it did before it was scaled. For example, if the stroke started out at 6 pt, and I scale the stroked object 200%, I can see that the stroke is much thicker, but the Stroke weight field still shows "6 pt."

☑ Step away from the computer. Take a deep breath. Now approach the computer, select the scaled and stroked object, and choose Reset Scaling to 100% from the Control or Transform palette menu. The stroke weight field will reveal its true weight, and the Scale X/Scale Y fields revert to 100%. (**Figures 6-10a, b** and **c.**) Why do you need to take this extra step? As your dad said, "it builds character."

By the way, if the frame you're scaling is a text frame and you're seeing this behavior, you'll have to use the Scale Text Attributes feature instead. (See "Reveal the True Size of Scaled Text," a few solutions earlier, for more on that feature.)

Other Transform Oddities

Master Your Proxies

? When I use the Scale or Rotate tool or those fields in the Control palette, I'm never exactly sure what's about to happen. Will the object rotate from the center or from a corner? Will the Scale tool grow the object up and to the right, or down and to the left? It usually takes me at least three tries to get it right.

✓ Ex-QuarkXPress users are constantly challenged by the subtlties of the reference point (also called "proxy"). Except for the Free Transform tool, all the transform tools and related palette fields rely on the selected point in the proxy, which lives at the far left of the Control palette, and in the top left corner of the Transform palette. This point tells them where to transform from.

The routine is this: Select the object, click a reference point in the proxy, then use a Transform tool or field to transform the object. For example, if you select the upper left hand point on the proxy icon, and enter a number in the Rotation field; the object rotates by that amount, but its upper left-hand corner stays put.

TIP: You can change the reference point using keyboard shortcuts by pressing Command/Ctrl-6 (to jump to the first field of the Control palette), then pressing Shift-Tab (to change the focus to the proxy icon). Now use the arrow keys or the numeric keypad to select a point. For example, the "9" key on the keypad selects the upper-right corner of the proxy. Press Enter to leave the palette and keep working.

The Scale, Rotate and Shear transform *tools* will honor an object's selected proxy point as well, but they give you more control over it. In addition to the 9 proxy points available in the proxy icon, you can set a reference point *anywhere* on the object. Just click the transform tool right on the object, exactly where you'd like the transform to "happen" from. You'll see a little non-printing icon jump to that position. Now drag the transform tool (or enter a transform amount in its equivalent palette field) and the object transforms from/around that custom proxy point.

Rotate The Drop Shadows

? Rotating an object to which I've applied a drop shadow (Object > Drop Shadow) doesn't rotate the shadow. I have to open the Drop Shadow dialog box to change the settings to match the rotation.

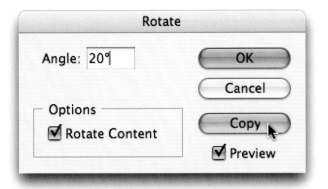

Figure 6-11: To rotate a copy of a selection, double-click the Rotate tool and click the Copy button.

on the pasted copy? That's a lot of steps for what should be a simple operation.

✓ Technically, InDesign is correct: It shouldn't rotate the drop shadow. Imagine a virtual light source casting a shadow on your object. You've already set the angle and position of the light source when you first made your drop shadow settings — size, offset and blur. Just because the object is rotated X degrees doesn't mean the light source changes, does it? It would be kind of weird if it did.

Still, you're the boss. If you want the shadow to follow the rotation of the object, the only way that we know of is to move your shadowed object to a new, blank page; export just that page to PDF (File > Export), and then use File > Place to place the PDF in the original location of the object, cropping it as necessary. Now you can rotate the PDF and the shadow will rotate with it.

Transform a Copy

? There's no "Copy" button in the Control or Transform palette. To scale, rotate, skew or move a copy of an object (leaving the original in place), do I have to select the object, choose Edit > Copy, then Edit > Paste in Place, and run the transform

✓ There's an easier way! It's your friend the Option/Alt key. Select the object, then hold down the Option/Alt key *after* you start dragging with one of the transform tools to create a transformed copy. Or edit any field in the Transform or Control palette and then press Option/Alt-Enter. When InDesign's spidey-sense detects the Option/Alt key, it does what you want (the transform) to a copy of the selected object.

By the way, InDesign does have the Copy button you're looking for: It's in each of the Transform tools' options dialog boxess. Double-click the Scale, Rotate or Shear tools to see it (**Figure 6-11**).

TIP: If you want to perform the same transformation on more than one object, InDesign CS2 has just the ticket: Transform Again — which you can find under the Object > Transform Again submenu (or press Command-Option-3/Ctrl-Alt-3). Or, if you have transformed an object in more than one way (such as scaling, and rotated, and shearing), you can choose Transform Sequence Again (Command-Option-4/Ctrl-Alt-4).

Fix Fills of Overlapping Paths

? Adobe Illustrator and Macromedia Freehand let you specify that a path that intersects itself multiple times (like a five- or six-pointed star) should be filled with either the "winding rule" or the "even-odd" rule. InDesign only offers the winding rule, so the middle of the star is always filled. How do I switch to the even-odd rule?

☑ Leave it to InDesign über-mensch Olav Martin Kvern to figure this obscure one out. First, copy the path and paste it in place (using Edit > Paste in Place). Next, select both the original and the duplicate (both are on top of each other), and choose Object > Pathfinder > Add (or click the Add button in the Pathfinder palette). That's all it takes. Olav adds, in his inimitable deadpan, "It's mathematically obvious when you think about what the Add path operation does."

7

Long Documents

Long Documents

*I*F AN INDESIGN EXPERT HAD A STAND-UP COMEDY ROUTINE IN THE Poconos, his bit about working on long documents might go something like this:

Well, I just laid out a 500-page file... and boy, are my arms tired! (pause for laughter) No, seriously folks. You know, it's always a joy to work on a project like that. When I get a chance to work on a long pub, something with some meat on its bones, I'm like, Yes! An excuse to use the Book palette! Can't get enough of them InDesign palettes, am I right? Bring it on! (laughter)

I remember once I had to do this really long document...

(Audience: "How long WAS it?!")

It was so long, I got a hernia moving the loaded text cursor!

So I spend like 3 weeks laying it out. And I'm into it, right? There's fifty docs in the Book palette, I've got automatic page numbering going on, style sheets are synchronized so perfect I'm thinking this thing could win an award, you know? And then two days before the job's due at the printer, the client calls and says, "Hey, the footnotes aren't in the right place. They're supposed to be at the bottom of the pages, not at the end of the chapters. Also, I forgot to mention that I'll need an index. I circled every word that has to go in it... not too many, about 3 or 4 on each page. And while you're at it, could you be a pal and change every 'your' to 'their' and make it italic in every chapter."

Oy. Take my client — please!

Book 'em, Danno

Paginate a Misbehaving Book Palette

? One of the documents in my Book palette show a page range of "1–28" even though it's in the middle of the book and *should* say something like "57–86." All the other files in the Book palette are paginating correctly.

✓ Select the misbehaving document's file name in the Book palette and choose Document Page Numbering Options from the palette menu (**Figure 7-1**) or just double-click the document's page numbers in the Book palette. Make sure that the Automatic Page Numbering radio button is selected—not the other choice, "Start Page Numbering At [x]"—and click OK. Now check the Book palette. Since Auto Pagination is turned on by default, the document should now show the correct page range.

Didn't work? Okay, try this: Open the document and scroll through its Pages palette and make sure there are no other little black triangle icons above pages (indicating a section start) besides the one on the first page. If you do find a section start icon, double-click the triangle to open that page's Numbering & Section Options dialog box. As above, make sure that Automatic Page Numbering is turned on for this and any other sections, not "Start Page Numbering At [x]." That should do the trick.

Find/Change Throughout a Book

? I need to change the copyright year that appears in the footer of every page of my 20 chapter book document. I was disappointed to see that "Find/Change in Book" is not an option in the Book palette menu, even though Print Book and Export Book to PDF are. Please don't tell me I have to run this simple Find/Change twenty times!

✓ Heaven forbid. It's true there's no dedicated Find/Change in Book command, but there's a different way to get this done.

1. Close any InDesign documents you happen to have open that aren't part of the book.

2. Now open all the documents in your book at once. One way to do this is to click the first chapter in the Book palette and shift-click the last one (that selects them all), and then double-click any of them.

3. Choose Edit > Find/Change. In the Search popup menu, choose All Documents. To InDesign, "All Documents" means "All *open InDesign* Documents" so the Find/Change only has to be run once to hit every open chapter. Enter your old and new copyright years in the Find and Change fields, add any Find/Change Format settings you might need, and click the Change All button. InDesign does

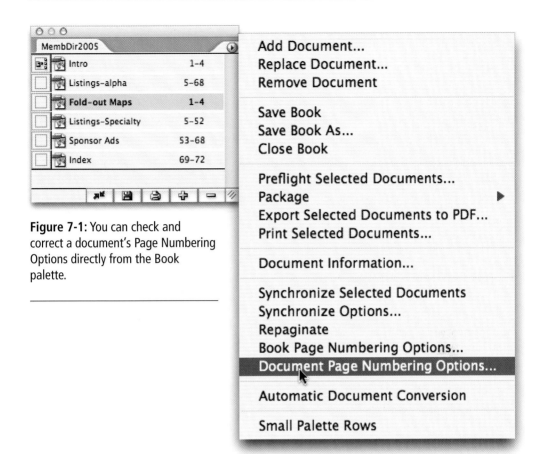

Figure 7-1: You can check and correct a document's Page Numbering Options directly from the Book palette.

its search and replace throughout every chapter in your book.

4. To quickly close all the chapters at once but leave the Book palette open, press Command-Option-Shift-W, or — on a PC — press Ctrl-Alt-Shift-W.

Get Page Palette Numbers to Reflect Book Page Numbers

? When I open a document that's part of a book, the Pages palette shows page numbers spanning from one to the last page. But in my Book palette, that document's Page Range shows up differently, such as "57–78." I want the Page palette numbers to reflect the document's actual page numbers as seen in the Book palette.

You need to change the program preferences while that document is open. In the General panel of the Preferences dialog box, change the Page Numbering View option from "Absolute Numbering" to "Section Numbering." Close the Preferences dialog box and you should see your Pages palette icons as well as the Current Page Number field (bottom left of the document window) update to reflect the book pagination.

Delete Empty Last Chapter Pages

? InDesign keeps adding a blank page to the end of some (not all) of my book documents. I'm positive I'm following all the correct steps to delete the pages, but they keep coming back. It gives me the creeps!

✓ InDesign is adding blank pages as necessary, and keeping them there, because you told it to do so. (You just didn't know you did.) If you don't want it do that, open Book Page Numbering Options from the Book palette menu and turn off "Insert Blank Page."

Think about it before you do so, though. The Insert Blank Page option only becomes available if you've chosen "Continue on Next Odd [or Even] Page" in the Page Order section of the same dialog box. If you end a chapter on an odd (right-facing) page, and the next chapter is set to "Continue on Next Odd Page," then where is that even-numbered, left-facing page that's comes between?

It's like a Zen koan — If a page is a thing with two sides, but some pages in a book only have one side, does it make a sound?

Generally, it's best to let InDesign add empty pages whenever it needs to. If it really bothers you, though, choose "Continue From Previous Document" in this dialog box and make peace with chapters occasionally opening on a left-facing page. (Or fine-tune your writing so the final text of each chapter appears on a left-facing page.)

Maintain Chapter Versions in a Book

? Our editors mark up their corrections on hard copy printouts of our book's documents. Before we (the designers) make those corrections to the InDesign file, we do a "Save As" to the existing chapter, adding "second_pass" or "v3" or whatever to the end of the filename. The problem is that the Book palette doesn't track these files — the newly-saved versions lose their association with the book and of course lose their correct pagination as well. We often end up with a Book palette containing a mix of current and outdated files.

✓ You can avoid this problem by adopting two habits. First, never open a document that's part of a Book in any way other than double-clicking it from the Book palette. (Don't use File > Open, for example.) Second, use the Replace Document feature as soon as you give a chapter a new name with Save As.

Here's how it should work. To open a document that you need to create a new version of, double-click its name in the Book palette. Choose File > Save As, give the document a new name, and click OK. You now have a copy of the old document open, but with a new filename.

Now check to make sure the old filename is still selected in the Book palette (it should be if you just double-clicked it to open it). If it isn't, select it now, and choose Replace Document from the Book palette menu (**Figure 7-2**). InDesign will display the Open dialog box; locate the document you want to swap in for the

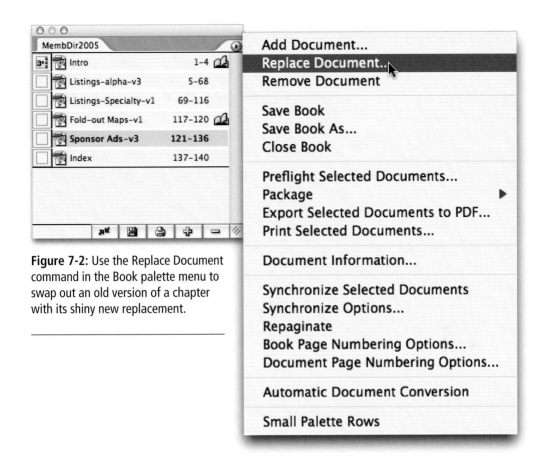

Figure 7-2: Use the Replace Document command in the Book palette menu to swap out an old version of a chapter with its shiny new replacement.

selected one in the palette. Choose the new document — in other words, the one that's open in InDesign right now — and click OK. The Book palette updates to show the new version's filename in place of the old version, and the new version's pagination is updated accordingly.

TOC Ticks

Locate Missing Entries for a Book's TOC

? After designating the first of my documents in my Book palette as the Style Source, I synchronized all the style sheets in my book's documents. But when I open that first chapter and choose Layout > Table of Contents to create and place the book's TOC, some style sheets that I need to include are missing.

☑ By default, the Table of Contents dialog box only lists style sheets in the current document. Synchronizing styles just makes sure that all the chapters in a book contain the same style sheets, with the same definitions, as those in the Style Source document. If one or more of the *other* documents contain styles that the Style Source one doesn't, InDesign ignores them. They're not modified or deleted, nor are they loaded into any other document that's part of the book.

The good news is that you don't need to manually load those other style sheets into your document. Just turn on the "Include Book Documents" checkbox at the bottom of the dialog box. InDesign then lists *all* the style sheets from every document that's part of the book in the TOC dialog box.

Note that the "Include Book Documents" option is only available when you have the Book palette open.

Use TOCs for Other Lists

? I really miss the "Lists" feature in my old page layout program. In addition to TOCs, it let me create illustration lists, advertiser lists, basically anything that I could identify via a unique style sheet. I could even maintain multiple lists in the same document.

✓ InDesign's Table of Contents feature can be used to create any sort of list, as long as it can be identified via a Paragraph Style. If every diagram in your document carries a title, and those titles are formatted with a "Diagram Title" paragraph style, InDesign's Table of Contents feature can create a list of diagram titles and page numbers.

You can create multiple "TOCs" in the same document, too — even if one is a "table of illustrations" another is a "table of advertisers," and so on. There is a workaround required, though, when you

want to update a single type of TOC in a document that has more than one. We'll get to that in a minute.

What if your layout doesn't include identifying text for the type of list you want to create? For example, most display ads don't include the name of the advertiser as a separate text frame next to the ad, but you want to generate a list of advertisers for the back page. Can you do this with InDesign?

Sure. Just create a new layer and enter your own advertiser names in new text frames on the same pages as their ads. Don't worry about making your text frames fit the design, because you'll be hiding the layer before you Print or Export. In fact, you can hide the layer anytime; the Table of Contents can still find it if you turn on "Include Text on Hidden Layers" which is in the More Options section of the dialog box.

Now you can choose Layout > Table of Contents and create a "TOC" that just includes the advertiser names' paragraph style. Choose your options for the list's formatting, its item order (by page number or alphabetically), and so on as usual. If you've already placed a TOC or another list, be sure to click the More Options button and *deselect* "Replace Existing Table of Contents." When you click OK, the cursor is loaded with the list of advertisers which you can place anywhere in your document.

Updating your list (after editing, adding, moving or deleting any of the advertiser names) is easy if it's the *only* TOC or list in the document. Just select the list's text frame and choose Layout > Update Table of Contents.

With multiple TOCs and TOC-generated lists in the same document, it's different. You can't use the Update feature to update just the advertiser list, for example, and not the front-of-the-book Table of Contents. (If you do, InDesign replaces *all* the TOCs and lists in the document with the same content, based on the last settings used in the Table of Contents dialog box. Yikes!)

Instead, when you need to update a particular list, delete that list's existing text (or entire frame) and make and place a new one from the main Layout > Table of Contents dialog box. If you've created Table of Contents Styles for each type of list (see the Tip following this entry), it just takes a couple seconds.

> **TIP:** You can manage multiple lists with TOC styles. After you've selected which paragraph styles to include in a TOC or list, and have specified how you want InDesign to format it in the Styles section of the TOC dialog box, save your settings by clicking the Save Style button and entering an identifying name like "Feature Articles" or "List of Advertisers." Now, if you accidentally delete the frame containing the TOC or list, you can easily make a new one by choosing its name from the TOC Style popup menu at the top of the dialog box. All your finely-tuned settings reappear. Just click OK to load the cursor with the new TOC or list, and place it in your layout. To import a TOC style that was saved in a different document, choose Layout > Table of Contents Styles in your current file, click the Load button, and double-click the InDesign file that has the TOC style you want.

Tweak a TOC for Perfect PDF Bookmarks

? **We create parts manuals in InDesign, then export them to PDF for distribution to our field reps. Linked Bookmarks in the PDF would really help these reps navigate the manual's numerous sections and subsections. The problem is that the bookmarks generated by the Table of Contents option, "Create PDF Bookmarks," aren't suitable. They're too detailed and they're not grouped (nested) into logical sections, among other things.**

☑ The solution is to create *two* TOCs, one to use in the document itself, and one just to generate the Bookmarks.

First, though, let's clear out old mistakes. Open your Bookmarks palette (Window > Interactive > Bookmarks), and delete any bookmarks you find there. (Shift-click all of them and choose Delete Bookmarks from the palette menu.)

Now you'll need to save the settings you're using for your "real" Table of Contents as its own TOC Style. Open the Table of Contents dialog box from the Layout menu, check the settings (which should reflect what you last specified when you created your TOC), and click the Save Style button. Name the style something like "My TOC."

Leave the dialog box open and adjust the settings for your soon-to-be-saved Bookmarks TOC style. For example, you may want to add or remove Paragraph Styles (to include/exclude Bookmark entries), or assign different Levels (**Figure 7-3a**) to the Paragraph Styles to custom-

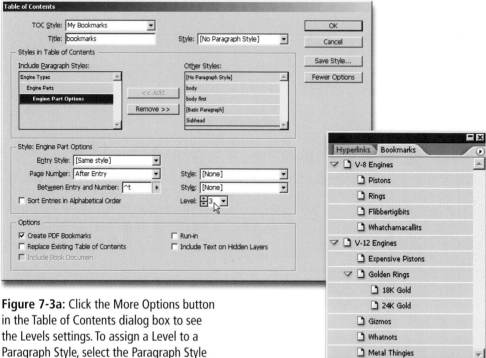

Figure 7-3a: Click the More Options button in the Table of Contents dialog box to see the Levels settings. To assign a Level to a Paragraph Style, select the Paragraph Style from the "Include" section and choose a number from the Level's popup menu (or just enter a number manually).

Figure 7-3b: Paragraph Styles assigned a Level 2 are nested underneath those with Level 1 assignments (and 3's are nested under 2's, etc.) when viewed in the Bookmarks palette and in the Bookmarks panel of the exported PDF.

ize how the Bookmarks will nest. Click the Save Style button when you're done, naming it "My Bookmarks."

From now on, whenever you're working with your document's actual Table of Contents, make sure that "My TOC" is the active TOC Style at the top of the Table of Contents dialog box, and that the Create PDF Bookmarks checkbox is *not* turned on before you click OK to create it or replace it.

To generate your bookmarks, choose Layout > Table of Contents and select "My Bookmarks" from the TOC Style popup menu. Before you click OK, make sure that the Create PDF Bookmarks checkbox is turned *on* and that Replace Existing TOC is turned *off*. Click the OK

button and place your "fake" TOC outside of the document in the pasteboard area.

Open your Bookmarks palette; ta-da! A whole slew of bookmarks appear (**Figure 7-3b**), possibly with different entries than those of your document's actual Table of Contents, depending how you modified the My Bookmarks TOC Style settings.

If a Bookmark's text is too lengthy, you can shorten it by selecting the Bookmark and choosing Rename Bookmark from the Bookmarks palette menu. You can also drag bookmarks around in the palette to reorder them, nest them differently, even delete existing ones and create new ones. Note that any changes you make in the Bookmark palette are overwritten the next time you create a TOC with Create PDF Bookmarks turned on. So save your customizations until the very end!

Perplexing Indexing

Delete All Index Entries

? Someone went and indexed a bunch of stuff in my InDesign document. Now I'm trying to get rid of it, but it's taking forever to remove each index entry one at a time. Isn't there a Delete All Index Entries feature?

✓ No, that would be far too easy. We do know of one way to remove all the index entries from a single story, but it's not necessarily for the faint of heart.

1. Place the text cursor inside the story and choose File > Export.

2. In the Export dialog box, choose Adobe InDesign Tagged Text from the Format popup menu and click the Save button.

3. In the InDesign Tagged Text Export Options dialog box, choose the Verbose option and then click the OK button.

4. Now open the file you exported in a text editor that supports GREP searching. On the Macintosh, you might use a tool such as BBEdit or TextWrangler. On Windows, you could use NoteTab or WildEdit. There are free or low-cost versions of all of these.

5. Perform a Find/Change in the text editor for:

    <IndexEntry.*>>

    (That's "regular expression" talk for "any string of text that starts with '<IndexEntry' and ends with '>>'.)

6. Leave the Replace With (sometimes called "Change To") field empty so that the program will replace the result with nothing.

7. Click Change All (or Replace All, or whatever the tool calls it).

8. Save the document under a new name.

9. Switch back to InDesign and use File > Place to import the new tagged text file into a new document. The index entries should be gone.

Note that this won't actually remove the entries or the topics from the original InDesign document; it just removes them from the story itself.

Figure 7-4: When you choose Show Find Field, the Index palette grows a new feature.

Where's That Index Topic?

? I have over 200 index topics in my index and now I can't remember whether I've indexed "spleen" as a secondary index topic under "organs" or "body parts." Isn't there some way to search through my index entries?

☑ Adobe decided that only the most die-hard indexers should be able to search through index entries, so they hid this feature. You can find it by choosing Show Find Field from the Index palette menu (**Figure 7-4**). Now type "spleen" in the find field that magically appears in the palette and click the Find Next button (that's the one that looks like a down arrow).

Correctly Place Cross-refs in Index

? InDesign always puts my cross-references (like "See also Elephants") immediately after the first-level index entry, but I want to put them at the bottom of my list of second-level index entries. That way, the reader will only see it after reading through the list of subtopics.

☑ No problem: make a dummy second-level index entry named "zzz" and set its type to cross-reference. Because of its name, it will fall at the bottom of the second-level index entries. Later, after you build your index, perform a Find/Change to search for "zzz" and delete them. The cross-reference will remain.

Footnote Finesse

Flow Word's Footnotes with Text Correctly

? **I have a big Microsoft Word document full of hundreds of footnotes. But when I import it into InDesign CS, all the footnotes show up at the end of the story as *endnotes*! How do I get them to the proper place.**

☑ You get these footnotes to the proper place very slowly and very carefully. The only fun part of placing footnotes in InDesign CS is when you fall into that recurring daydream of the day you get to upgrade to CS2. Yes, CS2 has a footnote feature which can read Word's footnotes and put them in the right place on the page.

But in InDesign CS, you're pretty much out of luck, you'll have to place them manually:

1. Select all the endnotes (the footnotes) and cut the selection to the clipboard.

2. Go to the document page where the first footnote reference appears. (You might want to temporarily change the footnote reference's Character Style so it's easier to spot in the text flow.)

3. Drag out a new text frame, roughly sized to hold the first footnote or two, at the bottom of this first page, right on top of the page text frame.

4. Don't resize the frame holding the page text, instead, apply a text wrap to the footnote frame so it pushes the page text out of the way, setting a top offset of a couple picas or a half-inch or so to the wrap so there's some breathing room between the page text and the footnotes.

> **TIP:** With the Type tool active but nothing selected, turn on Bounding Box Text Wrap and set the top offset measure. All the footnote frames you create from then on will wrap by default. (Don't forget to turn it off when you're done!)

5. Paste the contents of your clipboard (the endnotes you cut in Step 1) into the new footnote frame. Adjust the frame's height to reveal the footnote text for this page.

6. With the Selection tool, click on the footnote text frame's overset icon to load the remaining footnote text.

7. Move to the next document page with a footnote reference and drag out another footnote text frame.

8. Repeat steps 4–7 until all the footnotes are placed.

Since the footnote frames are threaded, you can enter Frame Breaks (Type > Insert Break Character > Frame Break) as necessary to help force footnotes to start at the correct page as you make adjustments. If you need to add a footnote frame in the middle of the thread, click the Out port icon of the footnote frame immediately preceding it, then with the loaded text cursor, drag out the new frame. The thread remains intact.

Sounds like fun, eh? And we haven't mentioned the issue of styling the footnotes and their references, nor what happens if you need to add a new footnote reference (it won't work). There *are* ways you can make this a little easier, including using master page frames for footnotes, and massaging footnote styling in Word before you ever bring it in.

But if you'll ever need to do this more than once, you should either purchase a Footnotes plug-in (such as InFnote from Virginia Systems, *www.virginiasystems.com*) or upgrade to InDesign CS2. Otherwise you'll go insane.

Get Your Footnote Number Back

? Ack! I accidentally deleted a footnote number at the bottom of my page (where the footnote text is). I can just type the footnote number back in, but then that footnote doesn't get renumbered automatically when I add or remove a footnote before this one.

☑ Yes, while InDesign CS2 offers a pretty powerful footnote feature, you can still get yourself in trouble pretty easily. In this case, don't type the footnote number yourself (if you already did, just delete it). Instead, place the text cursor at the beginning of the line and choose Type > Insert Special Character > Footnote Number. This only works when the text cursor is in a footnote text area (not up with your body text), and this special character will update properly.

Jump Between Footnote Number and Text

? I love being able to add footnotes in CS2. I click where I want a footnote, choose Type > Insert Footnote, and then type the footnote text at the bottom of the text column. But it's bothersome that I have to click back in the body of the text above again. Isn't there a keyboard shortcut for "go back to where I put the footnote reference"?

☑ It sounds like what you want already exists as a menu item: Type > Go to Footnote Reference. You may not have noticed this feature because it only appears when your cursor is in the footnote text. However, if you do this a lot, use the Edit > Keyboard Shortcut feature to give the Insert Footnote feature a shortcut. (That's under the Type menu product area.) When you give Insert Footnote a shortcut, that same shortcut applies to the Go to Footnote Reference feature.

Unfortunately, there's no equivalent command for jumping from an existing Footnote Reference in the text back down to its footnote for further editing. If this is something you do frequently, consider jumping to the Story Editor (Edit > Edit in Story Editor, or Command/Ctrl-Y) instead. If your cursor is at the footnote reference number in the layout, pressing Command/Ctrl-Y puts your cursor right next to the matching footnote text in the Story Editor (**Figure 7-5**). Slick!

Footnote text in the Story Editor appears in a cool little boxes in the text flow, directly following their reference

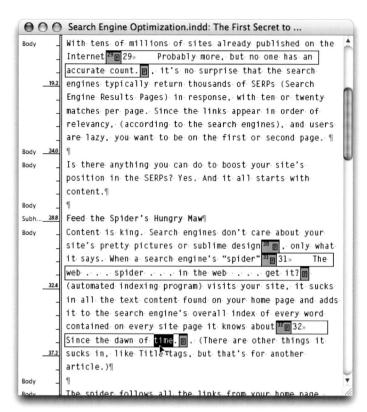

Figure 7-5: Editing footnotes in the Story Editor (Edit > Edit in Story Editor).

Formatting Footnotes

? InDesign always seems to put a tab between my footnote number or symbol and the text that follows it, but doesn't finish the job by setting up the indents properly so the footnotes "hang." It seems like I should be able to change that.

numbers in the text. They're expanded by default, revealing the footnote text, which you can edit just like regular text. To close a box, click on either side of it. (Closing a footnote box in the Story Editor just hides it from view, it doesn't delete the footnote.) You can also choose "Collapse All Footnotes" or "Expand All Footnotes" from the View > Story Editor menu. You can insert and delete footnotes in the Story Editor using the same commands as in normal layout view.

When you want to close the Story Editor and return to the layout, press Command/Ctrl-Y again. That way InDesign puts your text cursor in the same location as it last was in the Story Editor.

✓ The trick to fine-tuning how InDesign formats footnotes is to choose Type > Document Footnote Options. At the bottom of the Numbering and Formatting panel in this dialog box, you can assign a Character Style to the footnote reference (the number) in the text, and a Paragraph Style to the footnote itself. You can even edit the Separator field itself, which by default shows "^t" (that's the code for a tab character). Want to change it to a tab followed by an "indent here" character (so that the rest of footnote is indented to that point)? Just type "^t^i" (no quotes, of course). Want a period followed by an em space after the number? Type ".^m" instead.

Leaving the Nest:
Printing, Prepress, and PDFs

Leaving the Nest:
Printing, Prepress, and PDFs

IF YOU KEEP YOUR INDESIGN PAGES VERY BASIC, LIMITING YOURSELF to "old school" (circa late-90s) fonts, image formats, and page layout features, then you're probably thinking, "What printing problems? Why is this chapter even here?"

And we'd agree — basic InDesign functions shoot rock-solid PostScript to your desktop printer and PDFs to your desktop. Bang, zoom, there's your newsletter. But, is that why you bought InDesign? So you can add a couple CMYK colors, do a simple text wrap around a square-cut TIFF, and call it a day? We think not!

You're putting drop shadows over spot-colored text and exporting layouts directly to your hand-rolled PDF preset from the File menu. If there's a Blend Mode you haven't tried, by gum you're using it in the next project. Adobe wouldn't put these features in InDesign if they wouldn't print perfectly to every output device in existence, would they?

Well, okay, aside from a few kinks (which we'll cover as best as possible), Adobe has done a remarkable job in making sure that all the whiz-bang effects (and the more prosaic ones) make it through the printing and PDF process as intact and true to the design as possible. It is a feat of software engineering that a program capable of effects that not even the latest version of Postscript (Level 3) supports, namely transparency, can simulate the *exact same look* to older Postscript 2 printers, or even to inkjets, which don't speak PostScript at all!

Printing Issues in the Studio

Show Me the Printer

? **All our programs can print to our "Old Reliable" PostScript Level 2 laser printer except InDesign. The name of our printer doesn't even show up in InDesign's Print dialog box.**

✓ Could Old Reliable possibly be *Really Old* Reliable? Because officially, InDesign only understands PPD (Postscript Printer Description) files that are version 4.3 or later, as virtually every PPD made since the late 90s are up to. You can figure out the version of your PPD by opening it in a text editor and looking for a line that begins "FormatVersion:" (**Figure 8-1**). If you're not seeing the magic number 4.3 (or higher) after the colon, contact your printer manufacturer for an update. Most companies have a page on their web site where you can download the latest version of their PPDs free of charge.

Once you get your hands on an updated PPD, try to see if you can get away with just replacing the old one with the new one in your system's PPDs folder. Restart InDesign. If it didn't work — that is, InDesign still can't see the printer — you'll have the do it the official way. Quit out of all your programs, turn off the printer and remove its entry from your OS (via your system's printing utility). Then install the PPD where it belongs in your system, turn the printer back on and officially "add it" to your system with your printer utility. (Consult your Windows or OS X help files for detailed instructions on removing and adding printers.) Finally, start up InDesign again, and you should see your printer appear as a choice in the Print dialog box, as well as all your other programs.

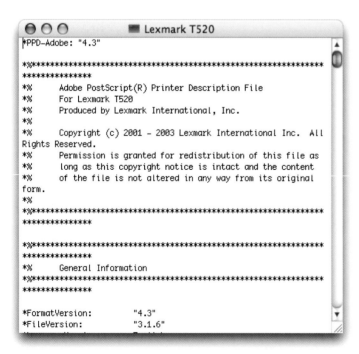

Figure 8-1: This Lexmark PPD is good to go: Note the "FormatVersion: 4.3" toward the bottom of the screen shot.

Kick Start the Print Spooler

? InDesign says it's printing the page, but it never actually prints. The job just sits in the print spooler, churning away, with no printout after almost an hour.

☑ Your printer might be having trouble with the fonts that are being downloaded for the job. Cancel any print jobs stuck in Print Spooler purgatory, and restart your printer to flush out any detritus left over from its struggles with the job.

Now, go back to the InDesign file and open the Print dialog box again. Select the Graphics category and in the Fonts area, change the Download type from Complete (the default) to Subset (**Figure 8-2**). This choice sends far less code for each typeface you've used in the document to your hard-working printer. Click OK and see if that didn't do the trick.

Make Your Apostrophes Reappear

? My printout looks fine except that in some of the text, there's white space where there should be apostrophes, trademark symbols, and other high ASCII characters.

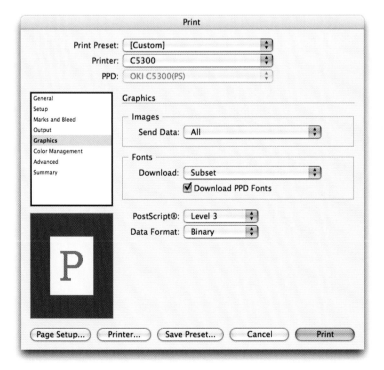

Figure 8-2: Tweaking the default settings in the Graphics panel of the Print dialog box is key to successful printing to your office laser printer or inkjet.

☑ Your printer is probably substituting its own built-in fonts for the ones you specified in your document, and having a little trouble with the substitution. To force the printer to use the robust Helvetica that's on your computer instead of its own 90-pound weakling version, make sure that the "Download PPD Fonts" checkbox is turned on in the Print dialog box's Graphics panel (**Figure 8-2**). Why did they sneak this font feature into the Graphics panel? Just to keep you on your toes.

Restore Quality to Bitmap Graphic Output

? **I don't understand why my photos look so beautiful in InDesign but come out muddy, blurry, and pixelated in my printouts. The Links palette says the image is up to date, and the Info palette confirms its Effective Resolution is 300 ppi. When I print the same image directly from Photoshop, it comes out great, so I know it's not my printer or the paper type.**

☑ Most of the time, the cause of this problem is InDesign getting a little too enthusiastic with "Optimized Subsampling" shenanigans when processing the images to send to your printer. You can turn this option off (it's on by default) in the Print dialog box's Graphics > Images area. Change the Send Data popup menu option from Optimized Subsampling to All (**Figure 8-2**, previous page). Printing pages with high-res images will take a little longer, but the results may be worth it.

This would be a perfect option to save in a Print Preset, by the way.

TIP: Are you the InDy geek in the office with the twelve custom Print presets? Share the wealth and set up your co-workers with the same goodies — they'll be extra-nice to you on your birthday. To create stand-alone presets (file type .prst) that you can put on a server or attach to an e-mail, open the "Define" dialog box for that type of preset. For example, choose File > Print Presets > Define to make Print Preset files. That's where you'll find the magical Save button that prompts you for a Save location (unlike the Save Preset button in the Print dialog box, which just includes presets in your InDesign preferences file). Your co-workers should use this same dialog box to Load the presets you've so generously sent their way.

Fix Disappearing Graphics

? **I can see all the images in my layout with no problem. When I print it out, though, some of them disappear! When I exported it to PDF, the images were gone there as well. According to the Attributes palette, they should print just fine (the Nonprinting checkbox isn't checked). The Links palette says they're up to date. They print fine when I "open original" and print from Illustrator. I can't figure it out!**

☑ This is a known problem with some QuarkXPress documents that have been converted into InDesign files. Somehow during the conversion process, any EPS images that were in the QuarkXPress document get set to "nonprinting."

Checking your layout in Preview mode (press the "W" key) will show you if any of your images inadvertently carry the nonprinting tag. Preview mode is true to its word: If an image isn't going to make it through the printing/exporting to PDF process; you won't see it in Preview mode either. The Normal (non-preview) mode, on the other hand, shows you every image regardless.

If you see some images disappear in Preview and you're in a hurry, you can do an end-run around the problem by turning on the Print Non-printing Objects checkbox in the General panel of the Print dialog box. If you're exporting the layout to PDF, turn on the [Include] Non-printing Objects checkbox in the Export Adobe PDF dialog box.

There's only one way to permanently fix the problem, though. Open the Attributes palette. Grab the *Direct Select* tool and click on the nonprinting image, not its frame. You'll see a checkmark next to the Nonprinting option in the palette. (Selecting the same image with the regular Selection tool won't work, as you've discovered. Only the Direct Select tool knows for sure.) Click the checkbox to turn off the Nonprinting attribute. Do this for each problem child image and you're good to go.

If you're on a Mac, you can go to the InDesign Scripts area at *http://share. studio.adobe.com* and download "Make all printable.scpt," a free AppleScript written by Rick Johnson. Running the script from the Scripts palette removes the Nonprinting attribute from all graphics in the active layout.

Batch Printing Without a Plugin

? We create over fifty versions of the same newsletter each month, each differing only by their masthead and banners, for dentists around the country to send to their patients. It's such a chore to have to open each file in InDesign and go through the Print dialog box fifty times to make print proofs. A batch print function would be a real time-saver!

☑ InDesign has secret Batch Print, Batch Preflight, Batch Package, and Batch Export to PDF commands. They're hidden in the Book palette menu. Who cares if your newsletters aren't really book chapters? Not InDesign.

Create a book file by choosing File > New > Book, naming it something like "Dentist Newsletters" and saving the .indb file where you won't lose it, like in the same folder as the newsletters. The Book palette immediately opens, empty for now.

Choose Book Page Numbering Options from the Book palette's menu and turn *off* the Automatic Pagination checkbox. If you don't turn this off, you'll have to deal with InDesign forever trying to change each documents' page numbers (see Note on page 207). Click OK to leave the dialog box.

Now choose Add Documents from the Book palette menu or click the plus symbol icon at the bottom. Then Shift- or Command/Ctrl-click *all* the newsletter files in the Open/Save dialog box, and

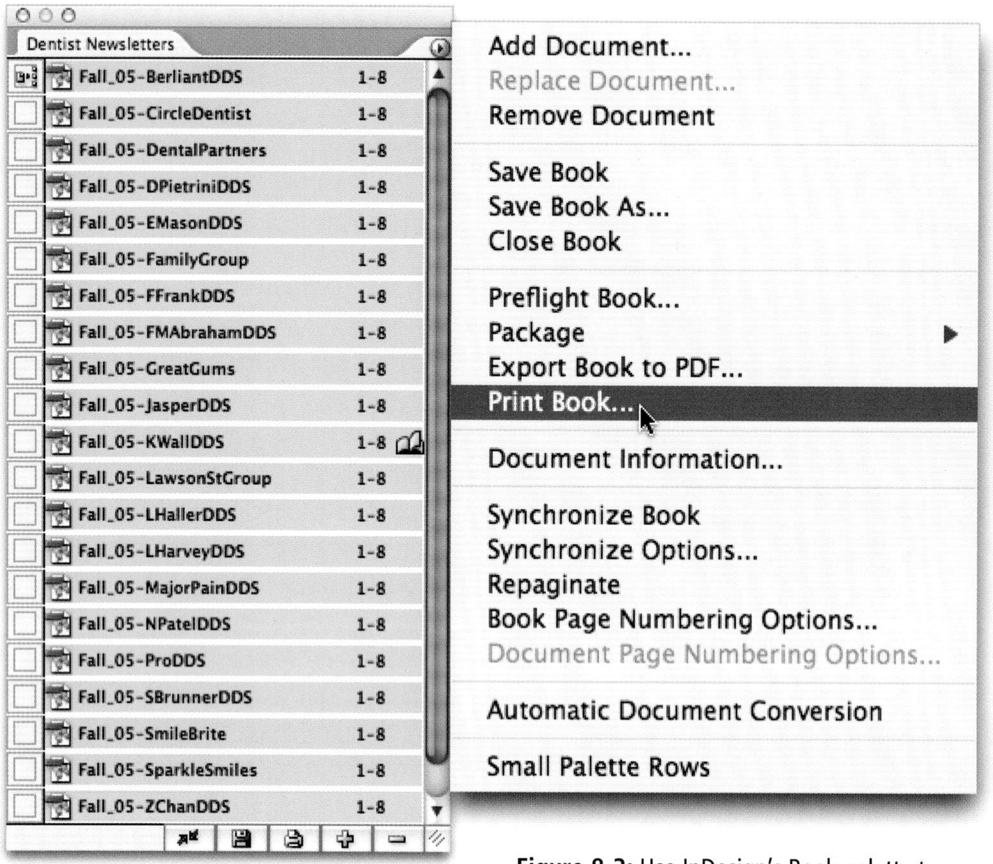

Figure 8-3: Use InDesign's Book palette to batch print multiple files, even if they're not chapters or sections of a single document.

click OK. Bam, they all appear in the palette (**Figure 8-3**). Didn't know it was that easy, did you? (This doesn't move or duplicate your files, by the way, it just collects references to them, sort of like the Links palette does with placed images.)

You can double-click any of the files listed here to open them in InDesign — the Book palette is like a miniature project manager. To print, export to PDF, preflight, or package a single newsletter, you don't even have to open it, just select its name in the palette and choose the appropriate command from the Book palette menu. And of course, to do the same to two or three newsletters, select them in the Book palette before you choose the command from the palette menu. (Or, if no documents are selected in the Book palette, InDesign assumes you want them all.)

Print Trim Borders in Page Proofs

? Our editors need to see page borders defining the trim edge when they're editing layout proof printouts. Before we switched to InDesign, we used a commercial XTension that added these for us, but there's no equivalent plug-in for our beloved InDesign.

NOTE: After you turn off the Automatic Pagination feature in the Book Page Numbering Options dialog box and add your documents to the Book palette, everything appears hunky dory. However, as soon as you add or remove a page from one of the documents and save the file, InDesign displays a warning icon in the Book palette.

The only way to make that icon go away is to choose Repaginate from the palette menu, but if you do that, then each document's page numbers will be reset sequentially (like chapters in a book). If you don't use the Automatic Page Number character in your document, then no harm done. But what if you do use automatic page numbering in a document and you actually wanted each file to start at page one?

The fix is to set each document to start at page one (or whatever page you want them to start at), which you can do by clicking on a file in the Book palette and choosing Document Page Numbering Options from the palette menu (or just double-click on the page numbers next to the file's name in the palette). It's tedious to have to do this for every document, but you only have to go through the process once.

✔️ How about something even better: a free, cross-platform Javascript? Cari Jansen, one of Australia's top InDesign trainers, offers a script called "1 pt. Stroke All Pages.js" (they're very literal downunder), free for the downloading at her web site: *www.carijansen.com*.

Drop the script into InDesign's scripts folder (Adobe InDesign > Presets > Scripts) and it's immediately available in your Scripts palette (choose Window > Automation > Scripts).

When you double-click the script name in the Scripts palette, it adds a one point border — actually a rectangle shape frame with a stroke of one point and a fill of None — to every document page. The script automatically puts the frames on their own layer ("The Border Layer") above any existing layers in the document, so they appear above any existing page bleeds. If you hide the layer, the borders won't print — exactly what you want to do when creating press-ready PDFs for your print vendor.

You *could* create trim borders manually (create your own border layer and add the frames to all the master pages, or to one parent master that all others are based on), but why go to the trouble? Just download the script and e-mail a thank you to Cari.

Add Page Numbers to Thumbnails

❓ **I can't believe that the Thumbnails option in the Print dialog box doesn't add page number labels to the output! When you're cramming sixteen miniature tabloid pages into a single letter-size printout, you need a microscope to see the pages' actual folios.**

✔️ We think this is one more confirmation that Adobe software engineers have super-human eyeballs — note, too, how the text in the palettes seems to get smaller with every upgrade. Fortunately, a normal human was able to

TIP: If you want some page items to appear on some printouts, but not others (as in the Trim Borders example above), consider selecting them and turning on the Nonprinting option from the Attributes palette. It's the only "print or not print" toggle that InDesign's Print dialog box offers. By default, objects set to Nonprinting will not print or appear on PDFs exported from InDesign. When you *do* want these items to print, turn on the Print Nonprinting Objects checkbox at the bottom of the General panel in the Print or Export dialog boxes.

Even better, if all your selective printing objects are on the same layer, you can Option/Alt-click the layer name to select them all, then set the selection to Nonprinting with just one click in the Attributes palette. But of course, if they're all on the same layer, you could just turn off that layer (hide it) before printing to do the same thing. Well, it's nice to have options.

sneak in a fix, and thumbnail pages are now numbered in InDesign CS2. Sell the microscope on eBay and buy everyone an upgrade.

Set up Printer's Spreads

? **Our in-house print department requires us to give them PDFs set up in printer's spreads (the last page is opposite of the first page, page 2 is next to page 7, etc.) instead of the normal "reader's spreads." We can do it by dragging pages around in the Pages palette, but it's** a bear to do manually with a long document. I looked in Preferences but there doesn't seem to be any way to change the default "spread type" for facing pages, nor any command in the Print or Export to PDF dialog box that makes printer's spreads automatically.

☑ If you're using InDesign CS, you can purchase Adobe's PageMaker Plugin Pack, which adds a number of handy features to InDesign, imposition (creating printer's spreads) being one of them. The specific plugin that offers the feature is called InBooklet SE, a "special edition" of a more fully-featured (and expensive) version of ALAP's InBooklet plugin. InBooklet SE can convert a copy of your reader's spread files into simple 2-up printer spreads (**Figure 8-4**) for saddle-stitched or perfect bound printing; letting you output the imposed files to your printer, to PDF files, or as new InDesign documents. More information on the PageMaker Plugin Pack and a link to order it from Adobe is available at *www.adobe.com/products/indesign/ pm_pack.html*

But before you buy, see if you already have it installed: Adobe began including the Plugin Pack with InDesign CS a few months after CS was released. If the good fairy installed the Plugin Pack, InBooklet SE appears at the bottom of your File menu. Instructions on how to use it and the other plugins from the Pack are in the InDesign online Help file (search for "Using InBooklet").

Plus, all the plug-in pack's goodies — including InBooklet SE — have been fully integrated into InDesign CS2 as regular features. More reason to upgrade.

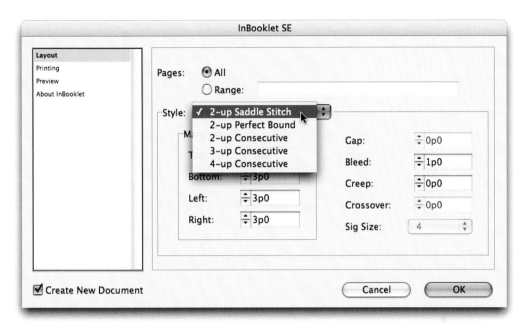

Figure 8-4: InBooklet SE makes it easy to create printer's spreads of your InDesign layouts.

Color Mismanagement

Understanding Color Management Differences

? I'm printing documents for clients (some use CS and some use CS2), but I'm finding huge differences in how these documents print color from when I was using CS.

✓ You're right, Adobe made big changes in InDesign's color management system in CS2. For starters, color management is turned on by default in CS2, so pretty much everyone is using it whether they know it or not. Second, InDesign CS2's "Preserve Numbers" feature is a huge step forward because it stops CMYK colors that don't have a corresponding color profile from being converted at print time (or when you create a PDF). The result: your 100% black text won't change to four-color text when this is turned on. Hooray!

On the other hand, Adobe also made a change that they didn't really document or tell anyone about — and it could cause major headaches. Each InDesign CS2 document can have its own document color management policies, separate from the application's own default policies. That makes it more like Photoshop. But the problem is that there is almost

Figure 8-5: You have to turn on the Ask When Opening checkboxes in Color Settings if you want to learn which document profiles have been applied to an InDesign layout file.

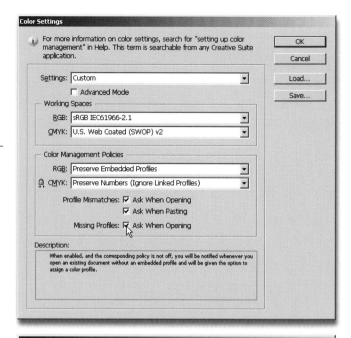

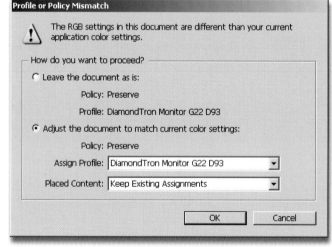

no way to find out what a document's conversion policies are! Oops. The only way to see a document's settings is to:

1. Close all documents.

2. Choose Edit > Color Settings.

3. Next, turn on the Ask When Opening checkboxes for both Profile Mismatches and Missing Profiles. (These are off by default.)

4. Click OK to save these new default settings.

5. Now open the document. If the profiles or policies in the document are different than your default application settings, InDesign will now inform you (**Figure 8-5**).

Is this a good system? No. Is it better than before? Probably, but it's still far too confusing.

That Ain't Black Text, it's CMYK!

? **Every now and then, when I print or export a PDF file, all my text (which is just set to 100% black) turns to a rich black—that is, it prints with cyan, magenta, and yellow, too. That sounds good, but it's a disaster on press, especially for small text that comes out looking fuzzy.**

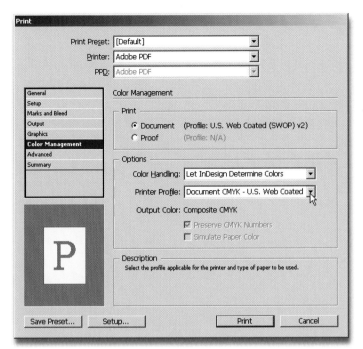

Figure 8-6a: Keep the Color Management output set to Document CMYK to avoid unwanted four-color Blacks.

If you specify any other CMYK profile when you print or create a PDF file, InDesign may convert the CMYK colors in your document to the CMYK equivalent for the output device. In other words, InDesign tries to make the magenta in your output match the magenta in your document, even if that means adding a little yellow or cyan to make it work.

InDesign CS also converts your 100-percent black text to an equivalent in the output profile's color space, which may mean adding a little cyan, magenta, or yellow to make it work. This is almost never what you want, but InDesign doesn't know that.

So, in InDesign CS the solution is to always leave the Printer Profile popup menu (in the Advanced panel of the Export Adobe PDF dialog box, or the Color Management panel of the Print dialog box) set to Document CMYK — at least when printing final separations (**Figure 8-6a**). If you decide you need to use a profile other than the default, then use Edit > Convert to Profile or Edit > Assign Profiles to change the document profiles before printing or exporting. (While this, too, may change your colors unexpectedly, it fortunately leaves

☑ Surprisingly, this is one of the most common printing mishaps in InDesign — so much so that Adobe spent a huge chunk of time adding a new feature in CS2 that attempts to eradicate it. The problem arises when you print to a different output profile than your built-in document profile. But don't feel stupid if you don't even know what a document profile is; most folks don't!

A document profile is what tells InDesign what the colors in the document look like. For example, you might specify 100-percent magenta, but there are lots of different magenta inks (some more red, some more orange). When you create a new document and color management is enabled (it is by default in CS2), InDesign assigns an RGB and a CMYK default working space profile to the file (as specified in the Edit > Color Settings dialog box). In North America, the default CMYK profile is usually "U.S. Web Coated (SWOP) v2".

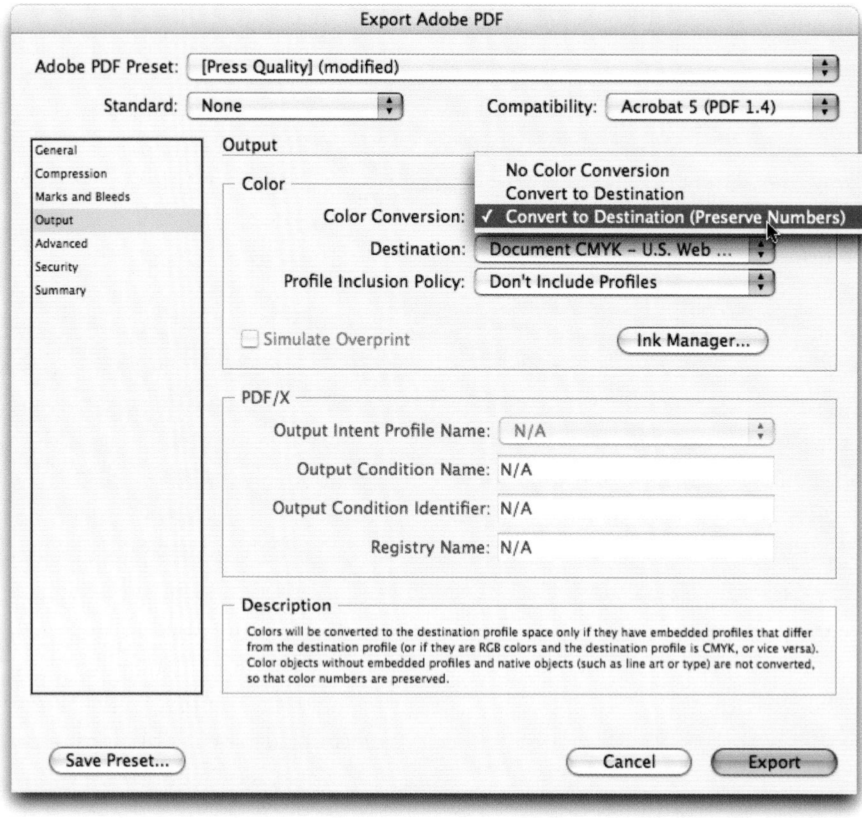

Figure 8-6b: With Convert to Destination (Preserve Numbers) chosen, you can be assured that the normal [Black] text in documents you're exporting to PDF will remain 100 percent Black in the PDF.

objects and text colored with the [Black] swatch alone.)

Another option is simply to turn off color management (in Edit > Color Settings) before you print or export a PDF file.

InDesign CS2 offers a new feature, called Preserve CMYK Numbers. When you choose an output profile that differs from the document profile, InDesign lets you turn on the Preserve CMYK Numbers checkbox in the Color Management panel of the Print dialog box. (When exporting a PDF, you can choose "Convert to Destination (Preserve Numbers)" from the Color Conversion popup menu in the Output panel of the Export Adobe PDF dialog box.)

When you turn on this option (**Figure 8-6b**), InDesign CS2 will not convert any CMYK colors to the new CMYK color space — except imported images that have a profile attached to them. (Actually, unless you change the defaults, InDesign's policies ignore profiles in CMYK images, too, because Adobe assumes that if they're in CMYK mode, they're likely "press-ready." So they, too, won't be changed when you turn on Preserve Numbers.)

We almost always leave this turned on, so our black text stays black no matter what profile we choose. Even better, if we specify 100-percent magenta somewhere in the document (or any other process color), it'll always print at 100-percent magenta, without any other colors muddying it up.

By the way, here are a couple other things to watch out for: Every so often we find someone who is using a black swatch based on RGB colors instead of the normal [Black] swatch in the Swatches palette (which is defined as 100-percent process black). In this case, the RGB black always becomes a four-color CMYK black when you print in CMYK (or print separations). Or, a newcomer to the graphic design field might naively use InDesign's [Registration] color (which is defined as 100-percent of each of the four process colors) instead of the normal [Black], because they look the same on screen. Tsk-tsk.

> **NOTE:** If you're using Distiller to create your PDF files, you should note that it, too, can convert colors — including converting 100-percent black to a CMYK black. Take a look at the Color settings in Distiller's Settings > Edit Adobe PDF Settings feature.

Colors Go Blah

? My color images and text usually look great on screen, but sometimes all my colors suddenly appear washed out—both on screen and when I print. Vibrant reds become dull rust; bold blues become, well, just blah.

 There are so many things that could be going on here, but most of them boil down to one unfortunate truth: process colors (CMYK) are usually more dull when printed than RGB colors display on screen. InDesign tries to give you clues about this discrepancy, but the clues (changing colors on you) often just make people more concerned than reassured.

For example, lets say you import an RGB image and then place an empty frame anywhere on the page. If you set the Blend Mode of that empty frame to Multiply in the Transparency palette, InDesign says, "Hey! I have to simulate a transparency effect!" It looks at what setting you have chosen in the Edit > Transparency Blend Space submenu. If this is set to CMYK (it usually is), then InDesign changes the display of all the colors on the spread to a CMYK preview. The result: The colors become somewhat washed out (**Figure 8-7**). Again, this affects all the colors on the spread, even if that object with a transparency effect is nowhere near them.

> **TIP:** Look at the Pages palette. If a spread has some sort of transparency on it (which will affect how it is displayed), its page icons will appear with a checkerboard effect.

If you change the Transparency Blend Space to RGB, then it'll look better on screen, but that's a mistake if you're going to print CMYK separations down the line. The only time you should use the RGB Transparency Blend Space is when your *final* output will be on-screen or on an inkjet printer.

Similarly, InDesign refigures its display using CMYK if you turn on View >

Figure 8-7: InDesign displays RGB images on screen differently depending on other page items or view features. The original image (above and left) is brash and bright. When a transparent frame (set to Multiply) sits anywhere on the spread, the colors dull slightly (top right). When you turn on Proof Colors (in this case, simulating newsprint for dramatic effect), the change can be massive (bottom right).

Overprint Preview or Separations in the Separations Preview palette. All your RGB images and colors will dull.

You'll really see the effect if you turn on the View > Proof Colors feature. This tells InDesign to display what your page will look like in the final CMYK workspace. If you choose View > Proof Setup > Custom and turn on the Simulate Paper Color option, you'll be amazed at how terrible your images will appear in print (**Figure 8-7**). Of course, seeing a "soft proof" like this (proofing on the screen) only makes sense if you have created a custom monitor profile. (See *Real World InDesign CS2* or *Real World Color Management* for more on that topic.)

The thing is that none of these change your actual output on a PostScript device when printing separations. They just give you varying degrees of accuracy on screen as to how the colors will appear.

Colors can also change radically when you print or export a PDF file. The key settings that control color in the Print dialog box are in the Output and Color Management panels. When exporting a PDF file, pay attention to the Advanced panel (in InDesign CS) or Output panel (in CS2).

If you're printing to an RGB device (and inkjet printers generally fall into this category even though they print with process-color inks), make sure

you choose RGB from the Color popup menu in the Output panel. Then choose an appropriate destination profile from the Profile popup menu in the Color Management panel.

When printing separations or to a PostScript RIP, you should probably choose CMYK or Unchanged from the Color popup menu. (Note that if you're using spot colors, InDesign won't convert them even if you choose CMYK; it generally only converts spot colors to process when you turn on Simulate Overprint or

tell it to separate spot colors using the Ink Manager.) Again, the choice of the proper destination profile is crucial so that InDesign knows whether and how to convert your colors.

By the way, if you really want bright, saturated colors on a color PostScript device (like a color laser printer), you should probably just choose to send it RGB colors rather than CMYK. It won't necessarily be an accurate proof of anything, but it'll be prettier.

TIP: The reason you're getting bland prints from an inkjet printer may have nothing to do with InDesign. Click the Printer button (or the Setup button, in Windows) inside InDesign's Print dialog box to see the printer driver's settings. Many printer drivers have their own color management controls which can greatly affect how color appears on the page. Try turning those off or adjusting them for better color.

TIP: When you prepare a PDF proof to send to a client, consider saving it in an Acrobat 4 format and convert all colors to CMYK or RGB, which flattens all the transparency effects and allows you to turn on the Simulate Overprint checkbox in the Advanced (in CS) or Output (in CS2) panel of the Export Adobe PDF dialog box. Otherwise, you'll have to tell them to choose Advanced > Overprint Preview in Acrobat, or in Preferences > Page Display in Reader. (In our experience, the fewer steps a client needs to perform, the better.) This PDF is not appropriate for a final print, of course — just for a rough proof.

Stop Overprinting the Black Already!

? I have to admit it: Sometimes I miss a feature or two from QuarkXPress. For example, there's no Trap Information palette in InDesign, so I can't specify the trapping value for a particular object. The place this trips me up the most is when I want to set some large black text to knock out instead of overprint. How can I do that in InDesign?

When you put large black text (or any other black object) over a color image, or overlapping multiple colored objects on the page, you may see those objects through the black — after all, in reality black ink is not nearly as opaque as you might think. The problem, as you discovered, is that InDesign automatically sets 100-percent black objects (applied with the default [Black] swatch) to overprint and there's no "knockout this object" feature.

One solution is to turn *off* the "Overprint [Black] Swatch at 100%" checkbox in the Preferences dialog box. (In InDesign CS, it's in the General panel of the dialog box; in CS2, it's in the Appearance of Black panel.) Unfortunately, this makes *all* your black text knock out, which causes untold headaches when printing small text or thin black lines.

Instead, you might consider using a rich black: Create a new CMYK color defined as 15- or 20-percent each of cyan, magenta, and yellow, plus 100% black. A rich black not only looks blacker in print, but it always knocks out all the colors behind it.

Another solution is to create a new CMYK color swatch that is simply 100-percent black. InDesign won't automatically overprint it, even though it's functionally the same as the swatch called "[Black]." Use the regular [Black] swatch most of the time, but use your 100-percent black when you want it to knock out.

The preference panel lets you control how black should appear on an RGB device, such as your screen or an inkjet printer. By default, InDesign CS2 is set to Display all Blacks as Rich Black, which means any color that is 100-percent black or darker will appear as solid black. But if you choose Display All Blacks Accurately (or Output All Blacks Accurately), then InDesign will use a dark gray for 100-percent black.

We tend to leave these set to the default. When we want an accurate picture of what colors (including black) will look like, we generally use the View > Proof Colors feature instead.

Overprinting Doesn't Add Up

? I have no problem using the Overprint Fill and Overprint Stroke features in the Attributes palette to set objects to overprint spot colors. However, when I try to overprint a process color over another process color, it's flaky: Sometimes I get what I expect and sometimes I don't.

✓ Overprinting has long been a misunderstood child. When you overprint a fill or a stroke, you're not actually saying "add this color to the background colors." You're just saying "don't knock this color out from the background." There's a subtle difference, but it has huge implications.

Where people get into trouble is in overprinting the same color. For example, let's say you have one light-green object colored 30-percent cyan and 20-percent yellow. You put it on top of a purple background that is 50-percent cyan and 80-percent magenta. If you set that green object to overprint, it *seems* like InDesign would add all the colors up and you'd get 80-percent cyan plus the other colors. But PostScript doesn't work that way.

In PostScript, whatever tint is on top wins. If you put 30-percent cyan on top of 50-percent cyan, you get 30-percent cyan — whether you overprint it or not.

The result in the above example would be a color *lighter* than the background: 30-percent cyan, 80-percent magenta, and 20-percent yellow (**Figure 8-8**).

When you want to *add* colors, consider using a transparency mode instead of the Overprint features. Setting the top object to Multiply in the Transparency palette will probably get you closer to what you want. Another good option is the Color Burn mode.

To see how the overlapping colors will mix, open the Separations Preview palette (Window > Output > Separations Preview), turn on Separations (viewing all the plates) and position your cursor above the overprinting color area. You'll see what percentage of each color will be applied to the same area.

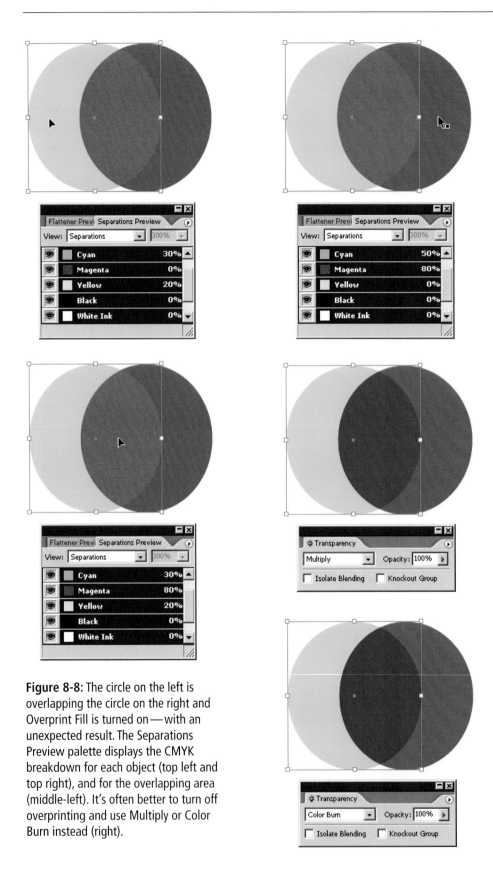

Figure 8-8: The circle on the left is overlapping the circle on the right and Overprint Fill is turned on—with an unexpected result. The Separations Preview palette displays the CMYK breakdown for each object (top left and top right), and for the overlapping area (middle-left). It's often better to turn off overprinting and use Multiply or Color Burn instead (right).

Separations Anxiety

Print Separations to PDF

? It's easy to print separations from the Print dialog box: I just go to the Output panel and choose Separations from the Color popup menu. But when I export an InDesign file as a PDF file, the Export to PDF dialog box is missing the Output panel altogether, and there's no other place where I can choose anything other than full CMYK composite output. I'd like to make a PDF of my separations so I could check them out onscreen instead of wasting a bunch of paper.

✓ Whassamatta, pal, the Separations Preview palette ain't good enough for ya? Just go to Window > Output > Separations Preview to open it up. Select Separations in the palette's View popup menu, and you're good to go.

Okay, okay, don't cry about it. To create a PDF of your color separations, you'll need Adobe Acrobat Professional. Open the Print dialog box, and print separations to the Adobe PDF printer (or to a PostScript file, and run it through Distiller). Don't forget to turn on Page Information in the Marks and Bleed panel before you hit the Print button, otherwise you won't know which plate of which page you're looking at in the PDF.

Where's the Trapping?

? I thought InDesign automatically applied trapping. But when I look closely at my color printouts, or zoom in to 4,000% on screen in InDesign, or to 6,400% with the Loupe Zoom tool in Acrobat, I can't see it, even with Overprint Preview turned on. Everything looks kiss-fit. I even tried changing the trap width from the default 0p0.25 to 0p6, and I see absolutely no difference.

✓ Yes, InDesign automatically applies quite intelligent traps (even to gradient edges), but only when you print out *color separations*. Composite, full-color printouts from

> **NOTE:** What's trapping? When objects overlap each other in a layout, like a small cyan frame on top of a larger, magenta frame, the cyan frame "knocks out" part of the magenta frame, leaving a hole. The edge of the top-most object perfectly abuts (kiss-fits) the edge of the knockout, like a jigsaw puzzle piece. If the two objects use completely different colors (inks), and the job is going to be color separated, there's a chance that the paper color might peek through in the final printed pieces, because few high-speed printing presses can maintain kiss-fit registration. Trapping is the practice of setting very thin lines to overprint each other at the edges of these sorts of abutments to compensate for a slight misregistration in film, plate, or press. You can see and modify InDesign's auto-trapping settings by choosing Window > Output > Trap Presets, and double-clicking the [Default] Trap Preset.

Transparency and Your Print Vendor

It comes down to this: InDesign, Illustrator and Photoshop all support transparency, but PostScript does not. Thus, an InDesign file containing transparency (placed images with transparency, and/or native transparency like drop shadows) will need to be flattened — not the layers, just the transparent elements — before it can be output on a Postscript device. Who should do the flattening, you or your print vendor?

Whenever reasonable, your print vendor should do it. Why? Because their equipment is more powerful than most end users' gear and can process high-res flattening better than yours; because they understand what flattening entails and how to tweak it for the best results on their RIP than anyone else; and finally, because if there are any unwanted artifacts created as a result of flattening, they would be the ones responsible for fixing it.

Just as output providers have purchased high-end trapping workstations (or hired expert pre-press staff to do it, or both) for optimum results in trapping, forward-thinking print vendors are now moving to transparency-aware RIPs or training their staff how to flatten transparency correctly for their press requirements. You want to seek out these people and give them your business! That way, you never have to worry about dealing with the Flattener Preview in InDesign, or fiddle with Transparency Flattener presets. Let your printer take care of it.

Get on the phone right now and ask your output provider if they'll accept either native InDesign files or press-ready PDFs *that have been exported from InDesign with Acrobat 5 or higher compatibility*. We put that in italics, because that's the only way you can create a "live transparency" (unflattened) PDF from InDesign. If they'll only accept Acrobat 4 files, you know they can't deal with transparency.

It won't work to print to the Adobe PDF printer, or to print to Postscript and then Distill it. Both of these methods are limited to creating Acrobat 4-compatible PDFs, which are flattened by definition.

Exporting to PDF/X1-a won't work either, because part of that format's requirements is that it's Acrobat 4-compatible. The PDF/X1-a format is meant for when you need to create a "blind" PDF (when you don't know who the printer is) such as submitting display ads in PDF format for magazines. Your PDF may end up being imported into a QuarkXPress layout for all you know, which as of this writing only accepts Acrobat 4-compatible PDFs. Unfortunately, a number of commercial printers are glomming onto this blind standard for *all* their clients. It's not necessary, and since designers can still submit bad PDFs (low res images, 50 spot colors) that pass the PDF/X-1a test, it doesn't do much good.

(continued)

InDesign are never trapped. When you turn over a press-ready composite PDF (also never trapped) to your commercial printer, *they* apply the trapping using their own software, when *they* output the PDF to separations. The only traps they may honor are any strokes you manually set to be overprinting via the Attributes palette, or in placed images where overprinting was included in the image file.

Thus, to see InDesign's trapping in action, choose Separations as the Output type in the Print dialog box, and inspect the edges of each color plate that gets printed. Or, print separations to PostScript and run them through Distiller (or print to the Adobe PDF printer) and look at each color's "plate" on-screen.

As an interesting experiment, you can also force InDesign to apply its trapping to a composite PDF, and inspect it in Acrobat or in a color printout of the PDF. Just remember that your print vendor will very likely *not* be using these settings, unless this is the final file you turn over. And in that case, you'd better warn them that's what you did, and then duck!

Here's the hack to create a trapped, composite PDF from InDesign, courtesy of Adobe guru Nick Hodge:

1. Choose File > Print, and choose the Adobe PDF printer as your printer.

2. In the Print dialog box, set up all your options as usual (page range, printer's marks etc.). In the Output panel, change Color output from Composite CMYK to In-RIP Separations, and set Trapping to Adobe Built-In.

3. Click the Printer button (or Setup button if you're on Windows) at the bottom of the Print dialog box. Change Adobe PDF options to the Press preset, and click Print to back out of the Printer Setup dialog box.

4. When prompted, name your PDF and choose a location to save it on your hard drive. Click Print again in the InDesign Print dialog box.

5. Open the PDF in Acrobat. To view the traps (the overprinting strokes), turn on Overprint Preview in the

Advanced menu. You may need to use the Loupe zoom tool if your traps are really small.

Trapping is Incorrect in Separations Preview?

? I have spot-colored 36 pt. type (that I created in InDesign) on top of a placed Photoshop image. When I view all the "plates" in Separation Preview, and zoom in closely, I can clearly see the traps (the colored strokes) InDesign has applied to the edges of the type. But when I move my cursor over the trap lines to see what colors are being used to create them (according to the Separations palette's ink percentages), the mix is incorrect. I'm not sure how to fix this.

☑ What you're seeing are *not* trap lines; they're the anti-aliased edges that InDesign applies to text characters to make them look smoother on-screen (**Figure 8-9**). When you move your cursor over the type edges, Separations Preview is being too helpful and is reading and reporting the mix of inks used in the anti-aliasing. (Actually, InDesign uses RGB colors for this, since it's just for screen preview. But Separations Preview always converts RGB colors to their CMYK equivalents.)

Weird, huh? To see for yourself, turn off the Enable Anti-aliasing checkbox in Preferences > Display Performance and check again. The diagonal and round edges of the text characters now look slightly pixelated, and as you slowly move your cursor over the color transitions, Separations Preview no longer detects any "traps."

As explained in the previous solution, the *only* way to make InDesign apply trapping is to output separations to a printer or to a PDF from the native InDesign file.

Show Spot Color Plates in DCS EPSs

? We have a lot of legacy Photoshop files that were saved as DCS EPSs because they contain spot color channels. When we place these into InDesign, the spot color gets added to the Swatches palette just fine, and it's listed in the Separations Preview palette, but when we view just that spot color's plate using the Separations Preview palette, there's nothing there!

☑ These symptoms point to one cause: The original Photoshop file contained at least one vector layer (a vector shape or live text layer). When the user saved the file as DCS, they left the Save Vector Data option turned on in DCS Format Options dialog box. We're not sure why InDesign has a problem with these, but it probably has something to do with lots of ones and zeroes.

The only way to fix the problem is to locate the original PSD file from which the DCS saved, and either re-save it as a DCS with Save Vector Data turned *off*, or just use the original PSD file in your document, since InDesign CS and CS2 support spot channels in PSDs. Either of these methods retains the spot color channel information and you'll be able to see the spot color artwork in Separations Preview.

Figure 8-9: The slightly-colored strokes you see around text when you zoom in are *not* trap lines! You're seeing InDesign's anti-aliasing at work.

If you try opening the DCS file in Photoshop, you'll lose your spot channel data when the base EPS format of the file is rasterized. Yet another reason to just stick with the PSD format in the future.

Reveal Mystery Colors in Separations Preview

? I'm wrapping up a 216-page magazine issue. The job is only supposed to use CMYK colors. Yet somehow, during the past couple weeks I've been working on this puppy, two RGB colors and three Pantone spot colors snuck their way into the Swatches palette. When I choose Select All

Unused from the Swatches palette menu, they *don't* get selected, ergo, they've been used someplace. But for the life of me, I don't know where. How do I find out which objects were filled or stroked with these unwanted colors? There's no "show me where this color is used" command.

 The Separations Preview palette (Window > Output > Separations

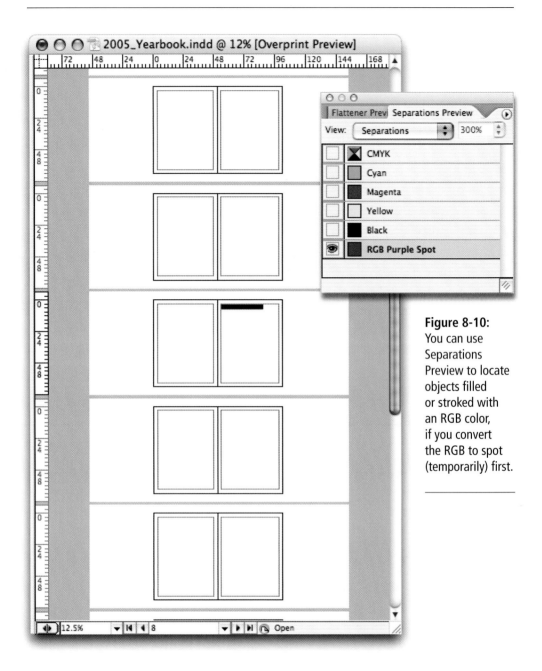

Figure 8-10:
You can use Separations Preview to locate objects filled or stroked with an RGB color, if you convert the RGB to spot (temporarily) first.

Preview) will show you all CMYK and spot-colored items. (We'll get to the RGB ones in a minute.) To see where you've used a spot color, change the View popup menu to Separations, then hide all the CMYK color separations at once by turning off the checkbox next to the first "color" listed, CMYK.

Zoom way out to something like 25% so you can see at least a few spreads at a time, and scroll through the document. Only the spot-colored items will appear (in their actual spot color), everything else will be hidden — you'll just see blank pages. If you're looking for a single spot color — you've turned off all CMYK and all spots except for one in the

Separations Preview palette — objects or type using that color will appear as black (**Figure 8-10**).

Once you spot the item (oh, bad pun!), you can select it, and change the View menu in the palette back to Off. Everything in the document reappears and your item is still selected. Now you just have to fix it.

What about the RGB colors? The Separations Preview palette is actually showing you what the separations will look like after it's been converted to CMYK plus spots. InDesign converts RGB images and colors to CMYK when you print separations, so the palette can't show you the RGB data. To work around it, double-click each RGB color in the Swatches palette and change it to a Spot color. Now they'll be listed in the Separations Preview palette and you can proceed as above. Once you locate the offenders, you'll probably want to change the RGB to a CMYK process color or use the Ink Manager to alias them to a spot color.

If your eyes start to roll back in your head at the thought of scrolling through hundreds of spreads looking for a speck of spot ink, try this slick technique suggested by InDesign master Peter Truskier on Adobe's InDesign forum:

1. If RGB colors are an issue, convert them to Spot colors in the Swatches palette before you begin.

2. Choose File > Print. Make sure that the "Print Blank Pages" option is turned *off* in the General panel of the Print dialog box.

3. In the Setup panel, turn on Scale to Fit, and in the Marks and Bleeds panel, turn on the Page Information checkbox.

4. Now go to the Output panel, and in the Color popup menu, choose Separations.

5. At the bottom of the Output panel, uncheck all colors (inks) except for the first single spot color you're looking for. (You'll repeat this process for each spot you need to track down.)

6. InDesign is now set up to output only those pages containing that spot color, and on those pages, only those items using that color will appear. (Saving you a ton of time if only one comma in a huge document uses that unwanted spot color!)

If you click the Print button, these pages will be sent to your local printer. To "save some trees," as Peter suggests, change the Printer to Adobe PDF, and print to that — you can view the pages in Acrobat.

On your printouts or in the PDF, look at the lower-left corner of each page. Since you turned on the Page Information checkbox, you'll see the page number listed here, giving you the information you need to locate that spot-colored object in your document.

Touchy Transparency

Figure 8-11: Not sure why InDesign thinks a normal-looking spread contains a transparent subject? Find the guilty party by asking the Flattener Preview palette to highlight Transparent Objects for you. Expect to see this technology in an upcoming episode of "CSI: Adobe."

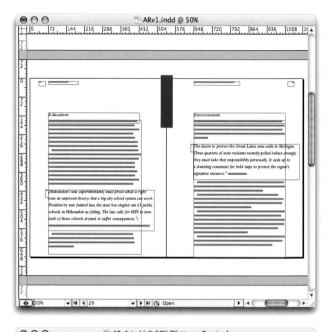

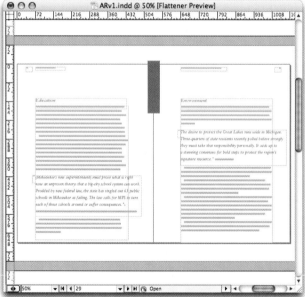

Where's the Transparency?

? A few of the page icons in my Pages palette are showing that gray-and-white checkerboard pattern indicating there's transparency on the page. As far as I know I didn't set or place anything with transparency there, so where is this coming from? I can't tell by looking at the page, everything looks 100% opaque to me.

☑ Many people don't realize that adding a drop shadow or using feathering adds transparency. Similarly, a PSD, AI, or PDF file that you imported may include transparency without you knowing it. To figure out where the transparency is, open the Flattener Preview palette (Window > Output > Flattener Preview) and choose Transparent Objects from its Highlight menu. Any object on the page that has transparency applied will appear with a red overlay, all the other objects will appear as a light screen of gray (**Figure 8-11**). Change the Highlight back to None to turn off the preview.

Transparency Harms Innocent Text, Story at Eleven

? Even though the drop shadow I've added to a rotated image doesn't touch the column of text it's next to, it appears to have affected some of it. A vertical strip of the text appears bold, just a small subsection nearest the image, in the proof print I made on my laser printer.

✓ InDesign creates a phantom, rectangular bounding box surrounding every object containing transparency, and everything on the page that ends up inside the bounding box is affected by the transparency being flattened — unless it's above the transparent object in the stacking order. Bounding boxes are never rotated — if the image is rotated, the bounding box just enlarges to enclose it completely. In this case, it sounds like the text was below (stacking order-wise) the image and that "bold" strip fell within the bounding box area.

The text becomes "bold" as a result of InDesign converting the text to outlines. Since you printed to your local printer, InDesign probably applied the default Medium Resolution preset for the Transparency Flattener (check the Advanced panel in the Print dialog box to see and change the Flattener preset).

There are a few ways to fix this:

- Export it to an Acrobat 5 or higher PDF, which maintains transparency (doesn't flatten it), and give that PDF to your print vendor. (See the sidebar, "Transparency and Your Print Vendor" on page 220.)

- Print with the High Resolution Transparency Flattener preset.

- Select the text frame and move it higher in the stacking order than the drop shadow box, to its own layer at the top of the layer stack if necessary. This is probably your best bet, because even if text lies right on top of a drop shadow, it won't be affected by flattening. You can verify this in the Flattener Preview palette, set to view All Affected Objects (**Figure 8-12**): The text appears light gray (unaffected), while the object and its shadow underneath appear with a red overlay (affected).

On occasion, you'll get bold text around transparency even if the text is on top of the transparent object. As far as we know, this only happens when you export a PDF file from InDesign and print it from Acrobat 6. It's actually an Acrobat bug, but the only solution we know of is to turn off the Overprint [Black] Swatch at 100% option in the Preferences dialog box (in the General panel in CS and the Appearance of Black panel in CS2). Now recreate the PDF and it should work properly.

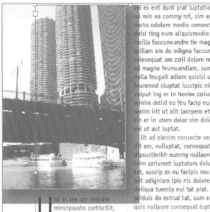

Figure 8-12: Our page (left) contains transparency (a drop shadow). When we turn on Flattener Preview, it turns some text red because it's in back of the image (top left). When we move the text frame above the image, it's no longer affected by the transparency (top right).

Remove White Boxes Behind Drop Shadows

❓ The drop shadows look perfect in InDesign and in our internal PDF proofs, but when my printer sent over the color proof (created from my InDesign file), every item with a drop shadow had a horrible white box behind it. He said that InDesign's drop shadows were "flaky" and that I shouldn't use the feature.

☑ InDesign isn't the flaky one here; it's your printer! InDesign's drop shadows and other transparency features are generally only "flaky" if you use older or quirky equipment to output the data. The majority of print vendors do use up-to-date hardware and software — fully compliant RIPs that understand how Adobe software handles transparency — and have no problems with drop shadows. Trust us, if this weren't true no one would be using the feature! (See the sidebar, "Transparency and Your Print Vendor" on page 220 for more info to help your current vendor or to find a new one.)

If your printer uses a composite workflow—their RIP does the separations—ask them to check that the RIP honors overprinting instructions in the file. Some backend equipment is set to ignore overprinting by default, and drop shadows (and other transparency features) depend upon it.

What's that Thin White Line?

? In Acrobat, with Overprint Preview turned on, I can see faint white lines or rectangles in the PDF I'm about to send to my print vendor. They appear to define the rectangular edges around certain objects that have drop shadows or other transparency effects. What are they? Should I be worried?

✔ Before you get concerned, zoom in very closely to see if they disappear. If they do, or if they stay the same tiny size as you zoom in, it's just a screen artifact and won't appear on the printout. You can typically get rid of them on screen by turning off the Smooth Line

WARNING: If you're seeing white boxes behind drop shadows or other transparency effects in *your* internal PDF proofs (**Figure 8-13**), turn on Overprint Preview from Acrobat's Advanced menu, or re-export the PDF with Acrobat 5 (or higher) compatibility.

If you're not seeing them, but your clients are when viewing your soft proofs in Reader or Acrobat, ask them to turn on Overprint Preview. Depending on which version of which PDF viewer they're using, the command will be in their Advanced or View menus; or in Reader's Preferences in the Page Display panel. If you have no idea which version of Reader or Acrobat they might have and you'd rather not encounter the problem at all, give them a for-proofing-only PDF that you've created with Simulate Overprint turned on in InDesign's Export to PDF dialog box.

Finally, if you're seeing white boxes behind drop shadows on your inkjet printer output, export the layout to PDF with Acrobat 5 or later compatibility, open it in Acrobat, and choose Print As Image from Acrobat's Advanced options in its Print dialog box.

Figure 8-13: Drop-shadowed text on a colored background sprouts awful white boxes behind it if Overprint Preview is off in Acrobat (when viewing a PDF proof on-screen) of if your print vendor turns off overprinting on their RIP (left). When you turn on Overprint Preview in Reader or Acrobat (and when your print vendor does the same on their RIP), transparency effects work as you'd expect (right).

Art and/or Smooth Images options in Acrobat's (or Reader's) Preferences.

Any lines that don't go away may be due to *stitching*, an Adobe term for a line that sometimes appears at the point of transition from a vector area to a rasterized area, when the rasterization is a result of the transparency flattening process. Stitching artifacts were occasional problems with InDesign v2 but became much more rare in InDesign CS. (And we hope will become virtually extinct with CS2.) Some manufacturers' RIPs are more prone to stitching than others because of how they interpret data, too. In other words, what creates a visible artifact on one printer (or one vendor's platesetter) may not on another.

If you're in charge of flattening the transparency, you should always use the High Resolution Flattener preset in the Print or Export PDF Options dialog box, which greatly reduces the chances of this happening. But the best solution, as explained in the sidebar earlier in this chapter, is to leave the flattening to your print vendor. Give them the native InDesign file or a press-ready PDF with live transparency (Acrobat 5 or later compatible), and ask for a composite color proof of the RIPped file.

PDF Export Exhaustion

Grayscale PDF From a Color Layout

? Our office periodically needs to create a grayscale PDF for one of our clients, even though their jobs are done in CMYK plus spot plates. There's no place to choose "grayscale" in the Export to PDF dialog box. We tried printing to the Adobe PDF printer instead, since the Print dialog box *does* offer Composite Gray as an Output choice, but some of the graphics didn't convert—they stayed in color. We *really* don't want to have to re-create these files in grayscale, as some are over 200 pages long!

☑ InDesign can convert colors to grayscale during the process you describe only if it can "get" to them. It does fine with any color created in InDesign itself (CMYK, RGB or Lab; process or spot), as well as placed color TIFFs and PSD files, even if the PSD has a spot color channel. However, InDesign won't change placed color EPS and PDF images into grayscale.

The good news is, through a simple hack, you can force InDesign to convert those recalcitrant images too. Nick Hodge first wrote about this trick for InDesign 2.0 and it still works in both CS and CS2.

He discovered that when any image is run through InDesign's transparency flattener, the program has a chance to adjust its colors to conform to the type of Color Output (in this case, Composite Gray) you set in the Print dialog box.

If you select one of your stubborn color images and set it to have a 99.9 percent opacity from the Transparency palette (Window > Transparency), it's enough to trigger the Transparency

Flattener when you output to a flattened format (**Figure 8-14**, next page). That allows InDesign to get in there and convert it to grayscale while it's at it, without changing the look of the image at all, since the .1 percent that is transparent is not detectable.

Apply that transparency setting to any placed PDF or EPS images first. Then, when you print to the Adobe PDF printer, make sure that changing the Color Output to Composite Gray is the *last* thing you change in the dialog box before you click the Print button. We've found that sometimes, the selection reverts to the Composite CMYK choice if you go elsewhere in the dialog box, or click the Printer (or Setup, in Windows) button afterwards, before clicking the final Print button.

Printers Can't Take Exported PDFs

? Oh, how I would love to use InDesign's handy Export to PDF presets and just choose one on the fly from the File menu. Alas, when I print to my old desktop laser printer, these PDF files always give me errors (or worse, just die without any error). My print vendor says she has trouble with PDFs created this way, too. I have to give them PDFs created "the old-fashioned way," by printing Postscript to disk and then running the .ps file through Distiller.

✓ No doubt the troubles your old printer and your vendor are experiencing are due to InDesign CS's penchant for encoding all embedded fonts in exported PDFs as "CID," also known

as "double-byte" encoding. While most modern-day RIPs do understand CID encoding — the format has been part of the Adobe Postscript specification for years — others choke on them. In contrast, when you write a file to Postscript (why are you doing that, anyway? You should be printing to the Adobe PDF printer, it's more convenient and does the same thing), fonts that don't require CID encoding are encoded normally as Type 1 or True Type fonts.

Fortunately, Adobe was listening, and the problem has been fixed in InDesign CS2. Exported PDFs are now no more nor less likely to contain CID-encoded fonts than PDFs created by printing to the Adobe PDF printer. Yet another reason to upgrade!

Export a Long Document as Single-page PDFs

? Our workflow requires that we output our final magazine files as single-page PDFs. Which, of course, InDesign CS can't do — EPSs sí; PDFs, no. When I heard that InDesign CS2 could *import* multiple pages of a PDF at once, I had my fingers crossed that it could work in reverse, too. Can I uncross my fingers now? Or must I still reserve two hours every month for the monkey work of exporting a single page after another to PDF, 272 times.

✓ Hmmm. Do you want to hear the good news or the bad news first? Bad news: No, with InDesign CS2, just as with all previous versions, you cannot split a document into multiple, single-page PDFs when you export it to

Good news: Open that behemoth PDF file in Adobe Acrobat Professional 7, go to Document > Extract Pages, and—are you sitting down—check out the new checkbox at the bottom of the dialog box, "Extract Pages as Separate Files." Yes dear, Acrobat Professional 7 can automatically split a multiple-page PDF into individual page PDFs and save them on your hard drive. Now you can uncross your fingers.

Placed PDFs Causing Postscript Errors

? **I'm in charge of producing our association's quarterly 4/C newsletter.**

PDF. (Without the help of a script, that is—check out Chris Paveglio's PDFBee at *http://chris.paveglio.com* if you're a Mac user.)

Part of this job entails placing display ads that our members send us. Before I place them into my InDesign layout, I always open each one in Acrobat and make a test print for our files (and to make sure they're stable). Yet I still sometimes have trouble with certain ads when I export the newsletter from InDesign to PDF for our print vendor. I get various, seemingly random Postscript errors, and the job quits, always when it's trying to process a page that has a PDF display ad (not every PDF ad, just certain ones). Is there anything I can do, short of rasterizing the "bad" PDF ads in Photoshop and replacing them in the layout?

☑ Yes. You can tell your display-ad-submitting members to please *disable* OPI Comments in the program they're using to create the PDFs they're sending you. Some programs have OPI Comments (used for OPI workflows, where low-res images are automatically replaced by high-res ones on an OPI server) turned on by default, as do some Distiller settings. These OPI comments embedded in the placed PDFs trigger just the sort of random Postscript errors you describe when exporting an InDesign file to PDF.

To flush out any OPI Comments in PDFs already placed in your layout, you could print the file to Postscript and then run it through a Distiller setting that has "Preserve OPI Comments" turned off. (Or print to the Adobe PDF printer, and specify the same Adobe PDF Setting in the Printer's PDF Options dialog box.)

Alternatively, you could try the Nick Hodge technique (described earlier) of applying a 99.9 percent transparency to the PDF ad that's giving you grief. When you export the layout to PDF, the Transparency Flattener will process the ad, but leave it looking virtually the same as before. We've been told (but haven't thoroughly tested) that the transparency flattener vacuums out OPI Comments in the process.

Index

X, Y, Z

Colophon

The body of this book is set in Adobe Warnock Pro Regular and Frutiger LT Std Bold Condensed; heads are set in Warnock Pro Light Display and Frutiger LT Std Black Condensed.

Text was prepared in Microsoft Word and laid out using Adobe InDesign CS2 (well, to be honest, we used beta software versions of CS2).

We used a Xerox Phaser 7750 for proofing pages.

The book was printed at Courier Corporation on 60 lb. Influence Matte.